TRADE MINDFULLY

The Wiley Trading series features books by traders who have survived the market's ever changing temperament and have prospered—some by reinventing systems, others by getting back to basics. Whether a novice trader, professional or somewhere in-between, these books will provide the advice and strategies needed to prosper today and well into the future. For more on this series, visit our website at www.WileyTrading.com.

Founded in 1807, John Wiley & Sons is the oldest independent publishing company in the United States. With offices in North America, Europe, Australia, and Asia, Wiley is globally committed to developing and marketing print and electronic products and services for our customers' professional and personal knowledge and understanding.

TRADE MINDFULLY

Achieve Your Optimum Trading Performance with
Mindfulness and Cutting-Edge Psychology

Gary Dayton, Psy.D.

WILEY

Design Credit: Wiley
Cover Image: top: © istock.com/Mak_Art;
bottom: © istock.com/agsandrew

Published by John Wiley & Sons, Inc., Hoboken, New Jersey.
Published simultaneously in Canada.

Charts created using TradeStation. ©TradeStation Technologies, Inc. 2001-2014. All rights reserved. No
investment or trading advice, recommendation, or opinions are being given or intended.

For general information on our other products and services or for technical support, please contact our
Customer Care Department within the United States at (800) 762-2974, outside the United States at (317)
572-3993 or fax (317) 572-4002.

Wiley publishes in a variety of print and electronic formats and by print-on-demand. Some material included
with standard print versions of this book may not be included in e-books or in print-on-demand. If this book
refers to media such as a CD or DVD that is not included in the version you purchased, you may download this
material at http://booksupport.wiley.com. For more information about Wiley products, visit www.wiley.com.

Library of Congress Cataloging-in-Publication Data:

ISBN 978-1-118-44561-7 (Paperback)
ISBN 978-1-118-99097-1 (ePDF)
ISBN 978-1-118-99103-9 (ePub)

Printed in the United States of America.

10 9 8 7 6 5 4 3 2 1

To Ning, with all my love,
To my parents, with gratitude,
and
To all traders who have struggled with trading's mental challenges—
which is to say, all of us

CONTENTS

PART I UNDERSTANDING YOUR MIND   7

PART II USING CUTTING-EDGE PSYCHOLOGY   95

CONTENTS

ACKNOWLEDGMENTS

Much appreciation goes to my wife and partner, Ning. She is known to traders by her American name, Helen. She read every word of this book when it was a draft and offered superlative editorial suggestions. For this and all her support during the lengthy period during which this was written, I am truly grateful.

To David Weis, Professional Trader and Market Analyst, for coaching me in trading. David taught me to read the markets through his interpretation of the Wyckoff Method. His careful and masterful tutoring helped me become technically proficient so that I could focus more on the psychological aspects of trading.

To Gavin Holmes, CEO of TradeGuider Ltd., for inviting me to speak on trading psychology at a seminar he produced in San Francisco. That experience taught me that not only did I have something of value to say to traders, but traders understood the importance of trading psychology and were eager to learn about the mental side of trading. Gavin had the foresight that psychology was a necessary part of trading and our continuing work together has brought psychology before many traders across the globe.

A special note of thanks to Dr. Charlie Maher, sport psychologist for the Cleveland Indians Major League Baseball Team and Professor Emeritus at Rutgers University, for generously teaching me his model for sport and human performance psychology which formed the foundation for the book's trading psychology process.

To Kevin Commins, formerly of John Wiley & Sons. Kevin made the initial contact and encouraged me to write this book and document my approach to trading psychology.

To all the psychologists and researchers whose work is referenced herein and upon whose shoulders I stood to write this book. I'm deeply indebted to their insightful research and their work on mindfulness, acceptance, and commitment. They deserve much credit for advancing the science of psychology and providing their work to other psychologists like me, who in turn distill it and provide it to you.

To the publishing team at John Wiley & Sons, including Meg Freeborn, Senior Development Editor; Claire New, Senior Production Editor; Tula Batanchiev and Tiffany Charbonier, Program Coordinators; and Evan Burton, Editor, for championing the book and for making what still seems like a daunting project a reality.

Thanks to Lane Mendelsohn, publisher of TraderPlanet.com, for the use of some of the graphics in the book.

And finally, I'd like to express my sincere appreciation to the many traders whom I have met, taught, and with whom I have worked. I have learned more from those seeking to better understand and improve their trading psychology than any other source.

Gary Dayton, Psy.D., brings together psychology and trading in his work as a trading psychologist, trading educator, and active trader in the S&P e-mini and currency markets. He teaches traders advanced trading skills through his Deep Practice program—a unique online weekly training in which traders face stimulating chart reading and psychological situations that take them to new levels of trading insight and learning. Gary is a popular international speaker who has presented to traders in England, Singapore, Malaysia, Australia, and the United States. A licensed psychologist, he earned his doctorate at the Graduate School of Applied and Professional Psychology, Rutgers University. He is president of Peak Psychology, Inc., a consulting firm that specializes in developing peak performance in traders.

Connect with Gary online at his website: www.TradingPsychologyEdge.com and Twitter: @DrGaryDayton.

If you have picked up this book and are reading it, chances are you have had some trading difficulties or have tried but have not yet been able to take your trading to the level you desire. You may have experienced one or more of the following in your trading:

- Cut winning trades short even though you know your trade setup is solid.

- Failed to pull the trigger on a perfectly good trade because of fear of loss.

- Let losing trades run hoping for a return to breakeven.

- Added to a losing position in the hope that the market would turn around.

- Made profits in the morning but gave them back in the afternoon.

- Became more aggressive after losing money.

- Took unplanned trades when the market suddenly moved.

- Stopped trading or reduced position size after a loss.

- Traded greater position size than prudent money management practice would advise.

- Held trades longer than they should have been held looking for a "home run."

- Failed to take a perfectly sound setup because the last two trades were losers.

- After a day of big profits, your confidence soared and your trading suffered.

- Consistently made small money but have been unable to elevate your trading performance.

These trading difficulties hurt. They not only hurt your account, but they also cause mental and emotional suffering. No other profession tests your psychology as does trading. These difficulties and unskilled trading behaviors arise from the underlying mental and emotional challenges traders face. Most likely you have made considerable effort to overcome these difficulties but the methods you tried have probably failed you. After a while, you may question whether anything will ever work, or worse, you may question your suitability for trading.

This book is different from the methods you have tried. It offers mindfulness, a state-of-the-art method backed by scientific proof, and a specific trading psychology process: together they can unlock the door to managing your mental and emotional challenges and to excellence in trading performance. If you are determined and are willing to commit to the effort, this book will definitely help you.

I am trained as a clinical psychologist. I became involved in trading and trading psychology more than 15 years ago. Like other traders coming into the market, I have experienced most of the difficulties listed above. Personal experience and the experience of working with other traders taught me that the conventional trading wisdom of controlling and eliminating one's emotions from trading does not work. Quite the contrary, the more we struggle to try and control our feelings, the more our attention is distracted away from our trading, and the more erratic our trading becomes. Not only does the conventional wisdom not work, it is wrong. Countless traders have traded poorly and failed to learn the trading skills following conventional wisdom because trying to get rid of our thoughts and feelings in the usual problem solving way actually is the cause of our problems. We become stuck in a rigid and intractable mental pattern and our trading suffers.

Albert Einstein once said, "You cannot solve a problem from the same consciousness that created it. You must learn to see the world anew." Einstein could have been talking about trading when he made this remark. We have to think differently to overcome the universal mental challenges of trading. This book will show you how.

I began to think differently about trading psychology when I saw something wonderfully mind-blowing at a psychology conference. A video presentation showed a psychologist treating a person who was depressed and suicidal. Within a single therapy session, however, the person had changed markedly. She was no longer depressed and no longer suicidal. She no longer needed psychological treatment. I couldn't quite grasp what the psychologist was doing because it was very different from what I had learned and practiced as a psychologist—it even seemed counterintuitive, but I knew deep in my bones that whatever it was, it was damned powerful.

The different way of thinking about psychology is called Acceptance and Commitment Therapy, or ACT. When I first saw that presentation, ACT was new. There wasn't much written about it and only a few had experience with it. That has all changed. Now there is an explosion of books, scientific papers, and conferences and more psychologists are adopting it because it is so effective. Settings outside the therapy room are also beginning to embrace it. Susan David and Christina Congleton, for example, have written about the *mental agility* that ACT promotes specifically for corporate executives and industry leaders in *Harvard Business Review Online*. Wouldn't you like some mental agility in your trading instead of mental struggle?

One of the core components of ACT is mindfulness. Mindfulness, as you will learn in this book, is incredibly important for traders. Although it has its roots in Eastern traditions, modern scientific research shows that it has powerful ability to positively impact us psychologically and even enhance the structure of our brains (as seen through neuroimaging studies). ACT's approach to mindfulness, along with its other advanced psychological techniques such as defusion and commitment to actions that bring high value to our trading, can dramatically change your trading psychology for the better. Instead of struggling to try and control your unwanted thoughts and feelings, mindfulness and other techniques allow you to be a sort of mental aikido master where you can sidestep them and redirect your focus onto what's really important, your trade.

It's not sufficient, however, just to develop mental agility if you want to achieve excellence in trading. At its core, trading is a performance-based activity. We develop trading knowledge, skills, and abilities and then apply what we know and can do by performing in the markets. The best performers in any field are guided by coaches, mentors, and specialized training. The structured guidance affords opportunities to learn skills and overcome mental challenges. Most traders do not have structured guidance. They are left on their own. This book sets out to change this.

What matters most in any performance activity is having and adhering to a process. A process is a well-defined series of actions or steps taken to achieve a desirable result. The more consistent we become in a sound process, the better we can apply our knowledge, skills, and abilities and the better our trading results will be, all other things being equal. My ideas about a trading psychology process were born in a graduate course on sport and human performance psychology taught by Charlie Maher, an accomplished sport psychologist. Charlie's course helped me shift my ideas of trading psychology. This shift involved moving away from traditional psychological methods and techniques of trying to change one's thoughts and emotions to applying psychology directly to the process of trading: how we prepare to trade, how we execute our trading, and how we evaluate our trading performance.

This is the first book about a trading psychology based on the power of mindfulness and the bedrock of process. The combination of a robust trading psychology process with mindfulness and other cutting-edge mental skills can help you excel in your development of both the psychological aspects and the technical aspects of trading.

■ How This Book Is Organized

This book is divided into three parts. Part I (Chapters 1 through 4) discusses the unique challenges traders face, both mental and emotional. In a very real sense, in order to succeed at trading, traders need to know how they fail. Part II (Chapters 5 through 8) introduces mindfulness, what it is, how it can help traders meet the mental and emotional challenges of trading, and how to do it. Part III (Chapters 9 through 11) presents a robust trading psychology process, made up of three distinctive time frames and the associated high-value mental skills traders can develop that can take them on a continuous improvement path to excellence and mastery of the trading game.

Part I

There are many psychologically influenced challenges to overcome on the path to trading success. The unaware trader can very easily be blindsided by cognitive biases and heuristics—mental rules of thumb we use effectively and routinely in our daily lives, but are inappropriate for trading. Emotions, too, can be a significant challenge for traders. Cognitive biases and emotions can cause you to hold onto losers, take trades at the wrong time and in the wrong direction, jump into unplanned trades, and other erratic trading. The chapters in Part I show you the root cause of erratic trading behaviors. Real-life examples of traders[1] in actual trading situations make the concepts clear and comprehensible. Practical exercises and forms are provided so you can begin to identify and constructively address the mental and emotional difficulties and erratic trading behaviors that you experience in your trading. All exercises in this book are available in larger, PDF format for download at the author's website (www.tradingpsychologyedge.com).

In Part I we also look closely at fear and its various forms, along with stress, other strong emotions such as anger and boredom, and emotional hijackings—those emotion-dominant states that cause us to act imprudently and can ruin a trader's account. We introduce Emotional Intelligence, an important psychological ability, which helps you identify your emotions, understand what they mean, and the patterns they generally follow. This alone can give you a significant advantage in your trading.

We review traders' default methods to cope with unwanted emotions, especially fear, and show exactly why many of these methods do not work. We review the psychological experience of loss aversion, why it is actually natural for us to cut winning trades short and what we can do to address this behavior. As we conclude Part I, we also show that trying to eliminate emotions from trading—what conventional trading wisdom advocates—is the exact wrong thing to do. After reading this section, you will never again think the same way about emotions.

Part II

Part II introduces mindfulness. Mindfulness is one of the most powerful skills all traders would be wise to develop. Robust research has shown that mindfulness has profound value to traders through its many benefits. With the enhanced focus and concentration afforded by mindfulness, you can see the market and the trading opportunities it presents more clearly. Mindfulness directly helps tame the fear response, strengthens internal emotional regulation, and significantly reduces stress. Mindfulness teaches that you can trade well even though you may have unwanted emotions. The practice of mindfulness along with the advanced psychological skills of defusion, acceptance, and commitment help you keep your focus on the high-value actions that best serve your trades so that you can execute them rather than be disrupted by anxiety, fear, and other unwanted emotions. Mindfulness also helps you reduce common trading errors caused by applying mental shortcuts (cognitive heuristics). It allows you to engage your deliberative mind and strengthens your decision making. Mindfulness also promotes learning and, together with deliberate practice (discussed in Part III), you can develop mastery in trading.

Several mindfulness practice scripts along with alternate suggestions of how to do mindfulness for you to use and develop your mindfulness skills are presented in Part II. Many of the mindfulness scripts have been recorded and are available on the author's website (www.tradingpsychologyedge.com) for download. There are examples to show you how to apply mindfulness in trading and how to use it along with other important techniques in overcoming psychologically difficult trading situations. When we are challenged by a trading situation that causes an emotional reaction, our attention automatically turns inward to our thoughts and feelings. We lose focus and our contact with the market and trade poorly. Mindfulness can correct this strong tendency. It helps us keep our focus where it should be: on the market. We also show you how to address both minor and major trading challenges with mindfulness and other state-of-the-art methods. You are given an explicit protocol for overcoming your specific, challenging trading situations along with the details of how two traders used this method to successfully resolve problematic trading behaviors of cutting winning trades short and oversizing trades after a loss, respectively.

Part III

To achieve excellence and optimum success in trading, in addition to mindfulness and other mental skills, you will need a sound trading psychology process that helps you continuously develop both your mental and technical skills. The trading psychology process we present here is a psychologically informed framework for your development into a successful trader. The framework is adapted from Charlie Maher's sport and human performance model. This trading psychology framework consists of three core psychological principles of the trading process: High-Quality Preparation, Effective Execution and Constructive Self-Assessment. Within each principle are four high-value mental skills every trader will find beneficial. The process of personal growth and self-development is made explicit by identifying your personal developmental needs, creating SMART goals to address your needs, implementing the goals, evaluating them, and adjusting them until you transform a limitation in your trading into a new skill and ability you can rely on. There are case examples from traders to help illustrate and clarify these concepts. Specific techniques, skills, and procedures such as mental parking, the mental STOP, the Trader's Performance Assessment, and other beneficial practices are explained.

Although this is a book, it has been set up as a manual or handbook for trading psychology. There are charts and forms you can use to apply the information you learn to your personal situation. I encourage you to not only read the book, but also do the exercises, practice and develop mindfulness skills, and apply what you have learned to your trading. Let this book be your coach, mentor, and guide in your journey to take command of the mental and technical sides of trading. Trade mindfully and achieve your optimum trading performance with mindfulness and cutting-edge trading psychology!

■ Note

1. Case examples of traders may be actual case examples or a combination of experiences from different traders presented as an individual trader to help better highlight concepts and techniques. All names have been changed and any potentially identifying information has been altered to ensure privacy.

PART I

Understanding Your Mind

CHAPTER 1

Traders' Mental Blind Spots

Colin had been watching the S&P e-mini futures all morning, waiting patiently for a trade. Finally, he saw one setup. He looked carefully at both the price action and the indicators he used to qualify his trades. Everything met his criteria. Price had turned bullish and all indicators were signaling long. "There's no flaw in the setup," he thought.

The trade started working almost immediately. The market moved up smartly, breaking a nearby resistance level and then moved into "clear air" where no other resistance was located. The S&Ps rallied for twelve points from the trade entry—an excellent intraday run for this market. But, Colin was not on board.

He didn't take the trade. When discussing this later, he said, "The same setup occurred yesterday. I guess I was thinking of that trade, which I took, but it didn't work out. I had a loss. There was even a slight difference in favor of today's trade. One of the indicators did not confirm yesterday. Today's setup was picture-perfect. I kicked myself for not taking the trade. I don't really understand why I didn't take it. I wasn't feeling any big emotions; I certainly wasn't fearful. I just thought that since yesterday's trade failed, this one would, too. I was wrong. Why didn't I take the trade?"

What failed Colin was not his emotions or misreading the market. What failed Colin was his thinking. Colin's mind entered a natural mental blind spot psychologists call the *recency effect*. The recency effect is a cognitive bias where our mind weighs the latest information with greater importance than other data when making decisions. In Colin's mind, yesterday's outcome weighed more heavily than today's "picture-perfect" criteria, leading him to shun the trade.

Many traders believe emotions are the most important aspect of trading psychology. This is only partially true. Feelings and emotions are certainly important. Traders cannot make reliable decisions without them. Strong emotions such as greed, anger, and especially fear can significantly influence trading and cause erratic trading behavior. However, emotions are not the only thing that can influence trading. Thoughts and the way we think also play a significant role. Sometimes, thoughts ignite strong emotions and thinking almost always amplifies them. At other times, as we see in Colin's case, emotions play little part in poor trading decisions. Less familiar to many traders is the role that our mind and our thinking plays in trading and the way we make trading decisions.

Our thinking can create mental blind spots that can shackle us, as the example with Colin shows, rendering technical skills useless at that moment. In fact, how we think and how we treat our thoughts are the most important aspects of trading psychology. A main objective of this book is to help you become more aware of your thoughts and how they directly influence your trading actions. Learning and applying skills related to cognitions described in this book may have the most decisive impact on our trading—they can be far more potent than some of the common things we try in dealing with emotions. Of course, this does not mean that emotions are unimportant and should be ignored. We discuss emotions starting in the next chapter. To begin, however, we focus on the natural constraints that arise from our thinking as one of the key aspects of trading psychology that traders need to become aware of and understand in order to trade well.

Thinking is integral to being human. It is so much a part of us that we usually don't think much about thinking. If we pause for a moment and observe our thoughts, however, we begin to become aware of the activity of our mind. This is a fascinating study. We soon realize that we have a near-constant, never-ending stream of thoughts. The mind is tirelessly commenting and telling us things. Unless you practice, you will find it impossible to quiet your mind and stop the flow of thoughts for all but a few seconds. Even with practice, quieting the mind for more than a few minutes before another thought involuntarily arises is elusive for most people. Two important characteristics of our minds thus emerge: thoughts are always with us and we do not have much control over them. This is essential data for traders.

Because we have experienced our mind's chatter every day for as long as we can remember, we are accustomed to it and rely on it heavily. We tend to accept whatever our mind tells us as an accurate reflection of reality. We rarely question or objectively evaluate our thoughts. Because thoughts are a natural part of us, accepting them seems natural, too, but in trading, this can be dangerous.

Part of the danger comes from natural limitations in our cognitive capabilities. There are certain mental boundaries that often constrain the way we think, distort the way we process information, and impact the way we make decisions that cause predictable errors in trading. These are our mental blind spots commonly referred to as cognitive biases and heuristics. The most important mental blind spots for traders include:

- The representativeness heuristic

- The recency effect

- Loss aversion

- Confirmation bias

- Base rate neglect

- The affect heuristic

- Hindsight bias

- The endowment effect

- Optimism bias

We discuss most of these mental blind spots in this chapter. Some—notably loss aversion and optimism bias—are covered in later chapters. Understanding these mental blind spots and becoming aware of them in one's own trading are crucial for the trader as they can directly affect trading performance and results.

■ Heuristics and Cognitive Biases

The term *heuristic* is just another word for mental shortcut. When faced with a complex or difficult decision, people often simplify their task by applying an abbreviated rule set to help problem-solve and make the decision. This streamlines the thinking chore into a more straightforward and manageable job. Heuristics shorten the decision-making time and reduce the mental load. Their use allows people to function efficiently and quickly without having to mentally process and make sense out of a large amount of data. These mental shortcuts are handy in many situations and produce reasonably accurate results much of the time. For an example, let's say we are planning a trip and need to budget gasoline expense for driving. To do this, we need to know how many miles can be driven on a tank of gas. One way to do this is to keep detailed records on gallons and mileage for each fill of the gas tank for the next six months and then calculate the average. It would produce an accurate figure of miles per tank of gas across many different driving conditions, which we can then use to calculate fuel costs. Alternatively, we can use a simple shortcut of setting the odometer to zero when the tank is next filled and apply the mileage gotten from that one tank of gas for our fuel cost projection. Will the shortcut be as accurate as gathering six month's worth of data? Probably not, but the simple approach produces a good enough result for our trip planning purposes. That's using a heuristic.

Heuristics are used all the time. When deciding to go into an unfamiliar restaurant, for example, we might use the restaurant's overall appearance in making our judgment. Rather than taking a survey of patrons' dining experiences as they exit, if the restaurant looks clean and inviting, and there are cars in the parking lot, we are apt to dine there. Note that an easier mental task is substituted for a harder one. This is a hallmark characteristic of heuristics. It's easier to assess the appearance of the restaurant than interview its patrons. Likewise, it is easier to calculate mileage from one tank of gas than to record and process mileage data over a six-month period for estimating driving expenses. Heuristics have value; they help us manage our world efficiently. Because they are effective and do have such value, we normally apply them as our default mode of thinking.

There are times, however, when heuristics and other abridged mental processes lead to significant errors and inconsistencies in our judgments. In their pioneering work on how we think and how we produce thinking errors, two psychologists—Nobel laureate Daniel Kahneman and Amos Tversky—found that when people make decisions under conditions of risk and uncertainty, they have a strong tendency to abandon careful rational analysis and, instead, apply heuristics and other cognitive short cuts. This often produces predictable errors and poor outcomes. Their research was in striking contrast to the conventional wisdom at the time it was published. This and subsequent work spawned a new discipline emphasizing psychology's influence on economic decision making now known as behavioral finance.

Kahneman and Tversky's research was followed by a long line of studies that demonstrate how natural limitations in our information processing—that is, how we observe, think, and problem-solve—automatically emerge in situations that involve the assessment of complex and often incomplete data and also entail risk and uncertainty in outcomes. The research is clear, robust, and their findings are significant for the trading world: in uncertain, risky conditions the application of heuristics and other cognitive biases in making decisions often results in significant errors and costly mistakes. Trading always involves risk. Trade outcomes are never certain, and traders confront complex and incomplete data in every trading judgment. When traders favor mentally efficient thinking shortcuts known to produce errors, they end up making poor trading decisions and these lead directly to poor trading results.

We saw this with Colin and his weighing of a recent trade outcome, which caused him to miss a sound trade. What makes it difficult for traders is that what works well in everyday life can lead to costly errors in our trading lives. Consider Jackie who has just moved into the city and now walks to work. Over the past two weeks she has enjoyed her walk in the warm, early morning sun. But yesterday, a cloud-burst drenched her and she arrived at the office sopping wet. Today, she carries an umbrella. This is an adaptive use of a recent experience. Contrast this with Colin's missed trade. Like Jackie, Colin also had an unpleasant experience in the form of a trading loss. The next day with the same type of trade setting up, Colin weighed yesterday's failed trade outcome—which has no bearing on today's trade and was irrelevant to his decision—as more significant than today's textbook trade setup because what happened yesterday was fresh in his mind. Jackie stays dry; Colin misses a good trade. Afterward, Colin could not understand why he didn't take a sound trade. This is the poignancy of using heuristics and cognitive biases in trading. Because we do use them so frequently in day-to-day decisions, it's natural that we readily bring heuristics and other cognitive biases into our trading. Because we also trust what our mind is telling us unquestioningly, we can be mentally blind to the serious trading mistakes we are making as we make them. It is crucial for all traders—from novice to the more experienced—to understand and become aware of these blind spots. We start with what is likely the most common trading heuristic called representativeness.

■ Representativeness

The *representativeness heuristic* means that we use a mental shortcut that looks for similarity between the current situation or event and its overall class as a way to judge probability. If an event is similar to our model or prototype, then we assume that the event has the same probabilities as the model. Representativeness occurs when something appears (or represents itself) to be likely, when, in fact, it may not be likely. An example from outside of trading will help clarify representativeness.

When buying a used car a buyer may look for dents, lift the hood, and kick the tires. If the engine looks clean, the car is shiny, and the tires look new, he may think, "This car has been maintained well." That's using the representativeness heuristic; however, mere appearance can be misleading. It is only by reviewing maintenance records and having the car checked out by a mechanic will the buyer be able to accurately assess the probability that this is, indeed, a well-maintained vehicle worth buying. Simply relying on appearance does not mean it is a sound car, even though it looks good. In our mind, the car represents itself as a well-maintained vehicle. Substituting the car's appearance for a thorough mechanical assessment is the cognitive error. In trading, representativeness is often seen in traders who scan the market action to see if it matches a prototypical chart pattern. For example, current market action might look to a trader like it is forming a bull flag, and he goes long. But that is like assessing only the car's appearance for its actual condition. If the chart formation is occurring after a lengthy trend, what appears to be a bull flag could instead be distribution. Simply matching market action to a chart pattern speaks only to pattern recognition. It does not speak at all to the probabilities of the next market direction.

It is very difficult for our minds to assess probabilities. Mentally, it is far easier to make a judgment that price action looks like a bull flag than it is to assess the probability that the market will act in a certain way or have a specific outcome. As we saw when evaluating the appeal of an unfamiliar restaurant or the condition of a used car, heuristics involve the substitution of an easier mental task for a more difficult one. We ask a question that is easy to answer: Does this look like a bull flag? The correct question is: What is the likely next move of the market? The easy answer to the easy question has us taking a long position. The correct question was never asked because it requires more involved thinking. The correct question may lead us to the conclusion that the market is overbought, has stalled at a higher time frame resistance level, and what initially looked like a bull flag is now seen as a market unable to rally farther and about to fall. We will use the following case example involving Zoe, a swing trader, to illustrate representativeness further.

Case Example: Zoe

Zoe was trading EZU, the Exchange Traded Fund for the MSCI European Monetary Union Index. She saw the weekly Bullish Engulfing Candle pattern in late June and went long. You can see what she had seen in Figure 1.1. She anticipated a continuation of the weekly uptrend, which looked strong to her. Zoe noted that every bullish engulfing pattern in this uptrend worked well. Thus, she expected a winning trade

FIGURE 1.1 Zoe's Weekly Chart Depicting an Uptrend
Source: TradeStation Technologies, Inc.

that would take price and her trading account to new highs. Shortly after taking the trade, however, she became despondent. Almost immediately, the market fell below her stop and she suffered a loss. Zoe couldn't understand why this happened. "Everything," she said, "looked perfect."

But everything wasn't perfect. Stepping up a time frame to the monthly chart, we see that this higher time period had recently produced a Dark Cloud Cover that caused this market to fall below the 2009 high just a few weeks before she entered her trade. Figure 1.2 depicts this vital monthly data. Zoe's mind didn't take this information into consideration.

Zoe focused only on the weekly chart with its bullish candle pattern. To her mind, the candlestick unquestionably appeared as another strong signal in the uptrend. Note that Zoe chose to answer the easy question: Is this a bullish engulfing pattern? Of course, the answer is yes. The more difficult and more important question—what

FIGURE 1.2 Higher Time Frame Dark Cloud Cover Pattern
Source: TradeStation Technologies, Inc.

is the likely next move of this market?—was never considered. Zoe committed the characteristic thinking of representativeness: she mistook appearance for probability and went no further than asking whether price matched a candle pattern. Remarkably, Zoe had no doubts about this trade. "I took one look at the chart and *I immediately knew this would be a good trade,*" she said. "I felt certain about it." She was so convinced and confident about what appeared to be represented in the weekly chart, she neglected the higher time frame information, and, of course, read the market incorrectly.

The bullish engulfing pattern had the appearance of a strong setup, but it occurred immediately after higher time period weakness. The *base rate* probability of the negative monthly price action trumps the odds of a weekly bullish setup. And, just because the bullish engulfing pattern was working recently in the uptrend does not guarantee it will continue to work. Again we see the recency effect extracting its toll on the trader. Recall that recency was the cognitive bias that caused Colin to miss a sound trade. When more weight is assigned to what happened most recently, errors in judgment increase. In trading, we tend to look at a lot of information: news, indicators, price action, morning calls, economic reports, newsletter recommendations, and the like. What tends to stick in our head is what occurred last and even what was looked at last. This can become overweighted in our decision process. In the ETF Zoe was trading, recent similar bullish engulfing patterns pushed the market higher. These preceding events were most salient in Zoe's mind and therefore weighted heavily.

You can see that it is easy to make these errors. The trade setups and price action look good, but are false. It is not that the market is trying to fool you, but that our minds frequently make quick, unstudied judgments by applying mental shortcuts that lead to errors and trading losses. Recall that Zoe said she "immediately knew this would be a good trade." She didn't carefully analyze the market. Her mind recognized the candlestick pattern, saw it had been working well in previous weeks, and applied a mental shortcut of assuming the current market action matched a choice trade setup when it did not. Zoe was affected by her mental blind spot.

Note that little strong emotional responses were involved here. Errors were made due to flaws in thinking; they were not driven as a reaction to fear or greed. She simply jumped to a conclusion without bothering to assess the full range of possibilities that a thorough market analysis would have revealed. Her mind locked onto the candle pattern and, in doing so, precluded any thought of further assessment. This is the representativeness heuristic in action. Had Zoe done the analysis, it would have told her that in this market context, the bullish candle pattern had low odds of working. Again, the base rate or statistical probability for this market context was neglected.

Keep in mind that cognitive heuristics and biases are not mental deficiencies. As we discussed earlier, these mental shortcuts are helpful and useful strategies in day-to-day decision making. They are efficient and usually work well. Because they do work well in many circumstances, we naturally rely on them and we tend to overuse them. Where they don't work well is under conditions of risk and uncertainty—precisely the characteristics of the trading environment. It is very difficult, however, to shift from something that is unconsciously used all the time to consciously overriding it. This is true for everyone and affects all traders from the novice to the experienced alike.

■ Intuitive and Deliberative Thinking

To help you understand the pervasive nature of our minds to almost automatically default to an error-prone mental shortcut, consider the two problems below. These questions come from cognitive psychologist Shane Frederick who studies heuristics and biases.[1] Frederick developed an enlightening test on how readily we apply mental shortcuts. Read each question and jot down your answers before reading on. Doing so will help give insight into an important psychological phenomenon highly relevant to your trading:

1. A bat and a ball cost $1.10 in total. The bat costs $1.00 more than the ball. How much does the ball cost? _____ cents
2. If it takes 5 machines to make 5 widgets in 5 minutes, how long would it take 100 machines to make 100 widgets? _____ minutes

Jot down your answers before reading on.

When answering these questions, the majority of people show a characteristic common in many problem-solving and trading errors: they jump to the first answer that comes to mind and spend little if any effort to assess whether or not they have arrived at the correct answer. In the first problem, was your answer 10 cents? Most people give this answer. The correct answer is 5 cents. The most common answer to the second question is 100 minutes, but again, this is incorrect. The correct response is 5 minutes.

In the ball and bat question, if the bat costs $1.00 more than the ball, then the ball could not cost 10 cents because then the bat would have to cost $1.10, which would have a total cost of $1.20. The ball costs 5 cents and the bat, costing $1.00 more than the ball, would have to cost $1.05. Combined, the bat and ball have a total cost of $1.10. In the second problem, since 5 widgets are made in 5 minutes by 5 machines, then it takes each machine 5 minutes to make one widget. Increasing the number of machines to 100 would produce 100 widgets over the same amount of time: 5 minutes. Take a moment to think these through if you need to.

If your answers were incorrect, don't feel badly. Most people answer incorrectly. In fact, when Frederick gave these same problems along with one similar problem to students from some of the most prestigious universities in the United States, including Princeton, Harvard, and the Massachusetts Institute of Technology, fewer than 50 percent solved all three problems correctly. It's less an issue of intelligence than it is an illustration of our natural limitations in thinking through complex problems.

In the research labs, cognitive psychologists Maggie Toplak, Richard West, and Keith Stanovich have shown that answers to Frederick's test are correlated with susceptibility to commit cognitive biases and errors. Incorrect answers on these mental problems indicate that a preference for using heuristics is likely to produce judgment errors when in situations involving uncertainty such as trading. When confronted with mildly challenging problems such as the ball and bat problem or whether or not the market is ripe for a trade, people often don't think deeply enough to arrive at the correct answer. Further, their shallow thinking keeps them from recognizing their error. This leaves them unaware that they are making *avoidable* mistakes. Zoe jumped to a trade decision and was unaware of her error. This has obvious and important relevance to trading.

Assuming you answered the ball and bat and widgets questions incorrectly, pause for a moment and think back to when you were answering the questions (before you knew the correct answers). In the first question, did 10 cents pop into your mind almost immediately? If it did enter your mind quickly, did you simply and almost automatically accept that answer as the correct answer to the problem without any further thought? The same query is relevant to the second question. Did 100 minutes jump into your mind and you felt comfortable with that answer, and so you settled on that? In both cases, once the answers came to you, were you satisfied with those answers and then quickly stopped trying to figure out the solutions? This is the experience of most people. Our minds seem to impulsively go to the erroneous answer and then look no further.

If you did answer the questions correctly, did the incorrect answers of 10 and 100 initially pop into your mind? Most people who do come to the right answers report that they at first came up with the incorrect answers of 10 and 100. The difference between those who solve the problems correctly and the majority who don't is that those who are correct suppress their initial answers and make a greater effort to think through the problem before settling on an answer. Incorrect responders simply accept the first answer that comes to them. This is exactly how heuristics work. Our minds accept the first plausible answer, and then quickly cease further deliberation. This is a mental blind spot. Notably, those who answer incorrectly typically feel that the questions were relatively easy, and it would seem that way because a mental shortcut was used and little energy was expended as they quickly came to an answer. Those who do answer correctly report that effort was required to come to the correct solutions. Maggie Toplak and her colleagues report that correct responders generally acknowledge that the questions were difficult and challenging.

Psychologists such as Daniel Kahneman who study cognition conceptualize our minds as having two parts or thinking systems. Kahneman calls these minds System 1 and System 2. We will be a little more descriptive and distinguish them as *intuitive mind* and *deliberative mind*. For most readers, it was your intuitive mind that came up with the (incorrect) answers of 10 cents and 100 minutes in the bat and ball and widgets problems above. Our intuitive minds are very quick in making judgments. They seem to operate almost automatically, if not impulsively. As many readers experienced in solving the problems above, little effort is expended when our intuitive minds are activated. We just quickly come to an answer. There is also little or no sense of voluntary control when our intuitive minds are managing our thought processes. It just happens naturally— which in trading with its risk and uncertainty can easily be a mental blind spot.

Our deliberative minds, in contrast, are distinctly different from our quick and impulsive intuitive minds. This part of the mind is active when we are thoughtfully absorbed in a problem or task. Deliberative mind is engaged when we are expending mental effort. Compared to intuitive mind, it works slowly and feels effortful. A sense of concentration, mental exertion, and choice are all associated with deliberative mind and not at all with intuitive mind.

Research by Kahneman and other cognitive scientists shows that intuitive mind automatically and effortlessly activates in response to things like:

- Determining which object is closer than another

- Calculating $2 + 2 =$ ___

- Completing common phrases such as "Curiosity killed the ___"

- Driving along a familiar road.

The response is automatic or nearly so; there is no conscious thinking involved. Contrast this with the level of concentration and effort needed to:

- Listen to a person speaking to you in a loud and noisy room

- Calculate $27 \times 93 =$ ___

- Drive an unfamiliar road with many turns

- Prepare a trading plan.

These mental tasks require mental deliberation and demand attention, sustained concentration, thought, and conscious reflection—all characteristics of deliberative mind.

You can see that intuitive mind is quick and essentially automatic in its response; it requires little thinking to come up with an answer. Deliberative mind is slow. Answers require effort and concentration. Intuitive mind activates with seeming ease, in part because we are born with certain perceptual abilities such as orienting to sudden sounds, recognizing objects, and avoiding threats. We can also become quick due to repeated practice (e.g., riding a bicycle or driving a car), and through prolonged exposure to cultural norms, social situations, and language such that we automatically know how to act in most social situations and can associate words with symbols and ideas and immediately understand what they mean, even if we haven't encountered them before. In trading, if we have studied chart patterns for a period of time, for example, it is our intuitive mind that quickly identifies a bull flag pattern.

However, it requires our deliberative mind to engage in the analysis as to whether or not that bull flag is in the right market context for a trade.

So why all this discussion about our two types of minds? Well, it turns out that understanding this two-part feature of our mind is vitally important for trading. Intuitive mind, quick and efficient, is exceptionally poor at determining probabilities, a key skill in trading. If it identifies a bull flag, it tells us to trade it. You might think then that our deliberative mind—which is good at assessing probabilities—would step in and curb the actions of intuitive mind. Not true. At best, our minds like to conserve energy and will employ deliberative mind only when necessary. At worst (and I tend to believe it is the worst), deliberative mind is lazy. This is Daniel Kahneman's considered view. Thinking is hard work, and at some level thinking is experienced by many as aversive. If there is a ready answer offered up by intuitive mind and the answer seems plausible, then the research shows that deliberative mind will tend to rely solely on intuitive mind and not question it. It takes the easy way out and avoids the uncomfortable experience of thinking hard. Think back to the widgets and bat and ball problems. Both of those tasks required the skills and abilities of deliberative mind, yet the vast majority of us give quick, intuitive answers without any serious consideration as to whether they were correct or not. In other words, in these tasks, deliberative mind simply accepted what intuitive mind told it, no further questions asked. Do you see how this characteristic of our mind can work against us in trading? Let's look at another case example and further our thought on this matter.

Case Example: Nathan

Nathan has developed reliable technical skills during the two years he has been a trader, but his results remain inconsistent. We'll take a look at one of Nathan's trading days, starting with his game plan for the day, a trade he took, and how his thinking—which included his misuse of the representativeness heuristic and his uncritical acceptance of what his intuitive mind told him in the heat of trading—caused trouble.

Each night, Nathan develops his game plan for the next day's trading. For this day, he saw from Figure 1.3 that both his higher time frame charts showed that the 10-Year U.S. Treasury futures market was weak. The daily chart had turned down at trend line resistance and the intraday chart was already in a downtrend. He decided that his game plan for the next day would be to sell the market short in the area marked E along the higher time frame intraday trend line at the right edge of the chart.

Early the next day, Nathan saw from Figure 1.4 that the market had made a new low at A, dipped under that low at B, and then held. After the market rallied to C, Nathan decided to go long at D. His thinking was that the selling had dried up at

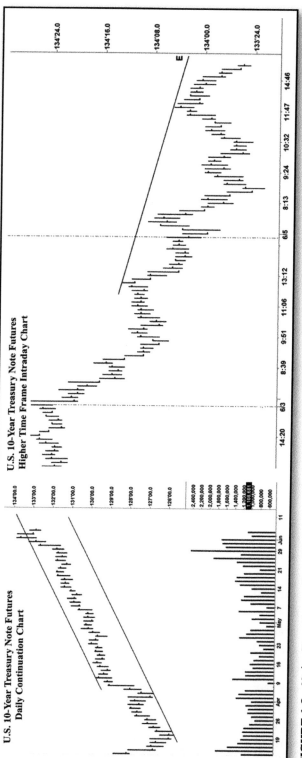

FIGURE 1.3 Higher Time Frames Show Weakness in 10-Year U.S. Treasury Futures

Source: TradeStation Technologies, Inc.

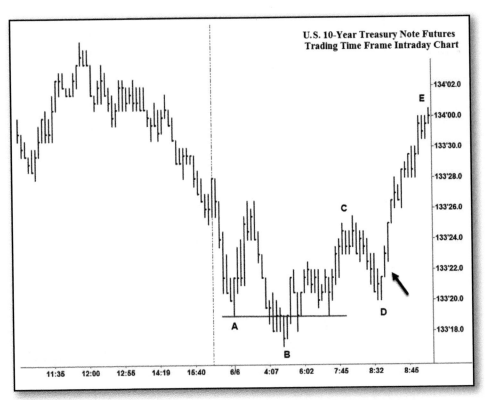

FIGURE 1.4 Nathan's Long Trade
Source: TradeStation Technologies, Inc.

this level, at least for the moment, and the market was showing some strength that morning. At D he told himself, "If the market begins to rally from here, I will go long." It did start to rally and he went long (at the arrow). The market then moved briskly higher.

His trade was a profitable one, and Nathan was happy. But then he ran into trouble. In his mind, the market had a strong response from holding the lows at A and B. "Clearly, there was aggressive buying on the rally [from D to E]. The market is very strong," he thought. Nathan decided to hold the trade. But holding the long trade was a poor decision. Figure 1.5 shows what happened. The profit made on his long trade was wiped out as the market quickly erased the morning rally.

How did this happen? Nathan explained it later that evening. "I was thinking at the time that it would be premature to exit such a good trade. I thought, 'Hey, I'm in a great trade and I don't want to cut a winning trade short.' I was feeling very good about my trade and I thought holding it was the right thing to do. I thought the market was obviously bullish and I should hold on."

FIGURE 1.5 Nathan's Loss Due to Representativeness
Source: TradeStation Technologies, Inc.

Nathan applied the representativeness heuristic, which led him to believe that the market was "obviously" bullish. Nathan jumped to the conclusion that the up move resembled strongly bullish behavior when, in reality, the market was not bullish. Similar to Zoe's candlestick pattern, mere bullish appearance does not necessarily mean the market is going higher. Nathan's intuitive mind mentally locked into the morning rally and its impression of strength. He was operating within a mental blind spot. Without further thought, he replaced his thorough nightly analysis with the easy question of: Did the market look bullish? Drawn to the salience of the morning rally, his intuitive mind was unable to detect that this was a mere façade in the larger downtrend. Although the base rate probability favored further downside movement, Nathan—as is typical with representativeness—took no notice of what was probable.

You might be asking how could this happen? After all, Nathan had developed a game plan to sell the market at E. How did that get ignored? Recall again the bat and ball and widgets problems above. Remember how quickly your mind came to the incorrect answer, and also, how swiftly and uncritically it was accepted? This is how our minds tend to operate when caught in a mental blind spot. Our intuitive mind swiftly develops a seemingly reasonable answer to a problem and our deliberative mind, rather than engaging in the effortful task of thinking through the problem, simply accepts what intuitive mind offers.

You might even say that there is a little mental sleight-of-hand being done by the mind. Intuitive mind can't really grapple with a question as complex as the probabilities of market direction. Deliberative mind is equipped to deal with the complexity of probabilities, but this is an involved question that takes mental effort to resolve. Instead of dealing with the difficult question, it gets replaced with a comparatively easy question, which then gets answered. According to Daniel Kahneman, this is a typical way intuitive mind operates. Nathan's intuitive mind asked, "Has the market rallied, moved up, and is it looking bullish?" The answer, of course, was yes. It did rally, price moved higher, and it did resemble bullishness. This made it easy for Nathan to believe that the market was bullish and led him to hold onto his long position. However, the more complex and appropriate question was, "Given the current position of the market, what is the probable direction of the market's next move?" That, of course, is a much more involved question requiring the use of Nathan's deliberative mind. Notice that this question was never asked; only the undemanding question, "Does the market look bullish?" was considered.

It may seem surprising that Nathan forgot all the work he had done the night before when he developed his game plan. He was interested in selling the market short at E. His deliberative mind worked this out after detailed consideration of the higher time frames, recent intraday trending, and other relevant market factors. This was a meticulous and thorough assessment that addressed the question of what the next probable move in the market would be and where it would likely take place. Rather than taking his long trade off at E and initiating the short position as he had planned, however, Nathan held onto his long. He committed a cognitive error and profit was returned to the market. Further, he forfeited all the profits he would have realized had he followed his plan to short at E because his intuitive mind took over. The quick rally stood out prominently, and in a very real sense, this one salient feature of market action captured his mind. We could say his mind was hijacked as he completely neglected his game plan and the short opportunity that had set up—a costly cognitive error!

Although Nathan recognized the weakness in his nightly analysis and also understood that a downtrending market will often see technical rallies, his intuitive mind simply and solely relied on the representativeness of the morning rally, ignoring the work he had done the night before. Kahneman refers to this as WYSIATI—What You See Is All There Is. It is a shorthand way of saying that the intuitive mind will focus on only a small, selective amount of information and confidently come to a decision. The information it considers is often incomplete, but it is nevertheless viewed as the only information relevant from which a judgment is then made. What is presently before the intuitive mind is all there is. Other important data—even highly relevant data like the detailed work done the night before—can be disregarded or unnoticed. Out of sight, out of mind.

Your intuitive mind has no difficulty stepping right up and voicing its judgment based on what it sees. This produces errors because this part of our mind is limited in what it can do. Trading decisions require a synthesizing of various pieces of market information that often are contradictory. And, trading decisions always involve probabilities. Intuitive mind cannot synthesize data or deal with probabilities. This type of thinking is the province of deliberative mind. But as Nathan experienced, deliberative mind is difficult to engage and it often acquiesces to intuitive judgments.

Nathan's mind was also highly influenced by other psychological factors. Once again, the recency effect showed its hand here. The most recent bullish price action was emphasized over both the fact that rallies tend to end quickly in a downtrend and the fact that price was coming to a known supply level. Also, Nathan's euphoric feelings in making a good trade decision early in the day producing quick profit over-shadowed his perception of reality. He felt delighted and even a little triumphant that he had just called the market correctly and was in profit. When we feel good about something, we tend to let down our guard. At these times, intuitive mind is especially free to reign. We aren't as critical or as analytical as when our mood is neutral or slightly negative. When feeling upbeat, we tend to expect positive results to continue. This is known as the *affect heuristic*, and it was evident in Nathan's decision to "let the trade run."

The representativeness heuristic and its associated biases are very common in traders. In every case, the trader misreads the features of the market as something authentic when it is not. This occurs because an easy task is substituted for a more difficult one. As we have seen in the case examples, in trading this often involves identifying a chart pattern, indicator, or price action as all that is necessary to make a trading decision because it resembles a prototype when a more deliberate analysis is needed. At the same time, what is most probable for the market—that is, the base rate—is neglected. Selected data that is usually conspicuous precludes other relevant data from consideration (WYSIATI) and recent events can be more heavily weighted in our decision making than is warranted. And, when things are going well and we feel good, we may let our vigilance slide, something we don't want to do when trading the markets.

Representativeness can arise in nonobvious ways. Michael Cooper, professor at the University of Utah, Eccles School of Business, has done some fascinating studies on representativeness. For example, during the frothy bull market leading into the twenty-first century, the Internet was new and exciting. Cooper and his colleagues show that companies that announced name changes during this period by adding "dot-com" to their corporate monikers saw their stock price outpace other stocks by a striking margin. Traders and investors apparently believed that the mere name of a stock was representative of sound management, a strong market share, sufficient capitalization, excellence in business planning, and a profitable and enduring line of products or services. Interestingly, Cooper continued this line of research after the dot-com stock market bubble burst. His research team looked at stocks that then removed dot-com from their names and found exceptionally high returns during the two-month period after the name change, showing again how representativeness can easily influence investor and trader behavior.

■ More Heuristics and Cognitive Biases

The representativeness heuristic is likely the most prevalent heuristic used by traders. There are many other heuristics and cognitive biases that have been identified by psychologists. Wikipedia, for example, lists over ninety biases related to judgment and decision making (there are also biases that operate specifically in social situations and others that are relevant in memory recall). You could drive yourself crazy if you tried to learn all of the biases and heuristics psychologists have discovered. Fortunately, for trading this isn't necessary. It is important, however, that you understand the more common ones and how they can undermine your trading. I highlight the ones most relevant to trading here with a few reserved for coverage in later chapters.

Confirmation Bias

Once an assumption is made, people tend to seek confirmation of their assumption, rather than look to disprove it. Thus, instead of looking for contradictory data—information that would call into question a trading hypothesis, for example, we have a natural tendency to seek out and overweight data that would be consistent with and supportive of our view. We have a strong need to be right and tend to look to confirm what we already know or believe. This is known as *confirmation bias*; it can be an important source of difficulty in trading.

A technical trader who uses the Stochastic Index as a major indicator to assess overbought/oversold conditions when considering taking a trade would be applying confirmation bias when she decides to also check the Commodity Channel Index, "just to be sure." Both indices measure essentially similar characteristics in price action and give the trader the same information. Not only is the trader basing her decision on methods that are correlated, she could fall into the trap of thinking that since both indicators are signaling, there is greater strength to the signal and it must, therefore, be a very good trade. This may promote unwarranted overconfidence and lead to unjustifiable actions such as increasing trade size or staying with a trade too long—two potentially costly judgment errors.

Focusing only on confirming data can also lead to greater than planned losses when in a trade and market action contradicts the position. In this common instance, the trader remains blind to the threat of loss because he continues to focus on and overestimate the indications that endorse keeping the trade. Thus, things like minor price action that, in isolation, appear positive to the trade are over weighted and used to confirm the original trade idea now under water. Significant negative price action that has emerged since the trade was taken is overlooked or ignored. In these instances, trades end by stops, if placed, rather than by an early exit prompted by objective assessment of the unfolding market. What is often the case when confirmation bias is present, however, is that stops are not placed and the trade exit occurs when the positive features of the trade are completely shredded and further pain of loss becomes too great to bear.

Legendary trader George Soros has commented that a trader's ability to sift through the data and search for disconfirming information is behavior that is rational and profitable. Searching for disconfirming data, however, is not common. It runs counter to our nature. Edward Russo and Paul Schoemaker, experts in judgment and decision making, suggest that confirmation bias acts as a type of psychological reinforcement. When we find confirming indications, it says we are right, and this strokes the ego; we feel good. You can see how intuitive mind would favor data that provides a quick and easy confirmation of a trade idea or market bias. Attaching the emotional reinforcement of being right makes it difficult to rise above this bias. Seeking, finding, and accepting disconfirming evidence is saying we are wrong. This is not natural for most of us. It also requires the active engagement of deliberative mind, which we have already experienced is not easy to do. No wonder Soros categorizes the ability to search for disconfirming information as rare.

The Recency Effect

We discussed the recency effect earlier. Because it can be so influential in trading, however, it is worth expanding our discussion of the recency effect. Recency bias occurs from our tendency to weigh the latest events more heavily than other data points even though other data may be equally or more important. What just happened lingers fresh in our minds and, thus, is more memorable than what occurred earlier. Mentally assigning more weight to recent events consequently influences our expectations of what will happen in the future.

Recency bias can affect trader behavior in a number of ways. As we saw with Nathan, traders can be susceptible to weighing recent market movement most heavily in their prediction of how the market will unfold in the future. Similarly, as we saw with Zoe, if a trade setup has just produced a successful trade and sets up again, a trader is likely to have greater confidence in the setup—more than its statistical track record would warrant. In contrast, if a trade setup has just produced a losing trade, many traders find it difficult to enter that setup again, especially when it sets up soon after the loss. Colin passed on such a trade setup.

In both winning and losing trades, the trader's mind can be overly influenced by the recent experience. It is as if the trader is thinking that the recent outcome of Trade A will directly affect the outcome of future Trade B. We know, or should know, that this isn't true. Each trade is independent of every other trade. Trade A does not influence Trade B, yet we act as if there is a relationship because of this cognitive error. Trader behavior becomes a function of the recency effect—a mental blind spot.

When first looking at a chart, the eyes of novice traders (and even many experienced traders) will rivet on the chart's right edge. They see the last few price bars and are quick to make a judgment about future market direction based on this limited information. The intuitive mind likes this approach. A few data points are selected, they are rapidly evaluated, and a decision is made. But this is also weighing the most recent market action as the only thing that matters in making a trading assessment. Without taking into account other background conditions and overall market context, the trader runs the real risk of making a trading decision based on random information. The recency effect has us neglecting market context and background data. What we pay attention to is determined by its newness, not by its relevance.

It's not just the recent things outside of ourselves like the market or our trade setups that we overweight, we can also overweight our trading performance. If we are trading well and string a few successful trades in a row or have an outsized gain, we run the risk of allowing this recent experience to influence our next trading actions. The tendency is to think we are on a hot streak or somehow our skills and abilities have rapidly improved or we are just reading the market better than others. This puts us at risk of committing several unforced trading errors such as increasing position size, overtrading, or entering marginally qualified trades. The affect heuristic—lowering our guard because we feel good—can reinforce and amplify recent positive performance. Overweighting recent performance can influence our current attitude and behavior, often leading us to act outside the bounds of our trading plan or, more generally, act outside the bounds of rational trading.

And, it's not just winning performances that can get overweighed; traders just as readily overweight poor performances, too. Recent poor performance can lead a trader to withdraw from the market in order to avoid the expectation of further poor performance, or they may do the opposite and double down with increased position size or take on additional trades in an effort to recoup what had been lost. Either way, the important point is that recent events or actions are judged as overly important and directly influence our next actions. This often leads to erratic trading behavior and increases the odds of committing unforced trading errors and producing unnecessary losses.

Hindsight Bias

Looking back is always with 20-20 vision. *Hindsight bias* is sometimes called the "I-knew-it-all-along effect," suggesting that people view events after they happened as more predictable than they were before they occurred. The benefit of now having the data influences how they recollect their initial view of the event. Judgment and decision-making researchers Neal Roese and Kathleen Vohs note in a review of the scientific literature of this well-studied mental blind spot that hindsight bias involves three levels of cognitive error: (1) flawed memories of one's earlier opinion or forecast making it seem as if the person predicted the outcome when, in reality, they did not predict it; (2) belief that the outcome was certain to happen and had to happen in the way that it did; and (3) that the outcome was foreseeable and knowable ahead of time.

In succumbing to hindsight bias, we tend to selectively recall only certain information that validates what we now know to be true and then create a story about it to make sense out of the event as we attempt to explain it to ourselves. If this story is relatively easy to construct it then seems that this is the way it had to occur and, therefore, the outcome must have been foreseeable. Again, as we have seen earlier with other cognitive errors, only certain, selected information is considered and our mind looks to take the easy route and substitute a story about the event that now seems persuasive rather than carefully considering all the available data and working through that data methodically to understand why the event occurred.

We often look at a market and will be able to make arguments why it might rally and also why it might react. Ambiguity is a frequent part of the trading game. When the market rallies, traders affected by hindsight bias will look back with seeming 20-20 vision. They will mentally set aside the ambiguity they experienced at the time, selectively cull information that supported the rally, and weave together a story of market bullishness, with thoughts and feelings that say, "I knew it all along."

Two significant consequences can arise from hindsight bias, as described by Roese and Vohs. The first is that hindsight bias can stimulate feelings of regret. Almost always, regret will be accompanied by thoughts of "I should have seen X" or "I could have done Y." If the trader is now thinking because of hindsight bias that they *should* have caught a strong move, they risk feeling bad that they missed profits. Worse, they may try to make up for it by now taking a marginal trade because they feel a self-imposed pressure from a faulty mental appraisal of what occurred.

The second major consequence of hindsight bias is that it prevents learning. As Roese and Vohs note, "If you feel like you knew it all along, it means you won't stop to examine why something really happened." For traders wanting to develop mastery and expertise, this is a significant roadblock to self-improvement and self-development. If we think the reasons a market moved were obvious, we won't bother spending the mental effort to review and study the move to understand why it occurred the way it did. This false belief can undermine our skills and abilities as traders. When a similar event reoccurs in the future, we are unprepared and likely misinformed. This, of course, can continue to adversely affect our trading.

■ Endowment Effect

A private stock investor acquired a long position in Apple, Inc. at an average price of about $350 per share. His personal research projected a target share price estimate of $750, based on what he thought revenue, profits, and other considerations would be in the near future. He was also enthralled with Apple's iPhone and iPad, and bought the latest versions. In September 2012, AAPL reached an all-time share price high of $705 before falling precipitously. This investor was also technically savvy and could see that the stock had become parabolic on the run up to new highs—an excellent technical reason to close at least a portion of the trade, if not all of it. This investor chose to hold his trade, however, despite the fact that he had doubled his investment and the technicals indicated it was now overbought. He said, "This stock will go to $750 or higher. I am not selling it for anything less." AAPL fell below $425. A year later the investor was still holding the position and still waiting for a $750 share price. This is an example of the endowment effect, another mental blind spot in which traders can become ensnared.

This cognitive bias is the opposite of cutting a winning trade short. Traders influenced by the endowment effect overvalue the stock, commodity futures, or currency contract that they already own, seeking a significantly higher price than if they did not own it and often a price well beyond fair market value. Mere ownership affects perceived value. They will become more emotionally attached the more they think about the things they like about it. Thinking about how much you like the Apple products (e.g., iPhone, iPad, Mac) and their features, for example, would tend to enhance the endowment effect. Thinking objectively about the stock (e.g., P/E ratio, earnings growth, price-to-book, technical condition) will help to minimize it.

As science becomes more advanced, we are learning that some mental blind spots are a part of our genetic make-up. Endowment offers a good example. Evolution has made us sensitive to scarcity, making us reluctant to give up what we already have, as there is risk in not having the object in the future when it might be needed. A team of scientists, led by Stamford professor of psychology and neuroscience Brian Knutson, has shown that a specific brain area, the anterior insula, will activate when vulnerable to the endowment effect. This brain region is associated with physical pain and the emotion of disgust, emphasizing that it is painful to give up or lose something of value. Consequently, we assign a higher value to it.

Turning a losing day trade into a long-term trade can begin with the endowment effect when the trader is unwilling to sell out because she believes it has greater value. When it doesn't meet the desired price level and the belief of higher value imprisons the trader's mind, the trader may continue to hold the position turning it into a longer-term trade.

■ What Traders Can Do

We include in this chapter short case examples from Colin, Zoe, and Nathan. Each committed unforced mental errors that led to poor trading actions and results. Each trader believed they were making correct decisions as they made them. The judgment mistakes made were costly. Each trader did not understand why they made the mistake they made. The three case examples reflect the experience of many traders.

It is very easy to make cognitive errors in trading. At the time they are being made, we are usually unaware that we are making them. Again, this is due to the ease and efficiency cognitive shortcuts bring in everyday life. What works in familiar situations is naturally brought into the trading environment, but trading is the kind of environment in which they are most likely to fail. The trader is then left wondering why. Cognitive shortcuts (heuristics) are natural mental blind spots that reveal themselves in the thinking traps and mental shortcuts discussed in this chapter. These are as much a part of trading psychology as emotions. As we will learn, trading psychology is more about understanding how our minds tend to work than controlling emotions. That is why I introduce this topic at the beginning of the book: to help traders of all levels begin to recognize that our thinking—and not just our emotions—is a vital aspect of successful trading. Understanding how our minds work may be more important to the more experienced trader who struggles less with emotions yet still finds consistency elusive. For the novice trader, understanding these blind spots and working to overcome them will help keep errors down. This along with development of other trading skills can build confidence and relieve the aspiring trader from some of the toxic emotional pitfalls that so many traders have experienced and suffered. Knowing and understanding the mental blind spots is the first step toward dealing with them. We conclude this chapter with some suggestions on steps traders can take to address their mental blind spots.

Because cognitive biases are mental blind spots, it takes special effort to avoid falling into their traps. Often, we realize our errors after the fact and it is too late. One important tool in making sound decisions is developing the mental skill of mindfulness. We discuss mindfulness in detail in later sections of this book, so I touch on it only briefly here. Mindfulness will help keep the trader centered and focused on the process of trading, which will significantly help her or him be aware of the decisions being made as they are being made and help avoid the mental blind spots discussed here. When we employ heuristics and other biases, we override the trading process in favor of mental shortcuts that provide mental effortlessness. Engaging deliberative mind takes work, and often we find ourselves accepting intuitive solutions to avoid the mental calculus needed to make carefully considered decisions. Mindfulness cultivates a mental space that can help us choose to expend the right effort rather than accept a beeline to a trading error.

In judgment situations where representativeness commonly appears—as in trading, Wesleyan University psychologist Scott Plous encourages decision makers to keep base rates firmly in mind. Many of the cognitive errors we can make in trading relate to ignoring statistics. In this regard, it is wise to know your personal metrics for all of your individual trade setups. This would include basic win-loss ratios as well as expectancy for each setup. Having these statistics at hand will help you avoid making important trading decisions based on one or two salient features of the market and remind you that each trade has a set of odds. Understanding trade setup base rates is useful in rising above representativeness and other biases, including the recency effect. If you are feeling reluctant to take a trade because you have had three losing trade events in a row, knowing that your trade setup has a win rate of 65 percent can help you remember that you are trading the setup's odds, and what it did the last time you took it is within the norms of its base rate and not a reason to avoid trading it when it next shows up.

Also important is to have a well-defined trade setup that includes the market conditions under which the trade works best. This will not only serve to remind you to pay attention to crucial background elements, it will also serve to filter your trade setups so that you take only those with the best background conditions for that setup. In this regard, you verify for yourself that you are taking only the choicest trades. This kind of qualifying criterion will not only help you avoid decision-making errors in trade selection, but it will also serve to increase your trade setup odds and expectancies.

To avoid distortion and bias in what you see in the charts, Russo and Schoemaker recommend that you deliberately ask appropriate disconfirming questions. This is useful for any cognitive bias and it is especially helpful in counterbalancing our strong tendency toward confirmation bias. For example, if the market is rallying and demand or buyers seem to be in control and you are looking for a long trade, it would be prudent to also ask yourself about supply. You might ask, for example, whether the last pullback showed lighter volume and narrower price bar ranges than the last rally and whether your key indicators are maintaining a bullish tone as the market pulls back. You are looking to disconfirm the presence of strong selling as you are about to take a long trade. When the market pulls back on light volume and lower overall activity and indicators fail to bend down, it shows supply is not dominant.

You can also test the alternative trade to the one you wish to take. Staying with the long trade example, you would look for evidence that a short trade was in order. You weigh this analysis against the analysis done for the long trade and assess which is the more compelling choice. At the very least if you are thorough and objective, you will identify anything overlooked. You will know whether your trade is a choice opportunity or not. This can be useful in more ambiguous trading situations and will also be of help with hindsight bias. It will pay you great dividends to develop a standard set of disconfirming questions for each trade setup you can routinely ask or by assessing its alternative before taking any trade. By doing one or both, you are not only actively working against confirmation bias; you are also actively engaging your deliberative mind.

Traders who use mathematic indicators in their analysis are well-advised to avoid auto-correlation. Multiple indicators can be useful, but not when they all measure the same thing. Make sure that the indicators that you do use are tapping into different market dimensions; otherwise you are committing confirmation bias. John Bollinger in his book, *Bollinger on Bollinger Bands*, provides a thorough discussion on multicolinearity among technical indicators and how to avoid it.

Paying attention to base rates, being clear on the best overall market conditions for your trades, and asking disconfirming questions or conducting alternative trade analyses are all designed to help sidestep the minefield of cognitive errors that our minds seem so willing to enter. Table 1.1 summarizes the cognitive errors covered in this chapter and some suggested tactics to counter their effects. The idea is to recognize that thinking errors are likely to occur in trading, to hold yourself back from accepting the first idea that comes to mind, and take specific steps to engage

TABLE 1.1   Common Cognitive Heuristics and Biases: Descriptions and Suggestions

Heuristic/Bias	Description	Suggestions
Representativeness Heuristic	Assuming an event is an accurate representation of a class (e.g., assuming a chart pattern represents a true directional play). Especially common in trading.	Pay close attention to the base rate of a trade setup. Be aware of the overall market context. Engage your deliberative mind before coming to a conclusion.
Recency Effect	Disproportionate overweighting of recent trading patterns or events and expecting them to continue into the future.	Make a special effort to look beyond recent events.
Affect Heuristic	Positive feelings promoting incautious and careless trading.	Use optimistic emotions as a signal to step back and engage deliberative mind.
Confirmation Bias	Using additional similar or comparable information to validate a preconceived trading action or idea.	Actively look for contrary indications and weigh against confirming indications.
Base Rate Neglect	Tendency to ignore trade probabilities in favor of representativeness, recency, salient features, and other nonprobabilistic reasoning.	Keep good records of all trades and generate individual metrics for each setup.
Hindsight Bias	Tendency to see past events as predictable.	Qualify trades and events by an objective assessment of features and attributes. Seek to understand why a market event happened.
Endowment Effect	Tendency to overvalue what is already owned. Focusing on associated features can amplify perceived value.	Pay attention to objective assessment data. Have objective profit target.

your deliberative mind. This is much easier said than done. All too often our intuitive mind presents what appears to be an attractive solution, does so effortlessly, and, without really being aware of it, we willingly (and confidently) accept the easy solution. Even Daniel Kahneman—perhaps *the* world's expert in this field—finds it difficult to avoid the cognitive illusions and traps that he has studied, researched, and defined for 40 years!

The best antidote to reduce judgment errors due to cognitive heuristics and biases according to Daniel Kahneman and his colleague Gary Klein is through the development of expertise. Even traders who are true masters and appear to rely on highly refined intuition in reading the markets and making trades are applying hard-won trading and chart-reading skills. The more skilled one becomes at reading markets and managing trades under varying market conditions, the fewer the trading errors due to heuristics and biases, and, of course, the better the trading results. This requires a protracted period of experience in which special forms of practice are carried out with clear, immediate feedback on performance. For a technical trader, this means a lengthy period of training through simulation or paper trading and a gradual immersion into actual trading so that trading knowledge, skills, and abilities are acquired, developed, and consolidated. In Part 3 of this book, we cover a proven approach for personal development and improvement as a trader, and in Chapter 11 we examine how expertise and mastery is developed through the psychological science of deliberate practice and how to specifically apply it to your training and expert skill acquisition and development.

■ Note

1. Shane Frederick, "Cognitive Reflection and Decision Making," *Journal of Economic Perspectives 19* (2005): 27.

CHAPTER 2

Strong Emotions in Trading

If you picked up this book and are reading it, it is very likely that you have experienced strong emotions in your trading and have struggled with them. It is also very likely that these strong feelings have caused erratic trading actions. You have had losses or missed profits because you acted too soon, acted inappropriately, or failed to act at all. Strong emotions have affected your trading.

You may have put extra effort into your trading to try to overcome this problem, learning more about technical analysis and maybe trading psychology. But that doesn't seem to matter. When you get into a trade you almost immediately feel your nerves rise. Your attention rivets onto price action; you feel like you are living or dying on every tick. Soon, your heart is racing and your muscles become tense. Your discomfort is palpable. If your trade is in a little profit, your mind is urging you to get out now—at least you will have a profit, it says. Certainly, you cannot have a loss. You might struggle a little longer and try to hold onto the trade, but your mind becomes insistent: "Get out NOW!" And, you do.

You feel relief. Whew! All that tension is over. And, you made a small profit. The relief feels good. Then, a few minutes later the market takes off and runs several points in your direction. A sizable profit was forfeited because you were mentally and emotionally hijacked. How many times have you repeated this or similar experiences? You promise yourself you will change but fail to follow through with your plan. Fear, or another strong emotion, gets the better of you—every time. You wonder if there is a better way.

Yes, there is a better way. The first step in learning how to deal with and overcome the erratic trading behavior caused by strong emotions is to help you bring clarity to your experiences so that you understand them on a deeper level than you do now. Let's get started.

Coping with fear and anxiety is a significant challenge for many traders. Even among those traders who say they don't struggle too much with fear or anxiety when trading, virtually everyone is interested in developing more confidence and reducing the trading-related fear and stress that they do experience.

Stocks, Futures and Options Magazine polled its retail trading readership on emotions in trading. The magazine asked a straightforward question: Which emotion is the toughest for you to control when trading? It listed fear, greed, and hope as possible responses. As Figure 2.1 shows, the response was revealing. Traders overwhelmingly endorsed fear as the most difficult emotion to control when trading. It was cited about twice as frequently as either greed or hope. Fear is a very common and frequent experience among traders.

Even successful traders with years of experience say they are never completely comfortable in making and managing trades. Tim Bourquin interviewed over 200 successful traders and distilled what he learned into common habits most traders follow that lead to success in trading. One surprising finding was that all successful traders came to realize that being uncomfortable when trading is okay. The traders he interviewed—some with over 20 years of trading experience—were "never really all that comfortable in their trading chair." They still had doubts, still had worries, and still experienced anxiety and fear. They felt the stress of trading and yet found that they could still make good, profitable decisions while feeling uncomfortable. Although these successful traders learned to "get comfortable with their discomfort,"

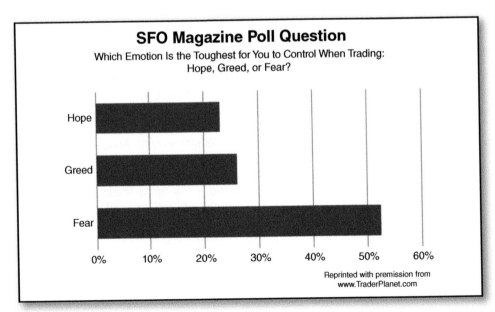

FIGURE 2.1 *SFO* Magazine Reader Poll on Emotions

Source: Stocks, Futures and Options Magazine 7, no. 8 (August 2008): 10.

the point is that they all experienced discomfort in the form of worry, doubt, and sometimes fear. The habit they created for themselves was not to try and get rid of fear and discomfort, but to keep fear and discomfort from disrupting their market judgments and trading decisions.

What is striking to learn from Bourquin's interviews is that successful traders eventually come to accept that trading will never be a totally comfortable pursuit. Because trading involves information that is incomplete and trade situations that are unique each time they arise, there is always a level of uncertainty and, thus, there will always be a level of psychological discomfort in taking and managing a trade. Over time and with experience, the discomfort diminishes, but as Tim found, even after 20 years of trading, it still arises. Tim's successful traders learned to cope with the discomfort, and so can you. This book offers useful techniques in this regard. Despite the useful techniques, it is crucial to understand that we can't really ever get rid of the fear and anxiety. It's a part of being human, and certainly very much a part of both life and trading. Even though conventional trading wisdom suggests otherwise, getting rid of fear and anxiety is really not possible, as Tim Bourquin's 200 successful traders found out on their own.

If you experience fear, stress, and anxiety when trading, understand that you are certainly not alone. Virtually every trader experiences these strong emotions. When a trader seeks help in developing their mental skills, it almost always involves dealing with fear and anxiety. Fear is the most common complaint seen in traders, and one of the most common issues that holds traders back from becoming successful in their trading. Two case examples from traders I have worked with can help give you a sense of the limitations that fear and anxiety can produce.

> Jennifer is a day trader with solid technical skills. Over the four years she has been trading, she has seen her equity curve begin to grow, having had periods of good profitability, especially during the past year. This is in contrast with the first two years of her trading where she experienced some sizable drawdowns. Because she is seeing greater profitability in her more recent trading, she wants to increase her position size. This is appropriate given her positive track record. However, when she steps up her position size, worry and fear seem to hijack her normal trading abilities.
>
> When trading a larger position, Jennifer becomes concerned that she might be missing an important technical consideration and she will suffer a loss. With larger trade size, she foresees larger losses. She recalls the pain of her early trading days from the drawdowns she experienced. Not wanting to have this occur again, she becomes hypervigilant of every tick of price after she has entered the market with larger size. She feels good, although "nervous" as price goes in

her direction, but becomes downright panicky when price reverses a little. "Although I want to trade bigger, I'm really, really afraid of having a big loss," she explains. "I don't want to live through another big drawdown. That would just be too hard for me." Her journal records show that she has been doing two things contrary to what she aspires to achieve: she cuts her winning trades short and, at times, she decides not to increase her trade size and instead trades small. She is struggling with her mind and what her mind is telling her about trading with larger size and the drawdown it could produce. Her recent trading performance reflects this struggle, despite her sound technical trading skills and abilities.

Marko has not been trading for very long. He says he "got bitten by the trading bug," and jumped in with both feet after attending a weekend seminar and reading a few trading books. Within seven months he wiped out a respectable trading account. He was devastated. He recognized that he "made every mistake in the book, trying to make a ton of money quickly." More importantly and to his credit, he also recognized that he didn't have sufficient technical skills or money management knowledge to be able to trade with competence.

He stopped trading and spent the next year learning to trade. He studied money management and developed solid procedures to protect his capital. He also spent months developing a sound trading plan and then traded it via simulation. Marko diligently kept records of every trade he took in simulation, and his records showed clear progress and improvement in chart reading, trade execution, and trade management. At the end of a year he felt ready to trade a real account again. When he went to put on his first trade, however, fear overwhelmed him. Doubts and worry about the outcome of the trade and remembrances of past losses prevented him from taking it. This occurred repeatedly. He identified valid trade setups—and many worked out profitably, but he was too fearful to pull the trigger.

Although Jennifer and Marko possess different levels of knowledge, skill, and ability, both experience similar emotions and both have similar responses. Fear and anxiety directly affect their trading behavior. The more experienced Jenifer wants to trade larger, but her fear is preventing her from going to the next level in her trading, despite the fact that she has a good track record and the requisite trading skills and abilities. Marko, a novice to trading, just wants to make a trade. It is hard to understand why he is unable to initiate a trade despite all the work he has done to learn the craft. Both are frustrated, both feel bad about their situations, and both are beginning doubt themselves.

We can see that fear and anxiety are not just experienced as feelings. Fear clearly affects trading behavior. For both Jennifer and Marko, their behaviors become narrowed and limited. Rather than seeing options and a range of choices, their actions are confined to trading small, cutting trades short, and standing aside. It is as if they are somehow imprisoned, limited to doing the same thing over and over, even though it isn't working for either of them. Their fear and anxiety about loss directly restricts their trading choices. As with many traders hindered by fear and anxiety, Jennifer and Marko find themselves involuntarily confined to erratic trading behavior: winning trades are exited prematurely, position size remains small, and valid trade setups are passed over.

It is worthwhile to note that scientists make a distinction between fear and anxiety. Fear is a response to an actual threatening event. For example, if we are in a city walking along a darkened street and confront a man with a knife in his hand, we experience fear. If a week later we are walking again at night along a similar street and are thinking that a dangerous man might confront us, we are experiencing anxiety. We have basically the same reaction (our brains do not distinguish between real and imagined in this regard), but the stress response is due to our imagining that someone could confront us, not that someone actually is confronting us. Most of the time in trading we are anticipating the threat of a loss. We are therefore experiencing anxiety, which induces a stress response. Although it is more accurate to say we experience anxiety, we will use fear and anxiety interchangeably. Just keep in mind that our fear in trading—however real it may feel—is mostly coming from our mind.

Fear arises in a few different forms for traders. Sometimes it is inconsequential; at other times it seems overwhelming. It is my experience that erratic trading and the vast majority of unforced trading errors arising from our emotions are due to fear or anxiety in one form or another (note well, unforced trading errors can also come from limitations in our thinking, as discussed in Chapter 1, as well as from a lack of trading skill). Moreover, virtually every trader is hindered to some degree by fear and anxiety in their trading. For these reasons, most of our discussion of strong emotions will center on fear. The term 'unforced trading error' refers to a preventable trading error caused by an action that is under the control of the trader. Jumping into a trade because the market suddenly looks as if it is about to take off only to find that the market reverses just as quickly and stops the trade out for a loss is an example of an unforced trading error. The impulsive trade was entirely under the control of the trader and, therefore, preventable or unforced. When a trader takes a trade that meets the standards of her trading plan and risk criteria, even if the trade is stopped out, the trader did not make a trading error. Taking an impulsive, unplanned trade that has no edge, in contrast, is an unforced error even when the trade produces a profit. Although other emotions can cause erratic trading and unforced errors, more often than not fear is the driving force.

■ Forms of Fear

Let's start to clarify fear and how it can drive our trading actions. This understanding will help us not only get a handle on the form of fear we are most vulnerable to, but the clarity will also help us identify when that fear is just beginning to occur. If we are able to identify fear as it begins to arise, with some practice, we can choose to take effective steps toward what is most important to us in our trading early on, before we become overwhelmed by emotion. This way we can begin to expand our choices and act in a way that is best for the trade, rather than being limited to making erratic, unskilled actions.

Trader and trading psychology author Mark Douglas identifies four principal trading fears. His breakdown is a useful way to categorize fear in trading. We will use Mark's categories and take them a step further by relating these categories to mental activity and trading actions. By doing this, we will clarify the various forms of fear by their essential elements, which can be helpful in your own dealings with this strong emotion. Knowing clearly what we are dealing with is always our starting point. The four fears are: being wrong, losing money, missing out, and leaving money on the table.

Being Wrong

The fear of being wrong may be the biggest trading fear. No one likes to be wrong. It pulls our ego in. If you make it a point to observe being wrong in your day-to-day life, you will hear people making excuses all the time to sidestep taking personal responsibility for mistakes, even insignificant ones. We all like to view ourselves favorably, and when we are wrong it hurts. Trading is no different.

Many times, traders will admit that being wrong is one of the toughest fears for them to overcome. They can imagine in their mind's eye what their spouses, trading friends, or other significant people in their lives would think of them when they make a losing trade and lose money. Many traders have a hard time accepting mistakes and being wrong about the market. One trader admitted how deep this can go, "If I'm wrong, what does that say about me?" One's identity becomes entangled in one's trades. There is a strong need to look good, even if it's only to ourselves. The fear of being wrong can cause erratic trading actions such as holding losing trades far too long, cutting winning trades short, moving stops, adding to losing positions, or jumping into the market in unplanned trades. It's a tough way to trade. We look more at how ego, self-justification, and other psychological considerations that affect our sense of self factor into our trading in later chapters. For now, just begin to become aware of how the need to be right may shape your trading behavior and how it may be affecting your trading performance.

Here is a valuable comment about being wrong from Marty Schwartz, a legendary trader who was interviewed by Jack Schwager in his book, *Market Wizards*. In this interview, Schwager notes that Schwartz lost money trading for ten straight years. He then asked, "When did you turn from a loser to a winner?" Here is Marty's reply:

> When I was able to separate my ego needs from making money. When I was able to accept being wrong. Before, admitting I was wrong was more upsetting than losing the money. I used to try to will things to happen. I figured it out, therefore it can't be wrong. When I became a winner, I said, "I figured it out, but if I'm wrong I'm getting the hell out, because I want to save my money and go on to the next trade." By living the philosophy that my winners are always in front of me, it is not so painful to take a loss. If I make a mistake, so what![1]

This workable attitude is one every trader should adopt.

Losing Money

No one likes to lose money, but it is an inescapable part of the trading game. There is no method that has ever been developed that doesn't lose money some of the time. The simple reason for this is that trading in all of its various forms is a probabilistic endeavor. This means that for any given trade that sets up, there is a probability that it will be a winner, and there is also a probability that it will turn out to be a loser. If our trade setup has a greater expectancy of winning over time, then we will be profitable trading that setup. Nevertheless, there will always be losing trades, the frequency of which will be based on the historical probabilities of the trade setup, assuming those probabilities hold into the future. Many traders understand this intellectually, but they still find, when in a trade or about to pull the trigger to enter a trade, their feelings take over and they are averse to loss. Loss aversion is a significant psychological hurdle for traders to overcome even though loss is a natural part of the trade setup probabilities. Loss aversion promotes irrational actions of cutting trades prematurely and holding onto losing trades—both actions done in the service of avoiding loss, not what is best for the trade. Such actions reflect a futile attempt to override the probabilistic law of trading. By tightly holding onto this fear, we try to undertake an impossible endeavor: to prevail over and invalidate a fundamental principle of trading, which just cannot be done. Nonetheless, it is a losing battle from which many traders find it difficult to disengage. Trading would no doubt be easier psychologically by adopting an attitude that losses are unavoidable and natural. We have much more to say about the aversion to loss in Chapter 3.

Missing Out

The fear of missing out is an aspect of fear that can cause traders to jump into unplanned trades. A trader sees the market begin to move and impulsively takes a trade. Their thoughts will run something like Jim's, a trader who leapt in and out of the market for fear of missing out: "The market is taking off," Jim says to himself. "I missed that last move; I don't want to miss another one. I haven't made any money today and I think this is going to run far. I can get in here rather than wait for a pullback. That way I'll get in at a good price and be in profit sooner. Plus, I'll make more money overall."

Notice that all of Jim's thoughts are in the service of justifying hopping into the market. Jim has no thoughts about whether or not the current market pattern is providing a sound trade opportunity. The fear of missing a move causes him to completely abandon his trading plan and act erratically. He rationalizes his reckless trading actions with irrelevant notions. Note that Jim's actions are different from Marko's. Marko has trouble getting into the market; Jim has trouble staying out of it. Both are plagued by fear and anxiety.

We often see that the fear of missing out occurs near the top of a market. Traders on the sidelines have watched the market rally and rally. It has gone higher and higher and they're not on board. Other traders are making money, but they are not. Frustrated and fearful of missing out on further gains, they either leap in as the market makes its final advance or they buy on the pullback after an exhaustion or climax. Either way, they are soon under water. The same fear-based pattern occurs at market bottoms with short sellers. Whether sidelined traders sell short at the bottom or buy at the top, emotion is driving trading decisions. Another signal that the fear of missing out is present is the tendency to enter trades too early. Jim represents this best: "If I don't get in now, I'll miss the move."

Leaving Money on the Table

Josh, an S&P e-mini day trader, was adept in identifying where trades would set up. He had no qualms about taking the trade and letting it run. Josh, however, overstays his trades, expecting them to produce very large moves. Josh's reasoning is, "I would have made much more money on the last trade if I stayed with it; I'm holding this one." Thoughts of big profits like Josh's cause traders to ignore important technical targets like resistance or support, extreme indicator readings, as well as market tells such as climactic action or the waning of participant interest marking the end of a move. Like Josh, many traders fear they "leave too much money on the table," and hold trades beyond the point of reasonable profitability. Of course, when price began to retreat, they view it as "just an expected pullback" that they would sit through. Many of these "pullbacks" retraced their entire profit; some ran to a loss.

A less obvious, but common trader behavior in the category of leaving money on the table is to increase position size after a few winning trades. The trader may think,

"Gee, I'm doing pretty well. I've had four winning trades in a row. If I traded with more shares, I'd have more money in the bank today." She then increases her size without a concrete plan typically exceeding sound money management/risk parameters. Of course, if the next trade is a losing trade, she has wiped out substantial profit from the last few trades—all because she thought she left too much money on the table.

We can see that the four forms of trading fears also have associated thoughts (what the trader's mind is saying) that reinforce the underlying apprehension and rationalize unconstructive trading. Importantly, each form of fear is also linked with detrimental trader actions or behaviors. For example, the fear of being wrong may trigger the thought, "I've had too many losses lately; I can't have another one on this trade." Such a thought is related to being wrong and losing money. The idea, "I can't have another loss," reinforces and amplifies the fearful feelings. Not having another loss certainly seems reasonable and serves to justify erratic actions such as moving a stop to avoid actually taking a loss. Please notice that the thoughts associated with the underlying fear have nothing to do with the market action. They are not objective thoughts about the trade or its management. Although they seem at the time to be directed at the trade, they are not. They are reflecting—and, therefore solely about—the trader's internal state.

Table 2.1 shows some common examples of the thoughts and erratic actions that can be associated with each of the four primary forms of trading fear. This is not an exhaustive list. Different traders may have different thoughts and different behaviors. Also, the lines between each form of fear are not always bright and clear. Cutting winning trades short, for example, may occur because a trader wants to avoid being wrong and also to sidestep losing money. There is certainly some overlap among the four categories.

In a study of 118 professional traders working for investment banks with offices in London, professor of Organizational Behavior at the Open University in England, Mark Fenton-O'Creevy and his research associates found that trading was often significantly influenced by the traders' emotional reactions to both their successes and setbacks. Big wins were responded to with euphoria and unwarranted confidence. When losses occurred, traders became more cautious and viewed potential trades differently from when they were making winning trades, a function of the recency effect discussed in Chapter 1. Less experienced and lower performing traders tended to be more emotionally reactive and had less adaptive responses when losses occurred. They refrained from taking trades or traded in lower than normal size. When emotionally upset, they would leave their trading desk and avoid trading altogether. Although Fenton-O'Creevy's research did not address thoughts per se, critical trading actions of the traders in this study were driven by emotion. Both experience and the research show there is a direct link between trader behavior and emotional state. It behooves every trader to understand how emotions affect their trading actions.

For each individual trader, it is also important to know that certain thoughts and corresponding actions are connected to the strong emotion of fear. These thoughts

TABLE 2.1	Examples of Thoughts and Erratic Trading Actions Associated with Fear	
Type of Fear	Examples of Thoughts	Examples of Erratic Actions
Being Wrong	"I can't have another loss." "I can't tell my spouse/significant person I've had another loss." "I can't be wrong, here."	Cutting winning trades short. Failing to pull trigger. Moving stops away from approaching price. Crowding stops. Averaging down. Ignoring money management. Avoiding trades.
Losing Money	"I need a better indicator/trade setup to reduce losses." "I must keep my losses to (a bare minimum) X percent." "You're in profit. Don't let this turn into a loss!" "I have to make up for this morning's loss."	Continuously looking for a better trade setup/indicator/analytical technique to reduce losses (holy grail quest). Seeking high frequency win rate/low frequency loss rate. Cutting winning trades short Crowding stops or moving them away from approaching price. Taking unplanned trades and doubling down to make up for a loss. Avoiding trades. Trimming position size after a loss.
Missing Out	"The market is moving without me!" "I missed the last setup like this; I won't miss this one." "I've got to get in here, I can't miss this trade."	Jumping into unplanned trades. Entering trade too soon. Oversizing position.
Leaving Money on the Table	"I can make real money on this trade." "The last trade ran far, so I'm holding this one." "I'm on a hot streak; let's increase size and make some serious money."	Holding trades far too long. Neglecting profit target objectives. Ignoring market signs to close trade. Oversizing position.

and actions are not related to sound, competent trading but solely to your internal state. It is crucial to begin to become aware of what your mind is saying. Is it about what the market is objectively doing vis-à-vis your trade, or is it about being wrong, losing money, missing out, or leaving money behind—all of which have nothing to do with making, managing, and exiting a trade. It is also critical to become aware of what your trading behavior is connected to. Is your action—such as entering a trade before it gives a clear entry signal—done to appease what your mind is telling you, or is it done because that is the right action for this trade at this time? These are crucial trading psychology considerations.

Typically, if your trading is adversely affected by fear, you will see one or more patterns in your trading. You might notice, for example, that you tend to cut trades short or place stops too close, because you fear loss or fear being wrong. It is important to assess your trading and identify erratic trading actions that may be caused by fear. The idea here is to shine light on the issue so you become aware of it. Trading out of awareness will keep you stuck in the same patterns. As we discuss later in this chapter, erratic trading actions do serve a purpose, but it is not a purpose that serves your trading. If your trading is erratic or overly influenced by the emotions of fear and anxiety, you can use the following exercise to help you become clear on the kind of fear that affects your trading and how it does so.

Exercise 2.1 asks you to identify and record personal erratic trading behavior you frequently experience. Record these under How You Act. You can use the examples of erratic trading behavior listed in Table 2.1 as a guide, and add any others you experience that are unique to you. Next, write down your thoughts—things your mind is telling you about the market or your trade. Then, determine the type of fear you are experiencing. You might find this exercise best to do while trading or just after trading. If you do it later you may miss important data. Our memory tends to be selective about things like this, so it is best to fill in the form as close to the event as you are able. Also, it will

Exercise 2.1 Becoming Aware of Fear and Other Strong Emotions

How You Act	What Your Mind Tells You	Emotion (if fear, note type of fear)

be more accurate and more complete when done over a week or two of trading. You will then have enough data to see your personal patterns and their variations. If you cut winning trades short, for example, you might hear your mind say that it would be best to take profits now, even if only a small profit, because you don't want to have the market turn against you or have a loss. You can then identify that as a fear of losing money or a fear of being wrong, or both. Begin to notice what fears may be operating, what kinds of things your mind is telling you, and the actions these influence you to take. Although you do want to be thorough, don't worry about being exact. Remember, there is overlap among the types of fears. Your thoughts and even your actions will be unique to you, so go with your experience. Also, the objective here is not to try and fix your fear, change your thoughts, or alter your actions, but simply to become aware of emotions and thoughts and how they are affecting your trading. We will discuss how to deal with your emotions and their associated thoughts as we progress through this book.

■ Hope, Greed, and Other Strong Feelings

All traders have heard that together with fear, hope and greed form an emotional trifecta, which adversely affects trading and must be controlled. As Mark Douglas has pointed out, however, and from a practical perspective, hope and greed—at least the way we think about them in trading—are usually fear-based emotions. They are not feelings that are separate from fear and have an independent effect on trading. Hope, for example, is usually experienced as holding a position well beyond reasonable risk parameters after the market has gone against the trade and the trader, now underwater, is hoping that the market will return to a breakeven or smaller loss level. That is not the hope of an aspirational desire as in "I hope to become a skilled and profitable trader." Rather, that is acting out the fear of not wanting to be wrong or not wanting to book a loss. Similarly, greed would have as its basis the fears of missing out and leaving money on the table.

Other strong emotions can also be important. Anger, annoyance, frustration, elation, sadness, shame, guilt, excitement, disgust, impatience, joy, boredom, and a range of other feeling states may factor into one's personal trading. Anger, for example, can breed the desire for revenge with trades made to "get back at" the market, often at inopportune locations and with too great a size. One trader would become so angry at some of the mistakes made in his trading that he would yell, curse, and spit at his computer screen! Destructive behaviors arising from non-fear-based emotions can certainly occur.

Becoming overly sad, ashamed, or guilty about your trading performance can lead to a withdrawal from the market and from trading. This is not necessarily unhealthy. A brief retreat from trading can be constructive. It allows us time and space to evaluate our trading and to consider how exactly we fell short and steps we can take to improve. Many wise traders enforce on themselves a brief retreat to reevaluate their trading when performance is down as a part of their trading plan. Avoiding the markets or a prolonged departure from trading due to depressive feelings and paralysis, however, are probably not going to be constructive.

Also not constructive is getting down on yourself for letting emotions control your trading. When we get down on ourselves, the inner critical voice becomes dominate and can be downright nasty. This can amplify other unpleasant feelings. If you listen to what your mind is telling you when you feel down, you might hear things like: "What's wrong with you? You'll never be a good trader!" or "You've done it again!" and, even worse, "You are so stupid; will you ever learn!" None of this is helpful. In contrast, a constructive critique of your actions can be beneficial. Acknowledge, for example, that you got into a trade too soon and for the next trade you say to yourself, "Be more patient … wait for the entry to trigger." This supports your trading and affirms your efficacy as a trader. For most of us, negative self-criticisms are highly toxic and have the opposite effect. We would never convey such things to a friend who was feeling low, but we seem to think it is okay to dish out nastiness to ourselves. Just as we can easily see this would be unhelpful to our friends, it does nothing but make us feel even lower when we do it to ourselves. For many, such unbridled self-criticism makes challenging emotions worse.

Not all emotions that affect trading behavior are negative. Joy and elation—strong positive emotions—can negatively affect trading just as easily as unwanted emotions. We saw this briefly in Chapter 1 with Nathan. He felt very positive for having caught a nice move in his morning trading. But his positive state allowed him to let his guard down, forgetting the plan he had worked out the night before, and causing him to become lackadaisical when he needed to exercise diligence and objectivity. Many traders find they blindside themselves when feeling positive, usually because they let their guard down and either allow their intuitive mind to take over or they ignore what they shouldn't. Strong positive emotion can also cause traders to assume greater risk than acceptable. One trader, Tomas, evaluated his emotions and his trading over several weeks. He found that whenever he had three or four winning trades in a row, he became very happy and overconfident. His excessive confidence led him to ignore sound money management. He started trading with larger size and also became casual with protective stops. He discovered through the exercise described earlier (Becoming Aware of Fear and Other Strong Emotions) that he was stuck in a repeating pattern of trading well, banking good profits, and then giving them back to the market in sloppy trading, all driven by positive feelings.

As with fear, other strong emotions can adversely impact your trading. Traders need to know their emotional patterns. If an emotion other than fear is impacting your trading, use the Becoming Aware of Fear and Other Strong Emotions exercise to note when that feeling occurs. Under Emotion, record what it is, and under the other headings briefly describe what you tell yourself, and how you act when in its throes as was done with fear.

■ Emotional Hijackings

When emotions dominate our decision making, we become subject to *emotional hijackings*—episodes where your trading actions are completely emotion driven. Such states are experienced by high levels of arousal, intense emotions, and an inability to focus on anything but a narrow range of objects—usually current price ticks and indicator fluctuations. It is also important to recognize that, when in this state, actions become rigid and restricted to a narrow range of patterned responses. As seen in many of the brief trader case examples, traders seem to be able to take only limited actions: cut a winning trade short, jump into a trade, fail to pull the trigger, persist in holding a trade, and other singular actions. They are unable to initiate more appropriate trading actions. When the hijacking is over, you feel as if something had possessed you and you were not quite in control of yourself. Here are two examples:

Warren, an exceptionally bright, young, and relatively new fund manager, had been operating his hedge fund for about a year. His investment management philosophy is based on fundamental value investing championed by Benjamin Graham and David Dodd. His edge is in identifying companies that are significantly undervalued by specific criteria he assesses. Once identified, he applies some of the techniques developed by Peter Lynch, including Lynch's "invest in what you know" principle by developing a deep understanding of companies that pass his initial screen criteria. In most cases, he builds a financial model of each company to test its sensitivity against key performance factors he believes critical for a successful investment in that company. He practices a deliberate, methodical approach. Once he decides to make an investment, he expects to hold that company for the long-term—years, if conditions permit it—to allow the investment to mature. It was quite an incongruity, therefore, to learn he had drawn the account down by day trading in the futures market.

In an overall market downdraft, some of Warren's investments were leading the way down. He was sure they would stabilize, and bought more stock in the falling companies, thinking he could sell out on a rally and recover the losses with the larger position. When the market didn't rebound, his losses began to accelerate. Thinking about his performance and the quarterly investor letter he soon would be writing, he began to watch the market throughout the day—something he never did, as he was normally focused on assessing companies. "Something came over me," he said. "I lost my way. I was gripped by fear. I started watching every tick of the market. I couldn't get away from the screen. I reduced and closed positions on several good stocks right at the bottom of the down move. Later, when the market did rebound, I was kicking myself as they all rallied smartly. Then, I started day trading! I'm not a day trader; I knew that, but I traded. I took positions in the S&P futures. None of those trades worked. I was very tense and anxious all the time. I couldn't sleep at night. All I thought about was the market and the losses. It was a nightmare. In the end, something good did come out of it. That was the realization of how important my investment process is to my work. When I was trading, I had no process. I was essentially acting randomly. I completely lost my way."

Billy, a position trader in the equities market, saw Ford Motor Company stock shoot up dramatically, easily clearing recent resistance. Although not a breakout trader, Billy bought this stock near the daily high just before the market close. Later, he admitted that his best trading play is "always to look for the low-volume pullback after a momentum move." Here, however, he acted impulsively. You can see the stock and his purchase labeled A on Figure 2.2. The next few days saw the stock drift higher, though the stock was no longer moving swiftly as it did

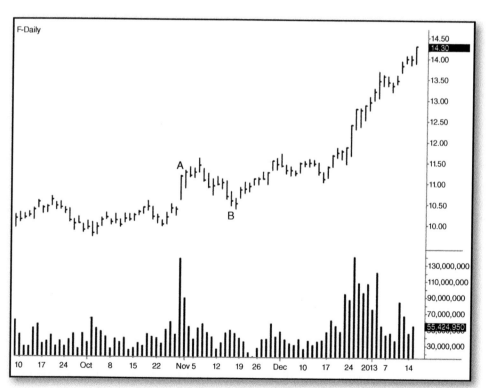

FIGURE 2.2 Billy's Impulsive Trade in Ford Motor Company
Source: TradeStation Technologies, Inc.

on the day that Billy bought it. A week after Billy entered this market long, it started to react against him. Billy wasn't concerned at first. He thought it was "just a normal pullback after such a strong move." Soon, however, Billy's trade was under water. He became tense and anxious. He couldn't look at other stocks while Ford was losing money. As it went lower, Billy's focus narrowed as he watched every tick of the chart. His attention was riveted to the smallest of intraday time frames searching for any evidence that the market was starting to move higher.

That didn't materialize for him. Although he put stop loss orders in the market each day, as the market approached them, he moved his stop lower to avoid taking the loss. Later, he said, "It's almost comical now, but sad, really. Every time the market moved close to my stop, I reset it lower. I felt miserable. My stomach was upset, my mouth was always dry, and I felt light-headed. I thought I might become sick. I really felt out of control." When price started to trade underneath the low of the strong day on which he bought, Billy was sure the market would now fall swiftly. It was at this point (B) that he sold his position for a loss. The next day, the market held and then began to move higher. Within a few weeks, the stock was up more than 25 percent from Billy's entry.

Both Warren and Billy had all the signs of an emotional hijacking. It starts when initial trading decisions were made on an emotional basis rather than in accordance with trading plans and careful assessments. One's trading process is completely abandoned. Initially, confidence may be high and risk is neglected. It then spirals downhill when the poorly planned trade fails to work out as predicted. As markets go against the trader, confidence withers and emotions become even more prominent in decision making. It causes feelings-driven actions that seemed correct at the time, but objectively and, of course, in hindsight, were obviously wrong. Attention concentrates on a narrow field, excluding virtually all other considerations and possibilities. Actions, too, become restricted. Trading actions are made to address internal states and the trader's runaway emotions rather than addressing the trading situation. Afterward, once the pressure is off, there is a recalled feeling of being out of control and with little, if any, personal power over feelings or actions. The term emotional hijacking seems apt for this kind of experience.

■ Emotional Intelligence

When under the spell of an emotional hijacking, we lose all semblance of emotional intelligence. Daniel Goleman, a psychologist and one-time *New York Times* science writer popularized the early research demonstrating that being aware of and understanding the emotions within oneself and in others is as valuable as—if not more valuable than—intellectual ability (IQ) in achieving life success. Today, emotional intelligence (EQ) is considered by psychologists every bit an intelligence, just as IQ is. Prominent EQ researchers John Mayer, David Caruso, and Peter Salovey have shown that EQ is a mental ability like other forms of intelligence, and it meets the standards set by psychological researchers and scholars for classification as an intelligence.

After 20 years of study, researchers conclude that, compared to others, persons who are emotionally intelligent exhibit more positive performance in work settings, can temper the burden of their own stress, and can positively impact others in stressful situations. They are less likely to engage in self-destructive behaviors such as alcohol or drug abuse. In the social arena, people with higher EQ have greater interpersonal competence, better social relations, and are perceived by others as socially adroit. Overall, emotionally intelligent people experience a higher quality of life and are happier compared to others. For traders, developing emotional intelligence is crucial.

Mayer, Salovey, and their colleagues have identified and described four important mental capacities in their model of emotional intelligence. These include the abilities to:

- Recognize and assess emotions—both in oneself and in others.

- Integrate the information expressed by emotions in decision making.

- Understand the meaning behind emotions.

- Conscientiously manage oneself.

Basic EQ skills begin with the ability to recognize and evaluate emotions. This includes being able to identify emotions as a feeling state, how they may affect one physically, and also being aware of the thoughts generally associated with certain emotions. To develop EQ skills for trading, we first need to break down and clarify unconstructive emotions. We will do this in detail with fear shortly. Being able to recognize feeling states in others is also a part of this basic EQ skill for traders. When the market is running hot and abruptly begins rising parabolically with a surge of volume, the emotionally intelligent trader will recognize not only the extremely high price levels but also the extremely high emotions of market participants. These are the times when the market is vulnerable to a reversal. Being attuned to the emotions of others in the market can help identify trade opportunities; it gives you a different perspective when thinking about jumping into a market because it has been moving and you have been on the sideline. The urgent feelings you are having in that moment are also being experienced by many other market participants. The emotionally intelligent trader will recognize this urgency not as a reason to jump into the market, but as a probable contrarian signal and patiently allow the market to unfold and present a trade opportunity in the opposite direction. This is one way of using the skills of EQ productively in trading.

A basic EQ skill for traders also involves using the appropriate emotions to aid in decision making. When studying the markets after the close, for example, the emotionally intelligent trader would use low-energy emotion to help focus attention on charts. If bored during the trading day because the market is narrowly trading sideways, the emotionally intelligent trader will recognize her boredom and take steps to refresh her energy and attention. The use of emotions as an aid in decision making also involves recognizing and honoring the feelings that come with identifying an exceptional trading opportunity, whether it is a patterned trade setup that meets every important criterion, or a company you have uncovered with excellent fundamentals and prognosis for near-term growth which no one on Wall Street is following. Likewise, the emotionally intelligent trader will acknowledge feelings that a trade isn't a great prospect even though the setup may meet basic criteria. Honoring both feelings of excitement and feelings of caution can help inform your process of prioritizing your trades, risking capital only for truly choice opportunities, or taking a second look at the technical aspects of a trade to evaluate whether something important was overlooked.

Understanding and comprehending emotions involves being able to label them once recognized and also understanding that emotions—especially strong ones—are rule-governed and typically follow a set pattern. Anger, for example, arises from an event experienced as unfair or unjust. As the emotion surges unchecked, we are likely to act rashly, only to regret it later, or feel ashamed or embarrassed when things eventually calm down. Some traders feel it unjust that stops get hit and they are taken out of the market for a loss, only to see price immediately turn and run in their anticipated direction. "They hit my stop on purpose!" is the hot thought that may run with the angry feeling that you didn't deserve to be stopped out. Acting rashly with an oversized revenge trade to show "them" you can't be pushed around is not only emotionally unintelligent trading, but the trade is likely to end badly with remorse and shame following quickly on its heels. The general rule-set here is: perceived unfair event taken personally → anger arises accompanied by hot thoughts → rash behavior → feelings of shame and regret. You can delineate typical rule patterns for any intense emotion: fear, sadness, frustration, and so on. Even feeling highly optimistic and joyful will have their patterns.

Feelings of sadness, for example, might arrive from the experience of a loss. As the blue feelings develop, a natural reaction for many is to withdraw from trading. Self-critical thoughts might emerge, finding fault with the trade or trader performance and even demeaning of the trader. These, in turn, encourage feelings of guilt, perhaps worthlessness (depending on how strident the self-criticism), and even a sense of hopelessness about future trading. For sadness, then, we see a typical pattern or rule-set that may look like this: loss causing feelings to be down → withdrawal from trading and isolation → self-critical thoughts → feelings of guilt, shame, and hopelessness. Rather than acting out these unproductive patterns over and over, it is emotionally intelligent for a trader to know how his or her personal patterns typically evolve when strong emotions are triggered. Once clarified, more productive actions can be taken.

Take a few moments and refer to your examples from Exercise 2.1 (Becoming Aware of Fear and Other Strong Emotions). Select a strong emotion pattern that you experience and define your own personal rule-set for this emotion. Use the next exercise, Exercise 2.2, to become more emotionally intelligent about your strong emotions and how they emerge and influence your actions.

As much as it may seem paradoxical and contrary to what you might assume, being able to manage oneself is not about controlling emotions as much as it is about being open to feelings, including strong emotions. Certainly, self-management involves being able to apply self-calming techniques and coping skills (which we discuss in detail in future chapters) to maintain a settled disposition when mildly anxious. Self-management also involves marshalling positive feelings to motivate us or to be able to delay the impulsive desire for immediate gratification for a larger reward later.

Exercise 2.2 Developing Emotional Intelligence: My Patterns for Strong Emotions

Event or Situation that Triggers the Emotion	Hot Thoughts That Ignite and Amplify Strong Emotions	How You Feel	Actions You Take	Results and Consequences

These are skill-based abilities that can be learned. It is very difficult, if not impossible, however, to purge or control emotions consistently for any period of time. Most people want to eliminate or control strong emotions, but this is almost always counterproductive. In their attempt to get rid of their uncomfortable feelings, ironically, they end up in a struggle with them. Attention gets diverted away from the market and placed almost entirely onto one's internal state as the unwanted emotions are battled. How can you manage a trade when your focus is on your internal state? This is not an emotionally intelligent response for trading. How one effectively responds to emotions as they arise is what emotional intelligence is all about. Indeed, it is a large part of what this book is about.

■ Clarifying Fear

Let's become more emotionally intelligent. We will continue to focus on fear as it is the most prominent difficult trading emotion, but you can do a similar clarification for any feeling that affects your trading. We want to develop the first mental skill of emotional intelligence and be able to recognize it when it arises. In order to do this we need to clarify it.

What happens to you when you become afraid or have another strong emotion? Pause a moment and think about this. Again, it helps to be clear on what we confront. If we can clarify the signs and symptoms of fear, not only do we understand better what it is we are dealing with, but we put ourselves into a position where we can recognize it early on. We have a much better chance of doing something constructive about it as it is just beginning to arise; we have less chance to act positively when we are already hijacked by it. So take a few moments before reading on to think about and try to clarify your own fear in trading. How exactly do you experience it?

For most people, fear and other strong emotions are experienced globally. By global, I mean that it affects our mind, how we feel emotionally, and also our bodies, or physiologically. If we are unaware of these features of fear, we leave ourselves vulnerable to becoming overwhelmed by it. It is critical to be alert to the signs and signals that forewarn a trader that he or she is entering a state of fear. The first step in learning how to deal with fear or any other difficult emotion that a trader may routinely face is to develop an awareness of its early signs and symptoms.

For many, the most obvious clues that a trader is anxious, stressed, and fearful can be found in the body. Because of the strong mind-body connections that exist with all emotions, what we feel emotionally is also felt in the body. When feeling anxious or fearful, we may feel our heart start to pound, our breathing increase, and our muscles tense. Once a threat is perceived, the amygdala—a region of the brain that has been described by Harvard professor and psychiatrist John Ratey as the brain's "panic button"—sets off an involuntary chain reaction in other parts of the brain and body that puts us into an alarm mode. Fear of a perceived threat triggers the *Fight-Flight Response* (FFR), an ancient, hard-wired reaction human beings and other species have evolved to contend with threat. When our ancestors were out walking in the forest, a flash of orange caught in the corner of one's eye would immediately set off internal alarms that a predator was near, automatically setting in motion internal processes geared toward dealing with the threat. This elegant survival response has been with us for thousands of years. It's ingrained in our DNA. Today in modern society, tigers aren't stalking around every corner, but our biology remains essentially the same. We still respond to threats we perceive with an automatic cascade of neurotransmitters, hormones, and proteins that cause an automatic, patterned reaction in parts of the brain and body.

It is not just fear from threat, but any intense emotional state can trigger a similar reaction: anger, sadness, and even the euphoria of being in a great trade can induce the stress response. I've witnessed more than a few traders holding a very profitable position pacing the floor, biting their fingernails, anxious and worried even though they are in good profit, asking themselves over and over, "Should I close this now or hold until the end of the day?" Also, the threat need not be external. Even a memory or thoughts of a stressful event, such as recalling a prior trading loss, can invoke the FFR. This is one of the major difficulties of being human. As far as we know, we are unique among the family of animals in that a threat does not have to be real to bring out the stress response. We can recall a previous threat, or imagine it, and put ourselves smack in the middle of the FFR.

Each of us will react a little differently to the Flight-Fight Response, but as Richard Blonna (professor at William Paterson University and expert in stress and anxiety) explains, there are universal actions that the brain and body perform when the stress response is triggered. It is the way we are genetically programmed. Although it feels uncomfortable, FFR automatically puts us into the best state to deal with the danger. Muscle tension occurs as the body prepares the large, stronger muscle groups to deal with threat. Blood drains out of peripheral regions such as arms and hands, which may cause us to feel numb or tingling sensations, but this is done to both nourish larger muscle groups with glycogen for explosive action and to reduce bleeding if bitten or cut. We breathe rapidly and more heavily to oxygenate the blood stream, which supplies additional oxygen and nutrients to muscles and the brain for a swift and sustained response, though the heavy breathing can make us feel a little light-headed and dizzy. Skin pores open allowing sweat to emerge, making us slippery in order to evade capture. Our digestive system shuts down. Eating isn't a priority now, it becomes secondary to survival, and energy is put to other uses. So, we may feel a little nauseous or feel butterflies in our stomach, and, because salivation stops, our mouths may feel dry. When sitting in front of our computer screen we feel distinctly uncomfortable, which is often experienced as a strong call to take action. This is Fight-Flight.

Mentally, our focus becomes narrowed. All attention is directed to the threat we perceive. We may have racing thoughts about the feared object; we can't stop thinking about whatever it is that is making us fearful. When deep in the throes of FFR, we aren't able to direct our thoughts elsewhere. Our DNA at this moment has us in survival mode. It doesn't want us to be thinking of anything else. We can't make detailed plans. We can't compare alternatives. In trading, this means that we often are unable to assess the market and evaluate potential options. These normally important executive functions of the brain require time and energy. In a mode of survival, these varieties of deliberative activities are shut down. Blood is shunted from the decision-making areas of the brain to the emotional centers as emotional reactions can be made with lightning-like speed and we need to act with dispatch. Thus, when FFR is triggered, it becomes difficult for us to think clearly. We lose perspective. Access to other choices and other actions vanishes once the trader enters this mode of responding.

All of this occurs within moments. When you think about it, it is quite amazing and quite elegant. This is our evolved, genetic heritage in action. It certainly can be life-saving, even today. If we were to step off the city sidewalk and suddenly, out of the corner of our eye, we see a bus racing toward us, it is our FFR that allows us to react virtually automatically and jump back to safety. The brain, however, doesn't distinguish well between the threat of being hit by a bus and the variety of other, lesser threats we face, such as a loss from trading. Because countless less important stressors can trigger the FFR, neuroscientists acknowledge a widening gulf between our biology and the kinds of threats we face in modern civilization. Modern life continues to advance at an accelerating rate; in comparison, our biology evolves at a glacial rate, taking thousands of years to instill genetic change. This disparity is amplified in trading.

We are stuck with our genetic heritage. Although traders talk about emotion as the culprit, in reality, it is our biology that plays a substantial role in the discomfort virtually every trader feels. This is why even highly experienced traders feel discomfort in their trading. When we perceive a threat or experience any heightened stressor, our brain automatically acts and does so with lightning-like speed. And it doesn't matter if we are confronting a tiger or a potential trading loss, the brain and body respond in a similar way. The brain automatically mobilizes the body to deal with the danger.

Among other neurochemicals, proteins, and hormones, cortisol—a powerful hormone—is automatically released under the stress response by the adrenal gland. Under stress, the brain and muscles have a huge appetite for glucose—a primary fuel. Cortisol rapidly makes glucose available to the brain as well as the large muscle groups. In addition, Harvard University's brain expert, John Ratey, notes that cortisol also triggers the hippocampus—a brain region that plays a crucial role in consolidating long-term memory—to begin recording the memory of this event so that we can avoid it in the future. Each time we confront a similar stressful situation, such as a trading loss, the brain records the event. Each recording solidifies the threat in our memory and creates an even faster signaling of the stress response in the future. In other words, the connections within the brain areas become stronger, fire more easily, and take over our mind and body more quickly each time the hippocampus records a stressful event. This is one important reason why the fear response can stay with a trader even after years of trading. A super communication highway is built within the brain that is difficult to dismantle. Also, the cortisol flooding our system causes our brain to ignore existing memories and focus only on the threat. This is why it is so easy to forget our trading plan when under stress. Under the stress response, cortisol is blocking those memories! So it becomes difficult to remember and learn. Our neurons become well-honed to respond to any threat of loss. Each time there is a potential for danger, the brain and body automatically respond.

This is a major reason why it is fruitless to try and suppress the feelings and thoughts about fear. We have no direct access over our amygdala, adrenal gland, and hippocampus, let alone neurochemicals and hormones like cortisol! Trying to directly control fear and other strong emotions is not the answer, as compelling as our culture and personal beliefs may make that seem. It's one of the great myths of trading psychology. We will discuss this in detail in the next chapter, including your own experience in trying to control emotions and how well that has worked. For now, we are simply looking at what is behind our experience of fear, clarifying it, and understanding how difficult it truly is to try to eliminate fear. So be sure to note the symptoms you experience that accompany the strong emotion of fear. What do you feel in your body? What is your mind telling you? And, emotionally, how do you feel? Keep in mind we are not trying to change these symptoms, just clarify them. In this regard, it is valuable to understand which of your symptoms occurs first. Do you first notice your muscles tense, or perhaps you detect certain thoughts come into your mind that then trigger other symptoms? You want to map how your emotion reveals itself. Like any good map, it will help you better comprehend and negotiate the territory you are traveling. Being aware of and being able to notice the early signs that fear is emerging will allow you to apply some of the coping techniques described in later chapters early on when they will be most effective, before the fear process turns into an emotional hijacking.

■ Note

1. Jack D. Schwager. *Market Wizards: Interviews with Top Traders* (New York: Harper Business, 1993), 264.

CHAPTER 3

The Struggle to Control and Eliminate Emotions

59

Traders experiencing strong, unwanted emotions such as fear and anxiety naturally try to control them. Because strong emotions interfere with trading, traders look for a way to get rid of them. This seems reasonable—what everyone would do. But therein lays the rub. Experienced traders know that doing the same things as everyone else puts you in the herd, not outside of it. Profitability and success in trading will be elusive when taking the same actions as others, especially when emotions are involved. We have already seen that we have little control over our amygdala and the internal, psychobiological events that fear and other strong emotions unleash when the fight-flight response is triggered. Aside from this trading axiom and our biology, there are sound psychological reasons why actively trying to control strong emotions will make matters worse. We will see later why this is virtually always a fruitless task. For now, let's look at how traders typically try and cope with the emotional side of trading. See if you can identify with the same or similar coping strategies that most other traders rely on. Again, bringing clarity is a first major step in dealing with anything related to psychology and that is what we will do here as we review how traders typically cope with challenging emotions.

There are many ways traders attempt to cope with strong emotions. Because little is known about this subject in trading, people try just about anything. Even though traders try many things, we can break coping down into three basic areas: an attempt to improve the technical side of trading, a quest to avoid losses, and the endeavor to exercise psychological control. We discuss each in turn.

◾ Improving the Technical Side of Trading

There is certainly nothing wrong with trying to develop better knowledge, skills, and abilities in technical trading. There is much value to be gained from continual improvement of the technical side and in Chapter 11 we detail a systematic process for developing technical trading skills. By the technical side, I am referring to improving knowledge, skills, and abilities in reading price bars and volume; increasing understanding and use of technical indicators such as moving averages, stochastics, MACD, and the like; and developing an understanding of market structure, intermarket relationships, internal market indicators, and other technical considerations in order to better anticipate the next move of the market you are trading. Developing a better understanding of the technical side of the market can have a positive impact on the trader's performance. It places the trader in a better position to read and trade the market.

When the effort to improve the technicals is undertaken in the service of coping with emotions, however, the trader is likely to run into trouble. Often, our first response to an uncertain situation that produces anxiety is to look for more and better information. This seems reasonable. Additional data that informs us about the next market move can give us a clearer picture of the future. If some information is helpful, then more must be even more helpful. The trader who finds additional information to support their hypothesis about the market's next move will feel better about making the trade. It may seem subtle, but the trader is seeking more information *to address feelings*. It is not done to qualify the trade, per se, but *to reduce uncomfortable emotions*. This is a very important distinction. Consider the experience of Jacques:

> After drawing down his account, Jacques looked for a better set of technical indicators to use in his trading. When that didn't work, he tried a different market, thinking "equities will be easier to trade than commodities." When that didn't work, he focused on developing a trading system. With each loss he experienced, he re-optimized his system. Although he believed he was "tweaking the indicators," he was really trying to tweak his emotions.

More and seemingly better information will not solve the problem of emotions. In this discussion, I am assuming you possess a valid technical edge in your trade setup. For example, if your trade setup has a win-loss ratio of, say, 60 percent and has an overall winning expectancy producing greater profit on winning trades than losses on losing trades, then your trade setup has a technical edge.[1] Additional information added to address emotions will do little to affect that technical edge. The trade setup's edge is due to its statistical performance; it has nothing to do with your feelings. Changing indicators or adding information to make you feel better will not improve the setup's outcomes. Many traders who struggle with strong emotions confuse this issue. On the face of it, it does seem reasonable: if the technicals can be improved, then outcomes will be better and anxiety will be eliminated. As we bring clarity, however, we can see that changing or adding information to an already valid setup often serves only as an attempt to control the internal state of the trader. What actually happens, unfortunately, is that traders entangle themselves in a futile struggle with their emotions. Because they are focused on the technicals, however, they don't even realize it! More importantly, they are doing nothing to address their difficulties with strong emotions. All their effort misses the mark.

In their book, *Winning Decisions*, Edward Russo and Paul Schoemaker discuss an unpublished study that can help illuminate how adding more information to the decision-making process isn't always helpful. The researchers in this unpublished study—Paul Slovic and Bernard Corrigan—asked experienced horse race handicappers to predict winners from a series of races with one condition: they were limited in the amount of information they could use to make their betting decisions. Four races were studied. In the first race, the handicappers were limited to five pieces of information from the horses' performance charts. The information could be any the handicapper chose, but only five separate items were allowed from which betting decisions were then made. In the next race, the amount of allowed information was doubled. Again, any information from the past performance charts could be selected, but only 10 items could be used. In the third race, the amount of information was again doubled to 20 pieces of information, and in the fourth and final race, the amount of information available was 40 items of data deemed relevant by the participants.

The researchers' aim was to see if predictive ability improved as more information became available. It did not. The pari-mutuel betters in this study did as well with only five pieces of information as they did with 40 data pieces. Over the four races with information doubling with each race, their accuracy rate was flat. More information did not improve outcomes. Slovic and Corrigan also measured the handicappers' confidence in their predictions. Their confidence did steadily increase as the amount of information grew. The more information they had, the more confident they became about their ability to pick winners. Their feelings changed, but performance was unaffected.

This raises an important consideration for the trader. Adding extra information to an already satisfactory trade setup will not affect the trade results, but can affect how we feel about the trade. It can make us feel confident. That may seem to be a benefit, but the confidence is false and hollow because adding information does nothing for accuracy. Where this becomes tricky is when we feel so confident that we overtrade the position because we have a lot of information pointing to a predicted direction. Again, we are wrongly using technical information as a way to regulate our feelings—in this case, promoting self-confidence. In the process, we can develop an unsound level of boldness. We then act not on the objective probabilities of the trade setup, but on how we have come to make ourselves feel about it.

Adding extra information to make a decision on a trade can easily cause traders to commit confirmation bias. As we discussed in Chapter 1, once an assumption is made, people tend to seek information that confirms their assumption, instead of looking for contradictory data to disprove the assumption. We have the natural tendency to commit confirmation bias by seeking out and overweighting data that is consistent with and supportive of our view. The reader is encouraged to review that section in Chapter 1 for the consequences of committing this cognitive bias and useful steps to help combat it.

Another side of the information coin is the issue of complexity. Generally, the most workable methods in trading seem to be the less complicated ones. Developing systems with large amounts of data and multiple indicators set to confirm one another can lead to "analysis paralysis." Such systems frequently have conflicting signals where some of the indicators are pointing buy, some are pointing sell, and others haven't signaled. One currency trader, James, explained, "I thought adding a few additional indicators would make the chart more clear, but now I find I can see both possibilities of the market moving up or down. I'm more confused than ever!" Like James, traders can become frozen by an overly complicated trading system and unable to initiate a trade. When missing trade after trade that yields nice wins because of conflicting indicator signals, the trader begins to doubt (and likely override) the system. Hours of effort designed to produce confident trading does just the opposite; it creates qualms and mistrust.

What we have been talking about in many respects is the search for the *Holy Grail* of trading. Improving the technicals, adding copious amounts of information, and designing complex systems can all be a part of the grail quest. The Holy Grail simply doesn't exist. What urges us on in this regard is our internal state. We seek to relieve the feeling of unease when dealing in an arena whose foundation is risk and uncertainty. Confidence boosted without an augmented edge paves a false road that could lead to financial loss and damaged self-confidence. Above all else, traders must accept the facts: we are operating with incomplete and uncertain data and every trade has a definite probability of loss. This means we must learn to be *open to* and *accept* the feelings that are associated with uncertainty and risk. Fighting those thoughts and feelings is delusive. It's like brawling with our shadow, over and over, again and again. We can never win that fight! The fundamental nature of trading the markets is risk and uncertainty. If we struggle with the thoughts and feelings that reflect the nature of trading, not only are we in conflict with the very nature of trading, but we also misdirect our attention away from the trading process and the tasks of trading. We must learn to accept the thoughts and feelings that go with loss and not try to eliminate them. Otherwise, success will be elusive. We develop these important psychological principles throughout this book.

■ Avoiding Losses: The Multiple Faces of Loss Aversion

Another way traders attempt to cope with fear is to try to control and reduce losses. This sounds reasonable. Who wouldn't want to minimize losses? Of course everyone in their right mind wants to curtail losses. But, it is the way in which traders act to reduce loss that creates the problem. Again, what seems rational ends up problematic. As the trader attempts to dodge losses, behavior becomes overly rigid. Actions taken to sidestep losses result in reduced profits, missed opportunities, and often greater losses—achieving exactly the opposite of what the trader intends to avoid. As you read this section keep in mind that it is not a loss itself that causes problematic behavior; rather, it is *our reaction to the discomfort felt at the thought of loss* that actually causes the trader to act erratically.

Daniel Kahneman and Amos Tversky—the two eminent research psychologists we met in Chapter 1—studied and described people's aversion to loss. They published their findings in the 1970s. Since then, it has been well-established through numerous studies that there is a bias in our mental machinery when it comes to losses. It is known as *loss aversion*.

We have a significant aversion to loss when making choices involving risk. Scientists believe that our brains are probably hard-wired to avoid loss as an aspect of our evolutionary heritage. Nature, it seems, doesn't want us to go around losing things without suffering the consequences for it. Frequent and constant losses would work against the survival of the species. The familiar saying of "A bird in the hand is worth two in the bush" captures this idea rather well. Throughout our advancement over the millennia, it was generally better for our survival as a species to hold onto what we already had and look for incremental gains rather than risk losing what we already had to strive for things that were out of reach or that we could easily lose. Thus, when we experience a loss, nature has made it painful for us so that we don't make the same loss again. Evolution, through our genes, has made us abhor losses, and because risk-taking involves the possibility of loss, it has made us risk-averse when there is a threat of losing something we already have (i.e., losing the bird already in the hand). We discussed this as an aspect of the endowment effect in Chapter 1. Like the genetically programmed endowment effect and the fight-flight response, loss aversion has certainly helped insure our survival, but it becomes a very difficult hurdle to surmount in trading.

Across many studies, scientists have been able to quantify that the psychological impact of loss is about two to two-and-a-half times the impact of a gain of equal size, depending on the study. What does this mean for the trader? Consider a successful trade that wins a profit of $2,500. That feels pretty good. Now consider a trade that sours and produces a loss of $2,500—the same size as the win. In order of magnitude, this loss will feel much worse than the win. Psychologically, it will feel as if the loss was $5,000, if not more. As Daniel Kahneman says, "losses loom larger than gains." If you weigh this out in your own mind from your own experience, you can see that how we are built genetically makes it difficult for us to trade well. Think about this question: In your own trading, what has been more significant for you—a loss or a gain? Which do you remember better? Which have you felt more intensely? If you are like most traders, you will remember your losses more clearly and with more recalled emotion than your wins (especially large losses). You will recall that you spent much more time thinking about and reliving a large loss compared to a big win, and if you let yourself relive the experiences in your mind, you will recall the intensity of the negative feelings of a loss more sharply today than the happier feelings produced by a win, even though the losses may have occurred some time ago.

As the size of the loss increases, so will its psychological impact. Several losses added together can also have a psychological meaning similar to a single large loss. If you are reviewing your trading for the week or the month and your tally of losses is sizeable, it can impact you psychologically and affect your next trades. A hedge fund manager running a small fund ran up a net loss of $80,000 in one month or about 4 percent of the fund's capital base. He was emotionally devastated and mentally exhausted from the losses he sustained. Although the losses occurred over a series of poor trades, the cumulative psychological impact was significant. For his budding investment operation, it felt like he had lost a very large percentage of his fund because, in his mind, he had psychologically doubled the size of the loss. What was $80,000 in actual losses felt like $160,000 or more in his mind. Fortunately, this fund manager took this experience and used it to look closely at his actions and what drove them. Once this was understood, he was able to create a more sound trading and investment process. Not everyone does this.

Another face of loss aversion in trading is seen in the search for trade setups with high win:loss ratios. People are happier when they are frequently right. In trading, this is seen when traders seek a high percentage of trades that are winners compared to losing trades. Most traders would love to have a win:loss percentage of 90 percent or more. In trading and investing, that's probably not realistic. While you may be able to achieve a higher win:loss ratio in very short-term scalping, in most trading circumstances a 65 to 70 percent win:loss ratio is excellent, and closer to 50 to 60 percent is more the norm. Searching for the high win:loss trade signal may be more of a Holy Grail escapade than a realistic investigation of reliable trade setups.

Informed traders know that more important than a high win:loss ratio is the expectancy of a given trade setup. A trade signal may have only a modest win rate, but if it has a positive expectancy, then the profit magnitude of winning trades is great compared to the level of loss on losing trades. Said another way, a trade indication may produce winning trades only half the time, but the winning trades produce outsized gains, more than compensating for numerous small losses. Psychologically, however, it is hard to sustain many losses waiting for the large win because of our natural aversion to loss. Remember, we double the size of loss psychologically, and they cumulate.

Loss aversion also has a paradoxical effect. Kahneman and Tversky studied gains in addition to losses and found that we become conservative when holding a gain. Consistent with the ideas of loss aversion, we seek to protect what we have. Rather than holding a winning trade for greater profits, we become defensive and quickly sell out to bank those profits, however small. This helps explain the common behavior of cutting winning trades short, the bane of nearly every trader striving to reach a higher level in their trading. When in a trade and we have some profit, it runs against our nature to hold the trade for larger gains. This is why cutting winning trades short is such a familiar and universal problem.

Paradoxically, as conservative and defensive as we are with gains, with losses, it's just the opposite. When in a losing trade, we are more willing to gamble and engage in riskier behavior (such as moving a stop) in order to avoid loss. Rationally, we know that risk is associated with loss. Psychologically, because we are so loss-averse, we are willing to take greater risk in the hopes of preventing a loss. This is why "letting losers run" is such a common behavior for traders. We know that failing to cut losing trades is not sound trading, but it is a behavior with which virtually every trader can identify. Most traders can cite numerous times when they held a losing trade far too long hoping the market would be forgiving. They end up taking a bigger loss than normal stops and money management practice would allow.

The observation of cutting winning trades short and letting losers run is legendary in behavioral finance circles. It is so familiar that it has its own expression: the *disposition effect*. Terrance Odean, professor at Berkeley's Haas School of Business, was the first to present empirical evidence for this trading behavior. He obtained and evaluated the trading records of 10,000 trading accounts over the period from 1987 to 1993. He found strong evidence for the disposition effect: investors frequently closed profitable stock positions and held onto losing stock positions. A notable exception found in the data occurred seasonally at the end of the year. In December, investors were more likely to realize losses as it was advantageous for tax purposes. During all other periods, however, they held onto their losses. Since Odean's initial work, the behavioral regularity of traders' cutting winners and riding losers has been well-documented.

Markku Kaustia, professor of finance at Finland's Aalto University, has reviewed the studies in this area and summarized the common themes on this stable trader behavior. He found that traders and investors are about 50 percent more likely to realize gains compared to losses. Further, the disposition effect is found for all types of investors: individuals, governments, nonprofit institutions, corporations, and even financial institutions. We might presume that financial institutions would be less vulnerable to cutting winners short and letting losers run since, as professional money managers, they have more knowledge and skills than others, but that just isn't the case. The psychology cuts across all traders more or less equally, though financial institutions are slightly more willing to cut larger losses (i.e., losses greater than 30 percent) than other investors.

In addition to organizations, Professor Kaustia reviewed the literature on individual traders. Studies of a large number of individual futures traders found strong evidence of disposition effect behavior. Day traders were prone to increase risk in the afternoon relative to their morning session performance. If the morning session performance was less than anticipated or involved losses, traders took more risk later in the day. Further, those who carried losing trades into the afternoon took longer to close the position compared to traders who carried a winning position into the afternoon trading session. Consistent with the disposition effect, winning trades were closed sooner than losing trades.

The disposition effect has been studied in several different cultures and has been shown to operate in each one studied. No matter where they are located or what their social and cultural traditions may be, traders in the United States, Taiwan, Scandinavia, Korea, and China are all more willing to close winning trades and hold losing trades.

There is some good news for traders. Professor Kaustia found that individual traders with more experience show a reduced tendency toward the disposition effect. Learning to hold onto winning trades and cut losing trades short may be difficult, but not impossible, and it improves with trading experience.

It is interesting to note that when people in a study on loss aversion were given instructions to "think like a trader," they experienced less aversion and reacted less emotionally (as measured by physiological indicators) to loss. Assuming a different perspective may help modify our normal reaction—both emotionally and physiologically—to the potential for loss. California Institute of Technology researcher Peter Sokol-Hessner and colleagues deliberately encouraged their study participants to take on a broader perspective than normal. When making a decision that could result in loss, participants were specifically told to "treat it as one of many monetary decisions, which will sum together to produce a 'portfolio.'" They were encouraged to measure their performance based on all trades taken together. This is the hallmark thinking of a professional trader. In the study, average people were able to adopt this attitude. They substantially reduced loss aversion both in terms of choices that they made and also in their arousal response to actual losses and gains. Taking on a perspective that measures performance across all trades made gave them more objectivity, helping them to reduce the psychological significance of any individual trade and the tendency toward holding onto losing trades and cutting winning trades short. This is the same perspective that any given trade has concurrent odds of winning and of losing, and that it is only over a large number of trades that an edge will play out. Each individual trade does not stand on its own. It is a part of a portfolio of decisions which will produce a level of profit consistent with the edge.

The focus on the individual trade rather than the larger perspective and the unwillingness to accept the fact that any given trade may fail and result in a loss is one of the biggest reasons why aspiring traders fail and why more experienced traders hold themselves back from reaching new levels in their trading. You can evaluate your own tendency to cut winning trades short and allow losing trades to run. Assessing losing trades is straightforward. If you are moving stops, not placing stops, or allowing your losses to exceed sound money management parameters, then you know you are acting to allow losing trades to run.

You will find it useful to check in with what your mind is telling you about your losing trade. Is it saying that you can't have a loss? Perhaps your mind is telling you that by giving your trade "a little extra room" you can avoid stopping out and taking a loss and, instead, sell out on the next rally? As with most psychological issues in trading, we find that we are taking actions not because the action is in the best interest of the trade, but to assuage our uncomfortable feelings.

The same is true for cutting winning trades prematurely. Is your mind telling you that a little profit is better than no profit? Is it urging you to bank the profit, however small, because holding the trade could result in a loss? Again, we see that trading actions are based on psychological considerations, not what's best for the trade. If you find that your winning trades would have been more profitable had you held them longer and the reason you didn't was due to the psychological discomfort you felt in holding the trade open, you know you are a victim of loss aversion and are likely ensnared in the disposition effect.

■ Psychological Control

Traders try a wide range of things to attempt to control strong emotions and thoughts. The belief is that unwanted thoughts and emotions and the discomfort that is associated with them negatively affect their trading performance. Thus, many traders work very hard at controlling their thoughts and feelings, thinking that restraining them is the only way they can reach the level of trading they desire. By control, I mean taking steps to eliminate, suppress, restrain, escape from, or get rid of unwanted thoughts and emotions. Interestingly, traders often set up a rule for themselves that goes something like this: "First, I must learn to get rid of my fear (or unwanted thoughts or other strong emotion). Once I accomplish this, then I will be able to trade well." As we will see, nothing could be further from the truth.

Harvard professor of psychology and researcher of mental control, Daniel Wegner, has studied the idea of controlling and suppressing thoughts for nearly three decades. His research has shown that attempts to mentally control thoughts can produce a variety of undesired consequences. When people try not to think about a thought (such as, "I don't want to have another losing trade") there is a strong tendency for that and similar thoughts to come to mind easily. This is especially true when they attempt to control their mental state under conditions of stress, which trading readily provides.

Although the intention to suppress the thought "I can't have another loss" may seem like a rational action when managing a trade, it is actually quite counterproductive. Wegner calls it an "ironic psychological process" because consequences occur opposite of what is intended. Rather than removing an unwanted thought from consciousness, the very act of suppressing it causes the thought to pop back into our conscious mind. The uninvited and unwanted thought can even become intrusive. On the one hand, our intention of attempting to consciously and vigorously keep the emotional thought out of mind may be supplanted by the mind's other hand through an independent and simultaneous ironic mental process that, acting outside of our conscious awareness, checks to see if we are being successful in controlling the thought. This checking has the unintended and paradoxical effect of reminding us of the emotional thought. In other words, while attempting to suppress the unwanted thought, our mind automatically searches for the unwanted thought and reminds us of exactly what it is we are trying to forget! The act of restraining creates searching and checking, which increases the mind's sensitivity to the very thought being suppressed. Therefore, the more we actively attempt to eliminate our unwanted thoughts and uncomfortable feelings, the more we have them.

Here is a simple, illustrative exercise from psychologist Kelly Wilson you can do now to see if suppressing thoughts works. You will be asked to not think about something. When told what it is, your only task is to keep it out of your mind and not allow your mind to think about it. Not even for a second. Do not even let it enter your consciousness. Okay. Ready? Do not think of ... rich, warm chocolate cake. You know chocolate cake, how luscious it tastes. If you are like me, you especially enjoy the chocolate icing ... creamy and sweet. But, do not think about that! You can recall your mother's kitchen and even now smell the aroma when her cake first came out of the oven, but do not think about that, either! Remember your task: suppress those thoughts of warm, scrumptious chocolate cake!

Most people smile knowingly when they do this exercise. They get the point right away. It's very difficult to control our thoughts, especially when it involves chocolate cake! Some people, however, insist that they didn't think of chocolate cake. I love it when this happens because they help me further highlight Wegner's principle of the ironic process in mental control.

When asked how they accomplish the task of not thinking about chocolate cake, they typically say that it was very easy. They simply thought of something else. One trader, for example, said he thought of "the snow-capped mountains of the European Alps." He was using the tactic of substitution, and it is a clever stratagem. But, when asked how he knew that thinking of the snow-covered Alps kept him from thinking about chocolate cake, he said, "Well, I was thinking about the mountains, and ..." "And, ...?" "Agh! I'm thinking of the snow-capped Alps and, therefore, I'm not thinking of *chocolate cake*." And, there it is: the ironic mental process checking to see if we are suppressing that chocolate cake!

This brings us to an important psychological point. As Steven Hayes—a brilliant psychologist we will be hearing more from in future sections—notes, the mind works by addition, not by subtraction. We can never completely remove something from the mind. Once it is there—be it a thought, feeling, image, or memory, it is there. We really can't get rid of it. This is why Tim Bourquin found that even after 20 or more years of trading, successful traders can still feel uncomfortable in trades. Although much diminished in intensity, they still had the faded memories of failed trades and significant losses. It is also why when you are now asked to think of the snow-covered Alps you also think of _____.[2]

Let's go a little further with this with an example that Steven Hayes uses to explain how thought suppression complicates things for us as we apply it to trading. Here are a few incomplete phrases. Read each one and see what you notice:

Don't beat around the _____
A fool and his money are soon _____
Don't make a mountain out of a _____
Look before you _____
Fight fire with _____
Where the rubber hits the _____

If your natural language is English, you most likely completed these phrases easily.[3] In fact, it probably seemed automatic. The word needed to complete the phrase readily came to mind without having to think about it.

Now, try it again. This time, read the phrase slowly and do not think about the word that fills in the blank. For example, slowly read "Don't beat around the" and do not think about "bush."

How did that go? Were you able to suppress the word that completes the phrase? Probably not. Like the chocolate cake example, it is difficult to keep our mind from thinking about something, especially when we are primed to think about something we have learned well.

So now let's apply this to trading. Instead of completing a well-learned phrase, suppose "bush" represented an unwanted emotional thought that you are trying to control. Perhaps it's the memory of previous large losses along with the anxious feelings associated with loss and the scary thoughts we might have of taking a loss. Just as "Don't beat around the bush" is well-learned, fearing a trading loss is also learned. Imagine yourself in the middle of a trade and then, like clockwork, "Don't beat around the _____" is triggered. But you really don't want "bush." You try to suppress it, but can't. The more we try to get rid of "bush," the more we have it. The more you try to get rid of the unwanted thoughts and discomfort of having a loss, the more you have them.

Can you begin to see that attempting to exert psychological control over unwanted thoughts and feelings is, in truth, a self-defeating action? Controlling thoughts and emotions is a myth. Not only is it unhelpful in our trading, it is harmful to trading because it keeps you stuck in unconstructive patterns where you take actions that don't work. In the above example where you are in the middle of a trade, and "bush"—the unwanted thoughts and feelings—comes into play, the likely action you take is to exit the trade. When we have intense feelings such as anxiety and fear, we tend to want to flee them. This certainly has an effect on the unwanted thoughts and emotions. It relieves them almost immediately. But it cuts the trade short. Because we struggle with what we can't get out of our mind ("bush") and that struggle only serves to intensify the unwanted thoughts and feelings, our only choice is to exit the trade. This is a variation on the fight-flight response, and is the usual psychology behind loss aversion and the disposition effect. As long as you continue to swallow the myth that we must exert psychological control over unwanted thoughts and emotions, you will be struggling against an impossible task and your trading will unquestionably suffer.

It is important to also know that having strong emotions and undesirable thoughts is not a sign of weakness. One trader who grappled with intense emotions said he strove to be "tough-minded and emotionless, like Clint Eastwood." If he couldn't act and feel like he imagined Clint Eastwood would act and feel from his heroic movie roles, he said, "I guess I'm just weak; something must be wrong with me."

That's just not true. In over 19 years in the field of psychology, I've never met a single person who can control his/her thoughts and feelings consistently over any length of time. It's just not possible. I've never met Mr. Eastwood, and I do admire his movies, but I would bet that even Dirty Harry has unwanted thoughts and strong emotions!

Perhaps you remember the commercial passenger jet (US Airways Flight 1549) that took off from LaGuardia Airport in New York City, hit a flock of geese, and was forced to land in the Hudson River? It was international news. Shortly after the remarkable landing, Captain Chesley Sullenberger, the heroic flight captain, was interviewed by Katie Couric on the popular CBS TV program *60 Minutes*. He told her of the experience, "It was the worst sickening pit of your stomach, falling through the floor feeling I've ever felt in my life. I knew immediately it was very bad." As the interview went on, Katie Couric asked Captain Sullenberger what was going through his mind. She asked, "Do you think about the passengers at that moment?" She also asked if he was praying. These are insightful questions because these would be natural thoughts we would have at the time of such great crisis. But Sullenberger said he didn't specifically think much about the passengers as the flight crew was attending to them and he assumed that the passengers themselves were offering prayers at the time. Understanding what Ms. Couric was really asking, he further said, "The physiological reaction I had to this was strong, and I had to force myself to use my training and force calm on the situation." He felt—physiologically—the muscle tension, sickened stomach, and other symptoms of fear that we discussed in Chapter 2, but he didn't struggle with them. He didn't try to control them or get rid of them. He didn't try to avoid thinking or suppress "bush." As heroic as he was in saving the lives of 155 passengers and crew, he also felt fear. Understandably so. It is natural to have strong, intense feelings, even for heroes.

There is more to learn from Captain Sullenberger and the Flight 1549 story. The takeaway message is this: Although he had strong feelings, had he fought those feelings and tried to eliminate them, it would have distracted him from the task at hand, which was landing that aircraft. Instead of fighting "bush," he turned his attention to those things he needed to do to land the aircraft safely *while having the strong physiological reaction.* "I needed to touch down with the wings exactly level. I needed to touch down with the nose slightly up. I needed to touch down at a descent rate that was survivable. And I needed to touch down just above our minimum flying speed but not below it. And I needed to make all these things happen simultaneously," he explained. Captain Sullenberger's attention was centered on the high-value actions that would land his aircraft, not his emotional response to a terrifying situation. This is what saved the 155 people aboard that unfortunate aircraft that day. This is what traders also need to do: keep their focus on the high-value actions of the trading task at hand even while having emotional reactions; not try to suppress, restrain, or control them. Learning to do this is a main purpose of this book.

There is a huge hurdle to overcome, however. We don't really believe it's impossible to get rid of strong emotions and unwanted thoughts associated with anxiety, fear, anger, and so forth. We still think that we have to get rid of them in order to trade well. You may yet feel this way, even after reading the last few pages.

Steven Hayes, a remarkable psychologist who, having himself suffered terribly from uncontrollable panic attacks, created not only a new approach to psychological training and psychotherapy but also launched the basic science to go with it, calls this belief the *control agenda.* The control agenda is the desire and goal of the trader who is frustrated by her or his inner state to get rid of it, suppress it, and control it, along with the belief that until it is under control, that trader will not be able to trade well.

It's very difficult not to want to get rid of uncomfortable thoughts and feelings. This comes from our culture. Until recently, even psychology believed it was the proper approach. Since childhood, we have received powerful social messages that we should be in control of our unpleasant thoughts and painful and scary feelings. As we grew up, we learned to believe that negative thoughts and emotions were dangerous and harmful and need to either be solved or eliminated. We believe that productive mental health for trading (and everything else desired in life) requires the absence of distressing thoughts and emotions. The implication of this belief is twofold: first, unpleasant thoughts and feelings like this are true (they must be or we wouldn't have such a strong reaction to them, both internally and culturally), and second, they must be dealt with, usually through some sort of problem-solving effort. We have already seen that the problem-solving method of exerting control over our thoughts is counterproductive and typically results in exactly what we are attempting to avoid. As for thoughts and feelings being true, simply consider how many times you have been absolutely convinced that the market was about to trade one way and it instead did the opposite.

As an independent trader, you need to make your own judgment on whether attempting to control strong emotions and unwanted thoughts has been workable for you or, instead, has been a fruitless endeavor and has actually been harmful to your trading. To come to your own conclusion, it is crucial that you look at your own experience. This involves doing a thorough inventory of the strategies you have used to try and control feelings and thoughts and how well they have worked. Exercise 3.1 contains a form to help you in this critically important exercise.

Exercise 3.1 is designed to help you clarify your own personal experiences with respect to attempting to control emotions such as fear, greed, anger, and other strong feelings, along with their accompanying thoughts and physical sensations. Take a few moments, think carefully about the questions on the form, and fill it out the best you can with as many examples as you can. It is likely, though, that you won't be able to complete it thoroughly from memory. Therefore, keep this form handy at your trading desk for a week or more. As situations come up where strong emotions arise, make your notes on the form. The idea is to help yourself clarify and understand the tactics you use to try and control unwanted internal states and, most importantly, how well these tactics work.

The first row provides an example of how to complete this form. In the first column, give a brief description of the situation that triggered the strong feelings and thoughts. In the example, the trader who filled this out was in a trade showing some profit. In the *Thoughts, Emotions, and Sensations* column, note unpleasant or unwanted thoughts, emotions, and physical sensations. The trader in the example noted that he became anxious and fearful (emotions) and noted that his mind was telling him, "This could turn into a loss. I should close the trade" (thoughts). Also noted were muscle tension and sweaty hands (sensations). In the next column, *Control Strategy Used/What You Did*, jot down any tactic used to try and control the unwanted thoughts and feelings and what actions you took. The trader in the example tried to stop his thoughts and feelings, but this was unsuccessful. He then got out of the trade. Under *Effect on Me*, note how you felt after the action you took. Pay attention to changes in your internal state here. How did your emotions change and did any new thoughts occur? In the example, the trader noted that he felt relief after closing the position and stated he made a little profit. Shortly afterwards, when seeing the market run further in his trade's direction, he felt dispirited and heard his mind tell him that he will "never be good at trading." This was noted in the *Price I Paid* column, which notes any costs that resulted from the strategy used. Costs should include things like lost profits, missed trade opportunities, and also any psychological costs paid as a direct result of control attempts. In the example, the trader noted he missed out on profit and also saw his mood and self-esteem change in a negative direction.

Exercise 3.1 The Price I Pay to Control My Thoughts and Feelings

Triggering Situation	Thoughts, Emotions, and Sensations	Control Strategy Used/ What You Did	Effect on Me	Price I Paid
Example: I was in a profitable trade	"This could turn into a loss. I should close the trade." Anxiety and fear, muscle tension, sweaty palms	"At first, I tried to stop the anxiety, then I closed the trade."	I made a small profit but mostly felt relief from the tension.	I felt bad when the market rallied. I missed profits and thought, "I'll never get good at trading."

List as many examples as you can; 10 would be good, more would be better. Keep in mind there are no right or wrong answers. It is your experience that is crucial here and that you want to clarify, as it is only your experience that will truthfully tell you how successfully thoughts and feelings can be controlled. You are doing some personal research on the effectiveness of controlling unpleasant thoughts and emotions. Just like when we research a potential trade setup to see how it has acted in the past so that we can get an idea about what to expect from it in future trading situations, we are doing the same thing here with our attempts to control emotions. You want to see how effective your strategies have been for you in the past to get a good idea about how effective they are likely to be in controlling your thoughts and feelings in the future. Because our belief about the necessity to control thoughts and emotions runs so deep, *it is vital that you include all the strategies you have used in your attempts to restrain, eliminate, or escape from them.* Take your time with this; you really want to be thorough.

Traders are inventive when it comes to attempting to manage strong, unwanted emotions such as fear, anxiety, overexcitement (greed), anger, and the like. Table 3.1 contains a partial list of methods, tactics, and strategies reported by some traders who have tried to control their uncomfortable thoughts, emotions, and related physical sensations associated with trading. Perhaps you have tried similar strategies?

Now that you have developed an inventory of the ways you personally try to exercise psychological control over thoughts and emotions, it will be helpful to next

TABLE 3.1 How Some Other Traders Have Tried to Control Unwanted Thoughts and Feelings

Tried to suppress thoughts and feelings	Snapped rubber band around wrist when angry	Didn't use stops	Used alcohol and drugs	Educated self on fear and greed
Read self-help books	Took medications	Tried to exert my willpower and discipline	Took an anger management course	Jumped into trades/ overtraded
Cut many winning trades short	Distracted self when upset	Did relaxation and meditation exercises	Used a brain synchronization machine; holographic/ subliminal message CDs	Held on to losing trades
Talked self out of anxiety and fear	Joined chat room to stay calm	Used herbal supplements and teas	Use positive affirmations to change how I think	Didn't take the trade
Overtraded my positions to make up for prior losses	Left my trading desk to try and calm down	Added to a losing position to get out at breakeven	Learned all I could about technical analysis	Tried to force myself to be tough minded

look at the benefits and costs of these efforts. If you find that you are getting a lot of benefit from your efforts to control undesirable thoughts and feelings, great! You can continue to do more of the same. If you are like everyone else, however, you are likely to find that you are paying a very heavy price for these actions. Any benefit is likely to be only very temporary, or hollow.

Exercise 3.2 will help you to assess the advantages and disadvantages of your psychological control strategies. In the *Control Strategy* column, list each strategy you used from the *Control Strategy / What You Did* column of Exercise 3.1. Then identify

Exercise 3.2 Short- and Long-Term Costs and Benefits of My Control Strategies

Control Strategy	Disadvantages and Costs		Advantages and Benefits	
	Short-Term	Long-Term	Short-Term	Long-Term
Example 1: Avoided pulling the trigger	Missed good profit; felt bad	Keeps me out of many good trades; not improving; feel like a loser	Feel less anxious	Not sure if there are any benefits
Example 2: Exit trade before it can go against me	Could have made 5+ points rather than 0.75 points; felt very frustrated	Significant lost profits; doubts about making it as a trader	Relieved the fear	Nothing comes to mind

TABLE 3.2 What Other Traders Say Are Advantages and Disadvantages of Psychological Control

Disadvantages		Advantages
Missed substantial profit	Always cutting profits short	Temporary relief from stress
Missed choice trade setups	Don't trust my system; losing confidence in my self	Did not have to confront my fear
Cancelled orders and missed good trades	Self-image is poor Feel like a failure No self-esteem	Stopped the stress—until the next trade
Thousands lost in profits	Failing to develop self as a trader	Absolutely none except avoiding dealing with my greed
Loss of income	Depression	No long-term benefits noted
Another setback to sticking to my rules	Lack of life balance	Feel better in the short term, but long term I am not achieving what I want

the disadvantages and costs from applying this strategy, both short- and long-term, then the advantages and benefits. There are two examples to help guide you in the process of completing the columns.

If you are like other traders who have completed this exercise, you are likely to find that the strategies you use to control unpleasant thoughts and feelings do have some short-term benefit. They tend to quickly alleviate the strong emotions. When a person is fearful of a loss, for example, closing the trade provides immediate relief of the fear because the threat of the loss has been discharged. A trader hot and angry after her stop has been taken out directly satisfies her desire for revenge by jumping back into the market. But these immediate benefits ring hollow when we consider that only emotions are satisfied and little else is accomplished. Those who do this exercise find that their control strategies are employed *in the service of their emotions*, not in the service of their trading. This becomes clear when they look at the disadvantages and costs involved and compare these against longer-term benefits. For most traders, disadvantages include missed trades and forfeited profits as well as feeling diminished in some way for not executing trades properly and sticking to their plans. Most find no long-term benefit in attempting to control their undesirable thoughts and emotions. Table 3.2 summarizes some traders' responses to the costs and benefits form in Exercise 3.2.

When we start to look closely at exerting psychological control over unwanted thoughts and emotions, we begin to realize that it is actually quite dysfunctional to our trading. Jamie, a trader who consistently cut winning trades short, had this to say about doing the above exercise:

> I never realized I was shooting myself in the foot. I mean, who wants to have a loss? No one, of course. But this became the all-encompassing

thought I had whenever I put on a trade. I just couldn't have a loss. I thought it would be terrible. I lost focus. I wasn't reading the market or managing my position. My body tightened up. I felt like I was in a vise. Each time I got into a trade, I felt overwhelmed. Everything was centered on avoiding a loss. The relief came when I closed the trade. Then I could relax and feel like I could get out from under the pressure cooker. But then I felt bad all over again. I wasn't trading. I wasn't getting any better. I wasn't making money. I felt like I'd never become competent.

Jamie is describing feeling both sides of the double-edged sword of attempting to solve trading problems by exercising psychological control. She notes all the signs of discomfort, tension, and suffering associated with fearing a loss and struggling mentally against that concern. But that's only part of the problem. She also feels the psychological pain of perfectly good opportunities to make money slipping through her fingers time and time again while she is caught up in the struggle for emotional control. She feels the pain of not improving her skills and being unable to improve her performance and not knowing what to do about it. She feels the pain of being stuck. This is exactly where attempting to suppress and control unwanted thoughts and feeling will put you and your trading: stuck.

■ Notes

1. The important concepts of trading edge and expectancy are only briefly touched upon here. For more information on these topics, the reader is referred to two useful sources: Corey Rosenbloom provides a very helpful discussion of edge and expectancy in his book, *The Complete Trading Course.* Also, Van Tharp discusses expectancy and R-multiples in his book, *Trade Your Way to Financial Freedom.*
2. Chocolate cake! Your mind has added chocolate cake to the mountains.
3. These are common idiomatic expressions in American English: Don't beat around the *bush*; A fool and his money are soon *parted*; Don't make a mountain out of a *molehill*; Look before you *leap*; Fight fire with *fire*; Where the rubber hits the *road*.

CHAPTER 4

The Necessity of Emotions in Trading

As we learned from Chapter 3 and likely from your own experiences reflected in the exercises in that chapter, we cannot really control or eliminate our emotions. Nor should we try to eliminate or suppress emotions from our trading. One of the great myths of trading psychology is that we should trade emotion-free. In this chapter, we will debunk that myth and show you that having emotions in trading is necessary. We will start with a story that begins in northern New England at a railroad construction site in 1848.

■ The Unusual Case of Phineas Gage

Our story of emotions begins with the unusual case of Phineas Gage. It highlights what can occur when we lose our emotional processing abilities, that is, when emotions are eliminated from decision-making. Gage, described by his physician, John Harlow, MD, as healthy, fit, and 25 years old, was a railroad foreman laying railroad tracks in Vermont in 1848. One of his responsibilities was to remove rock with explosives to clear the way for the rail line. He was skilled at the task, but on the afternoon of September 13, 1848, he made a perilous mistake. The blasting procedure involved drilling a hole into the rock, then adding explosive powder and a fuse. After this, sand was added to fill the hole, which was then thoroughly tamped down with an iron rod. Once everyone was safely away from the rock, the fuse would be lit. But on this day, Phineas Gage apparently became distracted. He placed the blasting powder and fuse into the hole as usual, but then tamped the powder firmly. He forgot to add the sand, which served as a buffer between the blasting powder and the rod. Striking the rock as he tamped, the iron bar threw a spark igniting the blasting charge. The premature explosion propelled the tamping bar up and out of the blasting hole, through Gage's head, entering under the left cheekbone and exiting through the crown of the skull, landing some 25 feet away. Miraculously, Gage didn't die. He was treated by Harlow and recovered physically in about three months. His case was so unusual that surgeons and medical students at Harvard University studied him extensively. Gage later became famous as a public attraction in Barnum's American Museum in New York, carrying his iron tamping bar and explaining his freak experience.

Although Phineas Gage recovered physically, his mental state was a different matter. The company for which he worked no longer viewed him as the capable and efficient foreman they had known before the accident. According to Harlow, Gage's change in mind was so profound, the company would not hire back its "most efficient and capable foreman," as Gage could no longer function in a normal manner. Dr. Harlow described Gage after the accident as "fitful, irreverent, … manifesting but little deference for his fellows, impatient of restraint or advice when it conflicts with his desires, … at times pertinaciously obstinate, yet capricious and vacillating.…" He was so completely changed, Harlow reports, that those who knew him said he was "no longer Gage."

Remarkably, his intellectual ability remained completely intact. He was as smart after the accident as he was before it. His memory for familiar people, places, and past events was also sound. He was able to learn new things. He showed no impairment in his movement, gait, or speech. The brain injury did not take away these vital abilities, yet he behaved completely differently. The accident left him with no self-control, which he never regained. As Harlow noted, Gage was impulsive, impatient, fickle, unstable, and stubborn. He acted more like an ill-behaved child than an intelligent and capable man who once supervised others.

Because of his lack of self-control, Gage was unable to live independently after the accident. He died several years later. After Gage's death, Harlow requested his skull from his family. Dr. Harlow understood the importance of Gage's case. At that time, there were exciting scientific discoveries being made about specific brain areas and functioning, such as Broca's area and speech. Dr. Harlow believed that Gage's case could add to the scientific knowledge, though he didn't know it would take over 100 years. The family granted Harlow's odd request and Gage's skull along with his tamping iron became housed in a medical museum at Harvard University.

Antonio Damasio, prior head of neurology at Iowa University's College of Medicine, his wife Hanna, also an accomplished neurologist, and their colleagues studied Gage's skull over a century later in the early 1990s. Aided by computer assessment and neuroanatomical imaging capabilities, the Damasio research team measured and analyzed Gage's skull and determined that the tamping bar had damaged portions of the prefrontal cortex, an important area of the brain. The Damasios became interested in Gage because his case fit the characteristics of a dozen other individuals with frontal lobe brain damage (specifically in the ventromedial prefrontal cortex) that the Damasios had studied—both in terms of the brain area affected and the behavioral characteristics they exhibited. Like Phineas Gage, these individuals, too, retained their general intelligence and memories, but their ability to maintain self-control and make rational, everyday decisions had deserted them. This unique group of people could work through problems of logic, make mathematical calculations, and apply their knowledge to abstract problem solving just like people with intact brains. What Gage and the others with ventromedial prefrontal lobe damage couldn't do, however, was observe, apprehend, and act within normal conventions. Moreover, unlike other people, these individuals were unable to make important personal decisions in ways that benefited and maximized their self-interest.

The researchers realized that those with prefrontal cortex damage lacked the ability to appropriately include emotion and feeling in their decisions. Because Gage and the other patients studied had brain damage in the same area, it led the researchers to conclude that parts of the prefrontal cortex—an area associated with a range of executive brain functions, including planning, evaluating, problem-solving, and determining the consequences of one's actions—also processed emotions and that our feeling states and emotions are vitally important in decision-making. Subsequent studies have demonstrated connections between the ventromedial prefrontal cortex and other areas of the brain involved in emotion, including the amygdala, hippocampus, and the peripheral nervous system. The prefrontal cortex is involved in several important functions. Notably for traders, these functions include the processing of risk and fear, as well as assessing emotional responses and integrating emotions into our overall decision making (see, for example, Hänsel & von Känel, 2008).

The takeaway message for traders is that emotions are important in decision making, including trading decisions. When the information provided by emotions becomes unavailable, as with the brain-damaged patients, actions become erratic and irrational. If you were somehow to find a way to abolish emotions from your trading decisions (which, as we have seen, is not possible, unless, of course, you suffer brain damage), you would end up without self-control and make impulsive decisions based on whim and caprice much like Phineas Gage.

Antonio Damasio developed a theory about emotion and decision making that has relevance for traders. It's called the *somatic marker hypothesis*. The term somatic refers to the body. We often experience emotions as felt bodily states, either unconsciously and instinctively (e.g., the fight-flight response and fear) or more consciously and explicitly (e.g., anger). Either way, our emotional experience shows up in the body and attending to bodily state helps us to be aware of our emotional state. Think of having a gut reaction to some situation. It is the felt emotion, according to Damasio's theory, that marks one alternative among other options in a decision. Our emotions color one choice above others making one option more salient to us and flagging it as the appropriate choice. Emotion is thus crucial for our decisions and for effectively negotiating the situations we face. Recent research conducted by Yuri Terasawa and colleagues at Keio University, Japan, shows specific brain regions activate (ventromedial prefrontal cortex and the portions of the insular cortex) when attending to one's internal state and evaluating emotions, indicating that awareness of one's feelings helps to integrate what you feel in your body and your perceptions of the current situation you face.

Interestingly, emotions do not seem to be stored as specific memories in our brain. They are not quite that tangible. Instead, the prefrontal cortex processes and stores associations of events and the emotions that were stirred by those events for use in new, similar situations. We remember how we feel about certain situations by this process. It helps us quickly and efficiently apply those feelings and make decisions in similar future situations. Because of this, we have tendencies or predispositions to feel and act in certain ways as similar situations arise. These tendencies are guided by our emotions rather than a calculated analysis of the pros and cons a given situation presents. In other words, it is our emotions that help create and inform our preferences. Without emotions, we wouldn't have preferences. If we don't know our preferences, how can we be guided when making decisions? An everyday example can help illustrate this:

> Needing a new shirt, Jeremy arrives at the men's clothing section of the department store and scans the numerous styles, fabrics, patterns, and colors of the shirts displayed. His eyes quickly settle on one shirt. He looks no further. Finding his size, he takes the shirt to the cashier and makes his purchase.

In this vignette, Jeremy was displaying his preference for a specific style, pattern, and color of shirt. There was no long, drawn-out evaluation of this style or that, which pattern among the many should he choose, or what color would go best with his current wardrobe. He simply made his choice.

Were we able to look into Jeremy's past experiences that involved his shirts (it sounds funny, I know, but these do exist) we would find that when Jeremy wore a similar shirt, he received compliments about it and about how he looked in it. Generally liking well-made clothing, Jeremy also enjoyed wearing similar shirts in the past. He liked the feel of the material on his skin. He also liked that a girlfriend had told him that it was her favorite shirt that he wore.

None of these prior situations were necessarily conscious in Jeremy's mind. He wasn't basing his decision on the recollection of specific compliments he had received. And, he didn't have to make a calculated study of each type of shirt offered by the store. He just had a preference for this kind of shirt based on the feeling linkages stored by his brain to previous situations that involved a similar type of shirt. His feelings—not a rational analysis—guided his selection.

Of course, preferences can be guided by negative emotions as well as positive ones. For example, Sally has a job opportunity that seems perfect in every respect. The salary is above average, the work is interesting with a chance for future promotions, and there is an office with a view. But something doesn't feel right and the offer is rejected. It may not be conscious, but a probe would reveal that the new job would involve working closely with a person who has characteristics similar to one of Sally's prior colleagues who treated her poorly. The feelings associated with her prior situations guided her present choice.

We also see this operating in trading. A trade setup that has produced good profits in the past will be viewed with a positive feeling state in the future. The trader's current feelings will be triggered from associations connected with prior situations involving similar market conditions and will help guide the trader in selecting and executing the trade. Just like Jeremy and his choice of shirt, our feelings create a preference for this kind of trade. If you removed emotions from the decision, however, you wouldn't know your preferences. Further, you would be unable to make an informed decision. As we will see clearly below, decisions made without emotional input result in poor outcomes. Emotions are an integral part of decision making.

Because there is such a strong myth that traders need to trade without emotions, I want to help readers become very clear on this. Fortunately, there is a series of solid studies that, while not involving trading per se, involves tasks very much like trading where emotions are clearly shown to add to the quality of the decision and lack of emotional input leads to poor decisions and chaotic outcomes. You will be able to see the implications clearly.

In one study conducted to further understand emotion-related learning, an Oxford University research team led by psychologist and neuroscientist Edmund Rolls enlisted 20 individuals with frontal lobe damage along with a group of individuals with undamaged brains to serve as a comparison group. The study participants were presented with patterns on a computer screen and were rewarded by points when they touched the screen to identify a correct pattern. They lost points for touching the screen when an incorrect pattern appeared. After participants correctly identified nine out of the last 10 patterns, the reward was reversed without warning. Now, participants received rewards for not touching the screen when a previously correct pattern was presented and touching the screen when a previously incorrect pattern appeared, though they weren't explicitly told this. No further instruction was given except that they should continue to try to gain points. Later, in a second trial of the study, the reward contingencies were again changed. In this second, unwarned change, participants were rewarded only when they refrained from touching both previously presented patterns; if they touched either, they lost points.

When the rewards were switched, the brain-damaged group continued to touch the initially rewarded pattern, even though this was the wrong response. They continued incorrectly despite the fact that points were lost. In the second trial, brain-damaged participants persisted in touching the screen when previous patterns appeared, even though the rewarded response was to refrain from touching it. Participants in the non–brain-damaged group easily switched behavior with few errors. *Those in the brain-damaged group were unable to change their behavior.*

Interestingly, the brain-damaged participants recognized when the rewards had changed, expressing comments like "they've switched" or "it's changed over." Nevertheless, they continued to respond incorrectly. Later, after the experiment was over, the participants could accurately describe the tests, how the tests had changed, and also how they were incorrectly responding to the changes, signifying that they fully comprehended the tests, at least on an intellectual level. They could not, however, explain the dissociation between what they knew and what they did.

They could not adapt their behavior and were at a loss to explain why they continued to make errors because they had lost their ability to process emotions. Rewards and the mild punishment seen here are associated with emotions—happiness or joy when rewarded and frustration and perhaps a bit of sadness when the reward points were taken away (the mild punishment). But the brain-lesioned participants experienced neither joy nor sadness. It was as if their emotions had been eliminated from their decisions. As a consequence, they were unable to stop acting in the way that was previously rewarded, but which now resulted in penalties. They had no emotional information with which to guide their behavior. It was as if they were repeatedly touching a hot stove, completely unaware that they were being burned.

According to Rolls, emotions are a crucial component necessary in making decisions, especially in controlling and correcting reward-related and punishment-related behavior because these kinds of decisions always involve emotion. These types of behaviors are critically important to traders. Were we to truly trade without emotions as the conventional trading wisdom erroneously suggests we should, we would be unable to respond to changing market conditions. Bullish trades that had been working in the uptrend, for example, would continue to be taken long after the market had turned down. Despite the punishment of loss after loss, we would be unable to adjust our responses if we detached ourselves from our emotions. We would continue to trade long as the market was falling, perhaps knowing it was wrong and being able to say it was wrong, but unable to act differently because we cannot do so without the information our emotions provide.

A related series of studies employed an exercise called the Iowa Gambling Task. The decisions called for in this experiment have many similarities with trading. Neuropsychologist Antoine Bechara along with Hanna Damasio and their colleagues studied decision making in individuals who had brain lesions in the prefrontal cortex area that compromised their ability to process feelings and emotions. With similar lesions and similar characteristics to Phineas Gage and the participants in the preceding study on rewards, participants in this study also retained intact IQs and memory, despite their brain damage. In this study, participants drew cards one at a time from four different decks (A, B, C, and D). Selecting a card from either deck A or B provided the player with a large reward. Selections from A and B, however, could also result in a stiff penalty. The occurrences of penalties could not be predicted. Selecting a card from either C or D decks resulted in a smaller reward and also a smaller loss.

A short time into the selection, normal participants avoided selecting cards from the high reward/high loss decks (A and B decks). These were considered "disadvantaged decks" because of the severe penalty when a loss card was drawn. After a small number of cards had been selected, normal participants also began to exhibit an *anticipatory skin conductance response* before their selection of a card from a disadvantaged deck. Skin conductance is a standard biofeedback measure that assesses psychological arousal through the electrical conductance of the skin. The electrical transmission of the skin varies with its moisture level. Under stress and anxiety (as we have learned from the flight-fight response), the body's sweat glands naturally open up and the skin becomes moist, readily transmitting nonharmful electrical impulses that can be measured with sensors attached to the skin.

Participants with normal brains had skin conductance responses when they anticipated taking a card from a disadvantaged deck indicating an aroused or stress state in anticipation of a potential large loss. Those with prefrontal cortex lesions had no such response. In fact, those with brain damage consistently preferred decks with high immediate reward over decks with a smaller reward, despite the fact that the decks with smaller rewards were more advantageous over the long run. Normal participants preferred drawing cards from the advantaged decks and exhibited a stress response when selecting a card from a disadvantaged deck. The brain lesioned participants did not show such an emotional response. Their emotions did not factor into their decisions.

The researchers went further. They manipulated the decks by varying the scale and frequency of rewards and losses causing disadvantaged decks to be even more disadvantaged. Despite increased large and frequent losses, lesioned participants continued to select cards from disadvantaged decks. Altering the losses and the rewards did not cause the lesioned participants to change their behavior toward disadvantaged decks. Because emotions had been removed from their decision-making process, they were unable to apprehend that drawing cards from disadvantaged decks was contrary to their self-interest. They had no emotionally informed insight. Normal participants did learn to adjust their selections and avoided the disadvantageous decks, and they again exhibited the emotionally-toned skin conductance reaction ahead of making their choices. Lesioned participants did not have the same emotional skin response. They lacked the feelings needed for navigating correct decisions. Because of this, they lacked emotional intelligence. Bechara, Damasio, and associates noted that the participants lacking emotional responses are "oblivious to the future and are guided predominately by immediate prospects" even in the face of increasing adverse consequences.

The conclusion to be drawn from this research is vitally important for traders: the idea that traders must trade without emotion and work to eliminate their emotions from their trading decisions is utterly baseless and wrong. We are unable to make sound decisions without our feelings. Acting without emotional guidance would be acting like Phineas Gage and other brain-damaged patients. Our trading results would be abysmal.

Some related research has been done with traders. Using biofeedback monitors that measured skin conductance response along with heart rate, blood volume pulse, and other nervous system measures, Andrew Lo and Dmitry Repin studied professional traders in their trading rooms making actual trades in the foreign-exchange and interest rate futures markets. Lo and Repin also tracked market price data and volatility. They found that traders' "emotional responses are a significant factor in the real-time processing of financial risks." This group of traders included highly experienced traders as well as traders with moderate and little experience. Traders with high levels of trading experience generally exhibited lower emotional responses than less experienced traders, but even the highly experienced reacted strongly to times when the market became volatile. We see professional traders do not eliminate their emotions and that these are felt during trading. Consistent with other studies on risk and decision making, Lo and Repin theorize that, although more experienced traders have less emotional reaction to price movement in their trading, they very likely apply emotions even when making rapid, expert trading judgments, although they may have difficultly articulating how emotions factor into their decisions. A trader's feelings are an integral ingredient in their judgments and become integrated as part of the decision process over time and experience.

In the study conducted on London traders functioning as proprietary traders and market makers by Mark Fenton-O'Creevy and his research team, the more seasoned traders also experienced emotions in their trading, including negative emotions. The researchers found that the more experienced and more accomplished traders were more willing to have negative emotions and didn't let their emotions distract them from their pursuit of their long-term goals. Some traders used their own emotions as a source of information about the emotions other market participants were experiencing as a way to inform their trades. Less experienced and less accomplished traders tried to avoid and eliminate their emotions by mentally attempting to control them or by behavioral responses designed to avoid them, such as trading with small positions after losses or removing themselves from trading by walking away from their trading desk when acute emotions were felt. The better traders were exercising emotional intelligence; they used the information their emotions provided to make better decisions. Less accomplished and less experienced traders acted without emotional intelligence. They tried to avoid, get rid of, and eliminate their emotions.

The Functions of Emotions in Trading Decisions

Thinking further about emotions and feelings in decision making, Hans Pfister, professor of business psychology at Germany's University of Lüneburg and Gisela Böhm at Norway's University of Bergen, developed a framework for how emotion functions in decision-making. They show that emotions are not a sign of irrationality; emotions are an integral part of rational decision making. They also emphasize that emotions don't all fit into a singular category and, therefore, should not all be treated in the same way. Further, categorizing emotions along a single dimension such as positive/negative or beneficial versus harmful is not particularly useful. For example, overindulgence in alcohol may be pleasant but can also be harmful. Holding onto a profitable trade may feel unpleasant but may be beneficial. Pfister and Böhm point out that categorizing emotion by a one-dimensional dichotomy is not supported empirically by the research and is not particularly useful pragmatically. When in a profitable trade and we view our emotional response as solely unpleasant, for example, we are likely to cut the trade short. When viewed more accurately as having multifaceted meanings, emotions hold a mix of connotations, such as the excitement of being in a trade with the potential for profit as well as putting us on notice that we have placed ourselves at risk and there is also danger of a loss. The unpleasantness felt can be interpreted as a signal to pay close attention to the market for signs that it is turning, which will be more accurate and much more constructive for a trader in a trade rather than being interpreted exclusively as a discomfort that must be escaped.

In any given situation in which a decision is made, according to Pfister and Böhm, emotion plays an integral part. Because emotions are multidimensional, these researchers have developed a model of how emotions function in shaping our decisions. They identify four primary functions:

1. Information—emotions provide information useful in understanding and appraising alternatives and options. As an example, emotions provide information when a trader identifies a choice trade setup. Feelings of heightened interest and excitement help inform our trade choice and shape the trade decision.

2. Speed—emotions can help us process information faster, giving the trader the ability to make decisions rapidly when time is a consideration. When in a short trade, for example, a trader sees her trade stall at support. Her feelings of apprehension that the market is no longer going down will help her to make a decision about the trade quickly, before price has an opportunity to rally against her position. The speed function also works in the opposite way. When a trader has only a little information on which to base a trade but knows it is a good trade and knows he must act quickly, it is his feelings—honed by experience—that can guide his actions to take the trade. In this way, emotions also provide a motivational function in trading decisions.

3. Focus attention—emotions help us evaluate a situation by directing our attention to the data that is most relevant to the decision. For example, an experienced trader will see what appears to be an excellent trade on their chart. Although it looks ideal, unsettled feelings about the trade causes the trader to consider the higher time frame before taking the trade. Emotions direct the skilled trader's attention to the highly relevant background conditions of the market before they act to take a trade.

4. Commitment—emotions help us to commit to a decision and to stay with that decision once it is made. Here, feelings of confidence in the decision or the feelings associated with doing what is most important to the trader help her take action and sustain her decision. A trader may be struggling with cutting winning trades short, for example, and she feels the unpleasantness of anxiety while in a profitable trade. But it is her feelings of confidence in herself and her strong feelings of desire to become a competent trader who holds her winning trades that form her commitment to see the trade through, despite her other, unpleasant feelings of anxiety.

In any given context, one or more of the four roles that emotions play in decisions will tend to dominate. Which ones dominate will change with the circumstances of the decision, but no one emotional function ever operates alone. For example, a trader might feel pressed by his discomfort to jump into the market because it has a sudden push up and he is missing out and at the same time have other important feelings associated with not taking that trade and remaining true to his trading plan.

So it is not emotions themselves that create trouble for the trader and successful traders are not the ones who somehow found a magic key to turn off their emotions. Smart, successful traders accept their emotions as a given in trading and also as internal aids in making decisions. Astute traders will see that Pfister and Böhm's model of emotions is a useful construct in becoming more familiar with their feeling states and recognize that emotions are not uni-dimensional but multifaceted and have direct influence on our decisions and trading actions. Pfister and Böhm's four functions of emotions in decision making can assist a trader in identifying how their emotions operate and influence their decisions. This model can help the trader add a level of emotional intelligence to their trading.

■ Becoming Aware of and Open to Your Emotions

It is beneficial for you to develop awareness of your emotions and the various influences on your trading decisions that emotions can have: Exercise 4.1 is designed for this purpose. Two examples are provided to guide you in making use of the form. We will walk through them.

Exercise 4.1 How My Emotions Function in My Trading

Situation	Information	Speed	Attention	Commitment
Example 1: Price begins to rally aggressively. Should I jump aboard?	*Feelings of excitement over potential quick profits.*	*The market is moving; I need to make a quick decision. However, I don't feel confident enough to take this trade.*	*Feelings of caution prevail. I know I am not seeing all the data. This is why I am not confident. I check my other indicators.*	*Feelings of pride. In the past, I would have jumped in, but paying attention to all my feelings kept me out of an unplanned trade.*
Example 2: Developing plan for tomorrow's trading: identifying trade locations.	*Feeling very curious about obvious selling in market today. Wondering what does this mean?*	*Feeling calm; there is no rush.*	*Continuing to feel very interested in the evidence of selling. I checked the higher time frame and was excited to find significant resistance!*	*Confident feelings that everything is coming together for a great trade tomorrow.*

In the first column of Exercise 4.1, jot down briefly a situation in which you were called upon to make a trading decision. In the first example given, the trader is deciding whether or not to take a trade at a sudden market movement. This trader notes in the *Information* column that his feelings reflect excitement over the fast profits he envisions. In the *Speed* column, he notes that he needs to act quickly, but doesn't feel the confidence he needs to make such a rapid decision. Feelings of caution continue and these draw his attention to his indicators; he notes that he has insufficient data to take a trade. Keeping himself out of the trade and doing what is most important for his trading and for himself as a trader (i.e., to refrain from jumping into poorly planned trades) gives him satisfaction and a feeling of pride that he is acting in the best interests of his trading. This helps him to commit to not only avoid jumping into an unplanned trade in the future, but also to continue to be aware of his emotions and to continue to work on his self-development as a trader. This trader's enhanced awareness of his emotions and his effective use of his emotions support him both in better trading and in remaining committed to the important process of self-development.

The second example is not an immediate trading decision, but a decision about where a trade may take place the next trading day. As the trader noted indications of selling in today's market, she was aware that she felt very curious about the selling. She noticed her curiosity was greater than normal and wondered what it might mean. She recorded this in the *Information* column of the exercise form. She also felt calm; not pressed to make a quick decision. This was entered under *Speed*. As she continued to check out her market with interest, her attention was drawn to higher time frame resistance. She suddenly felt excited. She now understood the reason for the selling in today's market. The excitement she now feels confirms her analysis and informs her decision making. All of her emotions lead to a high level of commitment for the next day's trading. Her skilled use of her emotions led her to a choice trade opportunity. Because she has strong feelings that "everything is coming together for a great trade," her commitment is high and she will be able to confidently execute and manage that trade when it occurs.

This is a very different way of looking at emotions. Emotions are not something to be avoided, managed, escaped, or eliminated. Certainly, they can be unpleasant and uncomfortable, but they provide much more information about the market and your trades than they are given credit for by conventional trading wisdom. Traders need to be emotionally intelligent. Begin to become aware of your emotions and see them as multifaceted and adding value to your decisions rather than as one dimensional, nothing but negative, and something to be controlled, turned off, or suppressed. Emotions are not the enemy. As you become more aware of your feelings, adopt an attitude of being open to whatever feeling may show up.

We want to be open to all our feelings as well as our thoughts rather than fighting them. We know fighting them makes things worse. We can get "anxiety about our anxiety" and amplify our arousal. Fighting our emotions also distracts us from what is important in our trading. Trying to get rid of or reduce our emotions takes us out of the trade. It turns our attention inward, away from the market and any trade we may have on. This is the true irrationality of emotions. It's not that emotions cause irrational decisions, but it's *trying to control emotions that causes erratic trading.* How can anyone be successful in trading if they are always engaged in fighting emotions? We know through our experiences that trying to control how we feel takes enormous effort. Because attention is finite, we can't place our attention on two demanding tasks—that is, controlling our feelings and managing our trade—at the same time. We can no longer be attentive to our trade when focused on our feelings. This is precisely why we want to work at being open to our feelings—even the unpleasant ones—and let them be just as they are.

■ A Few Words on Strong Emotions

While emotions have definite positive functions in trading decisions, traders nevertheless can also feel overwhelmed by strong emotions. All traders have had the experience that strong emotions negatively affect their trading performance. In a survey-type study of 80 online traders conducted by Lo, Repin, and trading psychologist Brett Steenbarger, traders recorded their day's trading results and also gave an assessment of their feelings. Strong emotional responses were found to be clearly counterproductive in real-time trading. Traders participating in this study who were more emotionally reactive to gains and losses had significantly worse trading performance than those with more even-keeled feeling states as they traded throughout the day. The authors note that our habitual emotional reactions can be "too crude" for effective trading. A different approach to our normal response to strong emotions is needed.

As a first step, we need to be more accepting of our emotions—the felt bodily states and feelings, or somatic markers as described by Damasio—that together with our thoughts and perceptions guide our decisions and consequent actions. When we are unwilling to have contact with our emotions, we tend to fight them. This is our "crude" and habitual reaction and it gives our unpleasant emotions additional strength. This is how we can become quickly overaroused and overwhelmed. When aroused and overwhelmed by our emotions, we can have difficulty in taking note of our somatic markers, logical thoughts, and rational perceptions about the market. We can become emotionally hijacked. It is as if one voice is screaming and we can't hear or even acknowledge other important voices in the crowd. As Lo, Repin, and Steenbarger found with day traders, hyperarousal overrides our normal ability to think rationally and respond to the market with care and consideration. High arousal leads to poor trading choices and inept trading actions. Most traders have probably experienced this.

In the next few chapters, we discuss in depth mindfulness and cognitive defusion—two potent techniques that will help us understand our thoughts and feelings in a different light. Through these methods we will see that we can step back from our thoughts and feelings, be more accepting of them, and begin to actually experience that we don't have to respond in only one, intractable way to our internal state; we can develop flexibility in how we deal with our emotions, even the strong ones. In later chapters, we also discuss the high-value trading actions that both reflect and bring more flexibility and consistency into our trading.

In Parts II and III of this book, we present many useful and reliable techniques and methods traders can learn to deal with fear and other difficult emotions. These powerful techniques and methods have been developed by psychologists and I have adapted them specifically for traders. I have taught these techniques and methods to traders who have used them effectively. They are practical and easy to do. But let's not get too far ahead of ourselves, as there is more to clarify before we get to techniques. For now, however, I do want to discuss one of the best things to do for fear, anxiety, and stress: regular exercise.

You may be surprised to read about regular exercise in a book on trading psychology, but it is a serious recommendation because regular exercise can be a very potent antidote to strong feelings. A recent cover story by Karen Weir in the American Psychological Association's membership journal, *Monitor on Psychology*, highlighted the strong research evidence on the mental benefits of exercise. The aim of the article was to encourage psychologists to include exercise in their treatment programs. Consider your own experience with exercise. If you have ever concluded a stressful day with a run or other vigorous exercise, chances are you felt better after the workout. There is a strong link between exercise and our state of mind, and the effect is immediate. It is a simple and very effective way to regulate mood.

In general, people who exercise regularly are less prone to mood problems than those who do not. This is well-established, but the research goes much further. In a revealing series of clinical trials, medical psychologist James Blumenthal and his colleagues show just how potent exercise can be. Blumenthal compared the effects of regular exercise against antidepressant medication in treating individuals with major depressive disorder, a very serious mental affliction. He and his research team found that regular aerobic exercise was *as good as medicine* in treating this serious mental illness. Moreover, when people maintained a routine of exercise, they continued to keep their depression in check after a year. This is significant because people who suffer with major depression are prone to relapse. Exercise not only alleviated symptoms as effectively as drugs, exercise also had a longer-term protective benefit, which no drug can offer.

Exercise is also powerfully helpful in reducing stress and anxiety and may be particularly beneficial in dealing with the flight-flight response discussed above. Psychologists Jasper Smits and Michael Otto have shown that regular aerobic exercise helps to desensitize a person from many of the physiological symptoms of fear and anxiety—for example, muscle tension, racing heart, feeling out of breath, and the like. As people become more accustomed to these physical symptoms through exercise, they become hardened and habituated to them. In other words, they become more mentally tough when it comes to uncomfortable bodily sensations because they routinely accept them in exercise. What earlier was felt as disagreeable becomes perceived as innocuous with exercise.

Exercise itself is a form of stress, requiring effort and adaptation. It puts your body into better shape, which empowers it to better handle other stress, including the stress from trading. Studies show that those who engage in a program of exercise have less physiological activation and intensity of common stress markers such as elevated blood pressure and heart rate as well as lower psychological markers of mood and symptoms of anxiety when confronted by stress. Exercise helps people adapt to stress. Those who persist in a regular routine of exercise also learn the same mental skills that help them to persist in holding a trade rather than cutting it short or delaying immediate gratification and holding back from jumping into a trade even though there is an urge to do so. In general, stress is a daily consideration in the trading environment and exercise will clearly help buffer you from its harmful effects—mentally, physically, and trading-wise.

As interesting as these findings are, it is what goes on inside the brain where exercise can really be of help to traders hindered by the discomfort of fear and stress. Harvard Medical School professor John Ratey describes these and other beneficial processes that arise from exercise as Miracle Grow for the brain. He reports that aerobic exercise does several positive things for body and brain. One of the most important is exercise elevates and balances neurochemicals. Remember that when we are stressed, the amygdala floods the brain and body with chemicals that prepare the body to escape or fight. Exercise restores balance. Exercise naturally increases serotonin, a neurochemical that has a calming effect on our mood and enhances our sense of security.

Regular exercise also increases GABA (γ-Aminobutyric acid) and ATP. GABA is one of the brain's main inhibitory neurotransmitters, meaning that it plays a large role in regulating excitability and arousal throughout the nervous system. Both GABA and ATP directly act to restrain the nervous system's fight-flight/stress response. Exercise naturally dampens our normal reactiveness to stress.

Physiologically, exercise reduces overall muscle tension, improves the cardiovascular system, lowers blood pressure, and lowers the resting tension of the major muscle groups that are automatically activated in stressful situations. Exercise helps to reset the stress threshold.

Through exercise, we harden the body and the brain to stress in a positive way. Exercise also has a psychological effect over and above making us feel better. Psychologically, we are actively doing something to cope with stress. We are taking action.

This gives us a sense of control over what we are able to influence. The combination of all these factors: increasing calming and mood enhancing neurochemicals in the brain, elevating our stress tolerance both physically and mentally, breaking down the feedback loop between muscle tension and fear, and generating efficacy over ourselves opens up the potential to take constructive action when in a trading situation that normally invokes stress or fear rather than the rigid, inflexible actions we might typically make. This can be potent for a trader hampered by fear and anxiety.

It is very hard to be a competent trader if you are plagued by anxiety each time you put on a trade or step up size. You can feel like a nervous wreck with no control over your anxiety and trading. Your trading world and how you operate within it shrinks. You are likely to find yourself repeating the same rigid patterns over and over, unable to break free. You may begin to doubt yourself as a trader and even as a person. Adding to the anxiety are feelings of shame, sadness, and maybe hopelessness. Developing a routine of exercise along with other suggestions in this book, can help you develop control over what you can influence. You may begin to see yourself as taking an active, rather than a passive approach to your trading. Things are not so hopeless. You can begin to lower sensitivity to anxiety, increase calming neurochemicals and hormones, increase your tolerance for stress, and provide an opening to use the other techniques and methods we will discuss shortly. As these techniques and methods are applied in your trading, continued exercise provides the growth and other factors the brain needs to develop and strengthen new pathways for trading actions, setting up new, flexible patterns in situations that in the past cause stress. Sound good? Well, there's more to be done.

PART II

USING CUTTING-EDGE PSYCHOLOGY

CHAPTER 5

The Traders' Psychological Edge Lies in a Different Kind of Thinking

Effective trading calls on traders to confront significant psychological challenges. Facing and overcoming these challenges is not an easy endeavor. The difficulty lies in the fact that our mind, our biology, and even our genes are not naturally suited for the mental demands of trading. In fact, our minds, our biology, and our genes tend to work against us in trading, as we have seen in the first few chapters. As we have also seen, the solutions traders develop to address these challenges—especially the notion that emotions should be eliminated—often compounds their troubles. We are not able to simply eliminate emotions or thoughts at will. That's just not possible on a consistent basis. Our minds are more complex; a simplistic, naïve approach not only does not work, it makes matters worse. We need to approach the psychology of trading in a different way.

■ Mind, Genes, Emotions, and Biology

One of the psychological challenges we face is the fact that our minds freely apply mental shortcuts that tilt toward cognitive biases in rendering trading decisions. Costly errors do not come from conscious intentional actions, nor are they always the results of emotions. Rather, many costly errors result from actions that appear to our mind to be correct at the moment and that later, on reflection, are seen as flawed and faulty. When we apply mental shortcuts, we ignore base rates and consider only the more obvious and recent information, and tend to address easily answered but woefully inadequate questions. The application of mental shortcuts to complicated trading decisions leads us to deficient market assessments and poorly constructed trades.

In Chapter 1 we distinguished between our intuitive mind and our deliberative mind. We noted that it is our deliberative mind that we need to engage in making trading decisions. In contrast to our intuitive mind, deliberative mind can assess probabilities, consider disparate information, synthesize data, weigh options, and override our tendency toward bias. Although more suited for trading the markets, deliberative mind is usually willing to accept whatever answers intuitive mind provides, however defective those answers may be. Deliberative mind is difficult to engage and maintain connection with. It takes effort and coaxing to engage deliberative mind in conducting the kind of evaluative calculus needed for trading. But traders must marshal their deliberate mind to engage in analytical thinking and reflect consciously on the data before them to make sure that nothing is overlooked and everything is weighed appropriately. Simply depending on mental shortcuts in trading is the source of many trading errors and losing trades.

Another psychological challenge for traders is the role our genes and biology play in our trading. Being ready to mobilize and either flee or fight a powerful forest animal has helped humans survive over the millennia. While today few confront hungry tigers, we continue to carry the genetic coding of the fight-flight response and automatically react with a strong call for action to more mundane threats, including perceived threats arising from our mind in everyday trading. During our evolution, we have also learned that it is usually better to hold on to what we have. We are innately averse to loss, and we confront the risk of loss every time we put on a trade.

As we have seen, emotions also present a significant psychological challenge to us in trading. Strong emotions—especially fear, as well as other emotions such as anger, excitement, boredom, and sadness—can cause unforced errors in trading. When under the influence of emotions, we may surrender our emotional intelligence and lose track of our trade. When our focus goes inward, we become unable to objectively assess the market or execute trading skills. The more we struggle and try to control our internal state, the more intense our inner world becomes, and the more our trading can suffer. Our struggles lead to mistakes and trading failure. When fear and other strong emotions kick in, they trigger specific brain areas that automatically send chemical messages to other parts of the body. Especially with the emotion of fear, we have seen that the amygdala and hippocampus are involved and we have no direct control over them once activated.

Is it any wonder why trading is such a difficult endeavor? In no uncertain terms, our biology, genes, mind, and emotions all can and do work against us as traders. Without a substantial and conscious effort on our part, our own nature and makeup can consistently undermine our ability to trade effectively.

■ Avoidance

Our thoughts, emotions, and bodily sensations will always play into our trading. Most traders generally experience their emotions most prominently and, perhaps to a slightly lesser extent, bodily sensations while trading. Because this experience can be uncomfortable and unpleasant, our instinct is to avoid or escape it. Avoidance and escape are natural and they work well in many day-to-day situations. But like many things in trading psychology, what is natural may not always be in the trader's best interest. Avoidance of unpleasant emotions almost always works against our trading. The control strategy examples you listed in Exercises 3.1 and 3.2 from Chapter 3 were likely all done in the service of escaping, avoiding, or reducing internal discomfort. Many of these strategies were natural reactions, and they seemed sensible at the time. When you weighed the costs and benefits, however, you would most likely find that these avoidance strategies generated little benefit, if any, to your trading, they had no lasting impact on your internal state, and they cost you in terms of actual losses, missed opportunities, and lost profits. Avoidance strategies undermined your growth and development in skillful trading.

Avoidance is seen in virtually all trading situations in which unpleasant bodily sensations, unwanted thoughts, and uncomfortable emotions occur. For example, fear might be experienced after a trader enters a trade and sees the market go slightly against her position. If the fear is strong enough, she might cut the trade short to escape the unpleasantness she feels. A less obvious example involves the trader who perceives the market starting to rally and jumps into an unplanned trade because of the discomfort he feels at not being in on the trade. Although subtle, he takes the trade to escape the unease he feels from being left on the sidelines. An even more subtle example is seen in a trader who identifies a valid trade setup and commits much greater size than normal. Odds are very good that this trader is responding with position size to an internal voice concerned with making up a previous loss, making more money that day than a trading friend, or some other irrelevant justification that is irritating the trader. Because relief from disagreeable feelings occurs through a trading action, the two can easily become linked and we can literally train ourselves to be poor traders—forever locked into escaping discomfort through maladroit trading actions. In psychology, this is known as *negative reinforcement*. It was originally described by behavioral psychologist B. F. Skinner as part of his highly influential theory of *operant conditioning*, that is, how humans learn through the consequences of their actions. Traders will find it worthwhile to understand negative reinforcement.

■ Negative Reinforcement Directly Affects Trading Performance

In general, we think of reinforcement in a positive way. For example, a trader on a proprietary trading desk receives a bonus for her outstanding performance. Her behavior is being positively reinforced. Because of the bonus (a consequence of her good behavior), she is likely to work hard to keep her performance up in the future. The reinforcement encourages and strengthens desirable behavior. Everyone can understand this. Negative reinforcement is a little different, conceptually. It is not about punishment. Negative reinforcement is *acting to remove or avoid something unpleasant.* Let's look at an everyday example to be clear:

> A mother and her child are in the checkout line at the grocery. It's 5:00 P.M. and mother has just finished shopping for tonight's dinner. Her child spots candy on the display stand and asks for a candy bar. Mother says, "No, it's too close to dinner." The child begins to cry. Mother tries to ignore the child, but the child begins screaming, "I want a candy bar!" Mother feels the eyes of other people in the line looking at them and tries to quiet the child, but the child will have none of that. Finally, mother acquiesces and gives the candy to her child who immediately smiles and stops her tantrum.

Mother's action of giving the candy bar to the child serves to take away the child's unpleasant behavior. Mother's action effectively removes something noxious. Mother's behavior is being negatively reinforced because the child stops crying. Of course, the next time the child wants a candy bar, what do you think will happen?

In trading, when we take an action to remove, avoid, or escape an unpleasant internal experience, we are rewarding the action that removes it. This is negative reinforcement. Giving the candy bar to the child (action) ended the child's tantrum (unpleasant experience). Jumping into an unplanned trade (action) removes the irritating thoughts and feelings of missing out (unpleasant experience). This may not be easy to understand, so let's walk through an example of cutting a winning trade short in detail as illustrated in Figure 5.1 to see not only the negative reinforcement, but also the discouraging consequences of such reinforcement.

Starting at the top, a trader identifies a trade setup. It meets his trade setup criteria, and the trade is entered. Shortly after the trade is put on, the trader begins to experience stress. The threat of a loss seems real and, because of prior losses that may be recalled or sensitivity to loss aversion or both, the stress response kicks in and the trader begins to notice discomfort.

The discomfort seems to confirm the threat of loss. Apprehension can rapidly rise into trepidation, then to alarm and fear. The mind becomes vocal, declaring

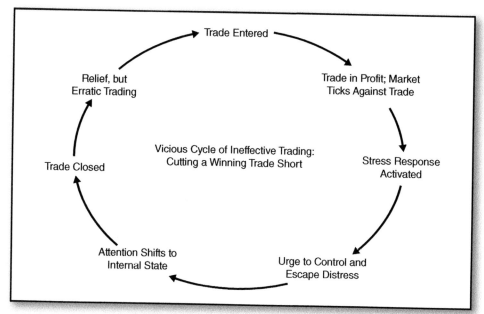

FIGURE 5.1 Vicious Cycle of Ineffective Trading: Cutting a Winning Trade Short

its concern. It tells the trader how bad a loss would be and how that just can't be tolerated. Emotions and bodily sensations seem to corroborate the internal voice and inflame the discomfort. Just like the child having a temper tantrum over the candy bar, the trader's inner voice becomes strident, urging the trader to exit the trade even though it has just begun.

Attention shifts and narrows. Just moments before, the trader was reading the market carefully, evaluating its current indications against trade setup criteria. That perspective has dramatically changed. Now, the trader's outward concentration is absorbed by negligible price fluctuations. Each tick against the position sets off new alarms. His main focus, however, has turned inward. The trader is acutely aware of body sensations and the inner distress he feels in both his emotions and his mental self-talk.

As attention shifts to the trader's inner state, not only is the focus on the trade lost, but the demand to escape the distress mounts. The trader may at first try to suppress the discomfort, but this only further misdirects attention away from the trade. The more the trader struggles with his unwanted thoughts and feelings, the more prominent they become. With internal feelings amplified, trade management is abandoned. All interest is now in fleeing the unease and discomfort of the internal state.

The simple and effective solution to alleviate the internal discomfort is to exit the trade, which the trader does. Note carefully that closing the trade is done solely to relieve distress. The trade is not closed because exiting is the right trade management decision or because this action is in the best interest of the trade. The reason the trader exits the trade has nothing to do with the trade. *The trader's action is done solely to regulate his internal state.* This is the crucial point. This is not trading; it's struggling with emotion.

Reinforcement comes as the trader is released from the grip of distress. As soon as the trade has been taken off, the trader begins to relax. The discomfort felt in the body melts away. The mind calms down. Emotions evaporate. The crisis is over. The action of closing the trade is reinforced by the relief. It is negative reinforcement because the action gets rid of an unpleasant experience. The removal of the distress is the reward for cutting the trade. Because the relief is direct and immediate, it is a very powerful reinforcer. Like the mother placating her child, the immediate relief from cutting the trade almost guarantees that when the trader is in a similar stressful situation in the future, he will address it in the same way.

Recall from Chapter 2 how the flight-fight response activates the hippocampus to remember threats and how to deal with them. The hippocampus will record and remember that cutting the trade successfully removes distress. Thus, an ineffective trading response pattern gets encoded in the memory center of the brain: feel uncomfortable in a trade → cut the trade → gain relief. The hippocampus doesn't concern itself with reduced profits. Because of our genetic heritage, the hippocampus is primarily concerned with removing the threat and knows that closing the trade effectively removes the threat and relieves the distress. The hippocampus—as the brain's memory center—stores this for future situations. The trader thus trains himself to escape trading discomfort by cutting winning trades short. Because cutting the trade is effective at removing distress and our brain codes it into memory, he is virtually guaranteed to do it again the next time. When repeated a few times, he will have conditioned himself very powerfully to cut trades in the face of stress. Avoidance of unpleasant internal states in trading usually leads to counterproductive trading behaviors. Once a counterproductive behavior becomes hardened through a few negatively reinforced trading episodes, it becomes difficult to change that behavior. This is a good example of why traders need to understand trading psychology. It's natural to want to avoid discomfort; but the things we do naturally can backfire in trading.

The obvious consequence for the trader caught in this mode of emotional trading is that he is blocking himself from learning to trade well. The development of trade management skills is sacrificed for the escape from unwanted feelings, thoughts, and sensations. This is what traders who struggle with strong emotions typically say about the costs associated with attempting to control and suppress uncomfortable emotions: getting rid of distressing emotions becomes the prime concern and their trading suffers. They leave significant profits on the table from cutting winners short. They never learn to trade skillfully. They become stuck in a cycle of unproductive trading. Ultimately, they feel bad about themselves as traders. This is a true vicious cycle that gets repeated trade after trade. If it is not somehow broken, it is easy to see that the trader will eventually burn out and leave the trading game along with their hopes for whatever lifestyle and level of financial independence they had envisioned.

Although the example above shows how fear can cause traders to cut a winning trade short, the same cycle can be applied for other erratic trading prompted by strong emotions. The trader who sees the market begin to move, for example, will feel similar stress at not being in the market and missing out on imagined profits. In this case, trade entry is made to appease the internal pressure felt at not being in a trade. Again, action is taken in the service of emotions and relief from one's internal state is achieved, making the impulsive action an almost guaranteed response the next time the trader sees the market take off. Regardless what situation prompts the erratic action, traders can teach themselves to be poor traders by trading in the service of their emotions and negatively reinforcing erratic trading actions that remove those unwanted internal states. Instead of developing sound trading behaviors that improve their skills at trading, they develop skills at fleeing emotion. This is one of the main reasons why so many traders fail at trading.

◼ A Different Kind of Thinking

Albert Einstein once observed that we cannot solve problems by using the same kind of thinking that caused the problem. This is very true with respect to our internal state. Attempting to control emotions does not work. You now understand that not only does this kind of thinking not solve the problem, it is very harmful to your trading, and harmful to your development as a trader. A different kind of thinking is needed to help traders understand that feeling unwanted emotion does not necessarily predict losing trades. Traders also need to recognize that what the mind says may not always reflect reality. We need to learn to pull back from our thoughts rather than buy into them. Moreover, we need a different kind of thinking approach in order to engage our deliberative mind. The usual way of thinking for the vast majority of us offers too much freedom for intuitive mind to operate: we tend to view the charts and our trades through the foggy lenses of heuristics and other cognitive biases.

An important and critical step toward a different kind of thinking is to develop the mental skill called mindfulness. Mindfulness allows us to be an observer of our own thoughts and feelings while keeping our mind in the present moment and our attention on the things that matter. Mindfulness skills can loosen the grip of difficult thoughts and feelings that derail skillful trading. Mindfulness can help traders develop a greater flexibility in responding to the market while at the same time strengthen their attentional capacity to engage deliberative mind.

◼ Mindfulness

I consider mindfulness to be the most important mental skill a trader can develop to address many of trading's psychological challenges. In this section, we present an overview of mindfulness and then go into some of the aspects—backed by scientific research—of why it is such an important mental skill for traders. In the next chapter, you will learn how to practice mindfulness through several mindfulness scripts which you can use to develop your own mindfulness routine and skill set.

Mindfulness is a quality of consciousness often described as "paying attention in a particular way: on purpose, in the present moment, and nonjudgmentally."[1] As you will see, mindfulness is a state of mind developed through practice to help increase attention and concentration. Mindfulness allows you to separate yourself from your thoughts and feelings; and it further helps you stay focused in the present moment rather than drift off into the past or future.

Mindfulness originated from the Eastern traditions of yoga and Buddhism. It has a very long history. Patanjali, a yoga master, wrote about the method in his *Yoga Sutra* (see, for example, Chip Hartranft's *The Yoga Sutra of Patanjali*) during the second century BC. Oral and other written material on meditation and mindfulness existed prior to Patanjali's manuscript, but his became the governing text in the yogic tradition. It is still used today. The practice of mindfulness is ancient.

Despite its age, mindfulness is relatively new in the Occident. Although new, mindfulness is rapidly changing the landscape of psychology in the West. It is becoming well researched and, in the last several years, scientists have documented several significant characteristics and benefits that mindfulness offers. I discuss some of the important research findings, as they are significant for traders.

The practice of mindfulness (sometimes referred to as mindfulness meditation) possesses several characteristics of value to traders. Through mindfulness, traders can develop better regulation of their attention and a heightened clarity of the various aspects of their environment. The mindful trader may see the trading cues signaled by the market clearer and more objectively. When mindful, it becomes easier for the trader to shift attention back and forth between the last few bars on the chart and the larger structure that forms the background. Mindfulness can support the trader in integrating the chart's right edge with overall market context and help the trader more clearly identify when conditions are ripe for a trade.

As a part of attentional management, mindfulness meditation also helps the trader stay in the present moment. The mind is a "frequent flyer" into the past and future. Notice, for example, how many times your mind has wandered while reading this text. While reading, you may have noticed that, on its own, your mind began thinking of other things. As you read about cutting a trade short, for example, you might have recalled a recent trade where you did something similar. Your mind then begins to think about and, perhaps, relive that past experience. Then, you might recall there is a new indicator you want to research, which you think might help you hold onto your trades, and you begin thinking about that indicator. You mind might start to think about this new indicator's components, comparing them with what you now use, and imagining how the new indicator might work for you on future trades. At some point, you might notice you have become hungry and your mind starts thinking about getting a snack. Is there anything in the cupboard, you wonder? "Yes! There is a bag of chips." But then you might think chips aren't so good for your diet and how you want to lose weight. "Losing weight has been hard," you think. "Maybe I should join a gym," might be your next thought. "That would be good for me." Your mind then starts planning. "I can work out Monday, Wednesday, and Friday after the market close...." And on and on it goes until somehow your attention is brought back to this book (remember, you are reading this book).

Usually, this aspect of the mind goes unnoticed. We slip effortlessly into past remembrances or into future projections without even being aware it is happening. When you begin to apply mindfulness and start to observe your mind, you will find it is rarely in the present moment. Mind wandering is our normal, default mode of cognition. We go from one mental association to the next, often in haphazard and random ways as the paragraph above highlights. If this is new to you, you need not be alarmed by this. It is just how the mind naturally operates.

Getting lost in thought also tends to activate emotions. We tend to live more in a self-constructed mental world complete with congruent emotions than in the actual world. Mindfulness helps us better notice when our mind is wandering and allows us to bring our attention back to whatever is important to us at that moment. Mindfulness helps ground us in reality rather than on what the mind is chattering on about. When trading mindfully, the trader becomes more self-aware and detects when he or she has left the present. Not only is attention to market action increased, but becoming aware of where attention is placed is also strengthened. All traders sometimes become distracted. When attention shifts off the market, we miss trades or important cues that the market is about to do something that may require our action. Mindful traders can better notice their mental roaming and bring themselves back to important trading-relevant tasks. This is a vital mental skill that enhances trading performance.

Perhaps the greatest benefit of mindfulness is its role in *defusion*. (Although we introduce defusion here, the concept is so important that we spend an entire chapter on it. See Chapter 7.) Mindfulness teaches traders defusion: how to see their own thoughts and feelings simply as passing events, rather than something that demands a response. Recall that attempting to suppress, control, or eliminate feelings and thoughts typically makes them worse. Mindfulness teaches the practitioner that thoughts and feelings arise and depart on their own, they are not always helpful and they are not always accurate reflections of reality. When we are not mindful of our thoughts and feelings, it becomes easy to get hooked by them. This was illustrated in the above example of the mind wandering as you read this book. Once hooked, we then follow whatever mental and emotional path the mind takes us down. Mindfulness helps us recognize that thoughts and feelings can be seen for what they are—mere internal events. Because our thoughts and feelings are typically about previous experiences, recalled images, projections, and predictions about the future, what the mind is telling us is not necessarily truthful, though the mind always represents its forecasts as true and correct.

Usually, the mind evaluates virtually all that comes into its awareness. We compare and contrast, evaluate what we see, and predict how this might affect our future desires. As the trader watches price bars unfold, for example, it is easy to misinterpret a bar or two and make a prediction about the future. Uncritically assuming that the mind always tells us the truth all of the time in all situations can cause emotions to stir and set off inept performance. Mindfulness extends the distance between what is seen and how we respond by helping us *look at* rather than *look though* thoughts and feelings. This aspect of mindfulness enables the trader to see and experience events before the mind has the opportunity to evaluate and react impulsively. As we discussed in Chapter 2, developing an understanding of how internal experiences influence our actions is a factor of emotional intelligence. Mindfulness directly promotes emotional intelligence. Difficult thoughts and feelings will still occur, but they are recognized as just that—momentary thoughts and feelings, not permanent and not necessarily reality. This is *defusion*. Mindfulness helps break down the belief that thoughts and feelings are always correct, always certain, and always unavoidable obligations to act. Through practice, mindfulness offers us the opportunity to develop a more skillful way of understanding and responding to our inner world.

These three characteristics of mindfulness—a heightened clarity of the market environment, focus on the here and now, and an understanding that thoughts and feelings are merely temporary events and not necessarily reality—can help the trader take action in the direction of what matters most in a given trade, as well as what matters most to him or her as a trader. When mindful we can create a distance between having a thought or feeling and reacting to it. This is a cultivated mental space where the trader can let go of internal events that wreak havoc on trading. At the same time, the ability to effectively respond to the market is broadened. Instead of rigidly patterned responses that address one's internal state such as cutting a trade short, jumping into an unplanned trade, or failing to take a trade, mindful traders place themselves in a position to choose more valued trading actions that address the needs of the trade. The higher level of awareness promoted by mindfulness can help traders experience undesirable thoughts and feelings without derailing their focus on the trade. We saw this with Captain Sullenberger's ability to not struggle with or be overtaken by the intense level of fear and stress he experienced and, instead, be able to direct his attention to the highly valuable actions needed to land Flight 1549 safely in the Hudson River.

■ Being in the Zone

In situations less dramatic than landing a damaged aircraft, such as in sport and trading, the mindfulness state shares characteristics of consciousness similar to what is commonly called "being in the zone," or what positive psychologist and former head of psychology at the University of Chicago, Mihaly Csikszentmihalyi, refers to as *flow*. Flow, according to Csikszentmihalyi, involves being fully focused and completely involved in an activity or task. Skills are matched to the task and are fully utilized. Time seems to fly by and internal mental dialogues become much less important. Because attention is sharp and concentrated, it brings clarity. Tennis players, for example, say that they "see the ball" better and can respond easily to the playing situation when they are "in the zone," fully absorbed in the match, and experiencing flow. Similarly, in this state, the trader is in clear, moment-to-moment contact with the market. Normally disruptive mental and emotional influences may still be present, but recede as if they were broadcast from a radio playing softly in the background. Emotional hijackings become less likely. The trader understands that thoughts and emotions do not have to dictate actions. The trader can follow his or her trading plan and fully utilize trading skills and abilities that lead to improved performance, consistency in trading, and growth as a trader. In contrast to the Vicious Cycle of Ineffective Trading illustrated in Figure 5.1 with the trader cutting a winning trade short, Figure 5.2 illustrates the Cycle of Mindfully Effective Trading. Through mindfulness practice, we no longer have to act as limited automatons, slavishly responding to the vagaries of our inner states. Mindfulness helps us approach the "zone" or flow state.

We will learn several different ways to do and practice mindfulness in Chapter 6. Before we do that, it is important for traders to understand a bit about the science behind mindfulness. Because mindfulness requires practice and is an investment of your time and effort, you should understand what it can do for you.

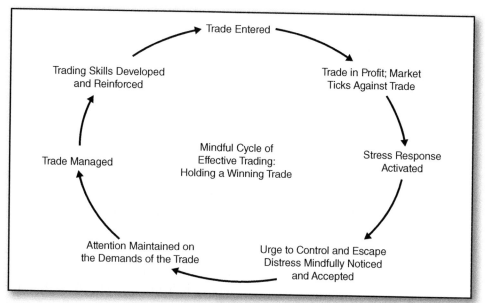

FIGURE 5.2 Mindful Cycle of Effective Trading

The Science of Mindfulness Meditation

Mindfulness meditation has been widely applied in clinical treatments with people who suffer from mental illness with much success. Mindfulness meditation has been shown to be effective in reducing stress, anxiety, and the frequency and intensity of chronic panic attacks. Research demonstrates mindfulness helps in lifting depression and preventing its relapse, reducing substance abuse, increasing attentional control in individuals with attention deficits, enhancing immune function as a defense for general health protection, reducing symptoms associated with chronic pain, and promoting adaptive emotional regulation. We make the assumption here, though, that most traders are not afflicted by mental illness. This begs the question: Is mindfulness of benefit to generally healthy individuals and specifically to traders? The answer is definitely yes.

General Benefits of Mindfulness

Peter Sedlmeier together with a team of psychology researchers at the Chemnitz University of Technology in Germany reviewed the psychological effects of mindfulness in generally healthy people across 163 high-quality empirical studies. This comprehensive review of the state of the science affirmed that mindfulness has clear and substantial positive effects for healthy people. The researchers identified a range of 21 psychological indicators that had been studied and, in all but a few, mindfulness meditation had beneficial impact. The largest effects were seen in reducing anxiety and negative emotions. Interpersonal relationship measures were also strongly and positively impacted. Slightly less strong, but categorically positive, were effects seen in measures of perception, stress, and attention.

Sedlmeier and colleagues state that the positive effects reported in their research are comparable to the levels produced by proven psychotherapeutic treatments for patients with mental illness. This gives the reader a sense of the potency of mindfulness for the healthy individual. Sedlmeier's team also compared meditation with relaxation. In the past, meditation and its effects have been considered similar to standard relaxation procedures because it often does produce a state of deep relaxation and calm. In fact, meditation was popularly described in the 1970s by Harvard Medical School professor Herbert Benson as the "relaxation response." But Sedlmeier and colleagues found differently. They state, "Meditation has an effect on the psychological variables analyzed that extends far beyond the relaxation response elicited by relaxation procedures." It is also noteworthy that the research found men and women of all adult ages benefited from the many positive impacts of meditation.

This research is great news for traders. Mindfulness has confirmed bearing on some of the most trading-relevant psychological considerations. It fosters improved attention, concentration, and perception, and offers protective effects from stress, anxiety, and negative emotions. This is good to know, but I want to go deeper into the research as I believe there is more to mindfulness that can be of tremendous benefit to traders and their trading. Understanding some of the specific elements of this story and how mindfulness meditation relates to trading is not only helpful in and of itself, but will also benefit you if you are struggling with unwanted thoughts and emotions: as we break down some of the details of mindfulness, it will simultaneously begin to give you an enhanced awareness of your thoughts and emotions. As you go through the recent research with me, we will break down thoughts and emotions into exactly what they are through the illuminating lens of mindfulness. The goal of doing this is to help you understand that there truly is a different way of thinking about stress, unwanted thoughts, and uncomfortable emotions that, when paired with high-value actions, which we will learn in Part III of this book, become a dynamic, effective, and hopefully profitable way of viewing your thoughts and feelings as you trade the markets.

Mindfulness, Fear, Loss Aversion, and Perspective

Recall from our discussion on strong emotions and fear from Chapter 2 that the amygdala—the brain's panic button—is strongly implicated in trading-related fear and is a significant actor in the fight-flight response. It should not be surprising that this brain area is also strongly linked to loss aversion. This makes sense because loss aversion is a fear-based bias.

Cognitive neuroscientist Benedetto De Martino used an fMRI (functional Magnetic Resonance Imaging) scanner to measure brain activity as study participants made decisions that involved loss aversion under a cognitive framing effect. Framing is a cognitive bias that influences our decisions depending on how information is presented or "framed." In this study, participants were given £50 and then were asked to choose between a "sure" option and a "gamble" option presented in two different ways. The key was the way the options were framed. The sure choice was stated as either *keeping* money (e.g., KEEP £30) or, alternatively, as *losing* money (e.g., LOSE £20) from the initial £50. The gamble choice was identical in both frames. Participants were more likely to choose a sure bet in the KEEP frame and a gamble in the LOSE frame. Astute readers will recognize that this is also describing loss aversion and the disposition effect: we are more likely to be conservative and risk-averse when we have gains by banking profits (the KEEP frame) and more likely to seek risk when we have loss by holding onto losers (the LOSE frame). The simple framing of KEEP or LOSE induced loss aversion.

As participants made their choices, De Martino's research team observed the participants' brain activity through the fMRI scanner. When participants responded with loss aversion, the amygdala became active and it did so rapidly, indicating emotion was highly involved in the choice. In reviewing De Martino's research,

Daniel Kahneman reported that this brain response indicates that the intuitive mind (his System 1 mind) was engaged in the decision. In those instances when participants overrode the normal loss aversion response and took on appropriate risk with gains and cut losses quickly, however, a different region of the brain—the anterior cingulate cortex—lit up on the fMRI scanner. The ACC is a region of the brain's prefrontal cortex and is involved in decision making and inhibiting inappropriate and impulsive responses. We have already discussed the prefrontal cortex and how it modulates emotional information in decision making when we discussed the case of Phineas Gage and other individuals with prefrontal cortex damage in Chapter 4. We talk further about the importance of the prefrontal cortex and what it means to traders shortly.

As interesting as this research is, De Martino went further. He found two very rare individuals who had lesions (tissue injury) in their amygdalas. They had normal intelligence and normal cognitive abilities; but their fear-processing center was damaged. For valid comparisons, they were matched in age, education, socioeconomic status, and other relevant characteristics with people with normal amygdalas. They were then studied for loss aversion. Like their matched counterparts, they could assess the expected value of a decision involving the potential of a gain and a loss. Unlike their matched controls, the individuals with damaged amygdalas failed to exhibit loss aversion. They held gains and cut losses. It is important to note that the individuals with injured amygdalas disliked losses and the risk of loss just as much as their counterparts; they were not cavalier in their risk taking. Nevertheless, they were significantly more willing than those with intact amygdalas to place appropriate amounts at risk for a potential larger gain, and reduce risk rapidly by eliminating losses. This rational perspective is the opposite of loss aversion and was seen only in the actions of those whose amygdalas did not activate when making choices under risk.

We see again that the amygdala is a critically important brain region for the trader. Not only is it our internal panic button that launches the fear response, it is intimately involved in loss aversion—a chronic psychological dilemma all traders face. Let's go deeper.

Remember the research demonstrating that those who thought like a trader showed less loss aversion tendencies than those who acted without that perspective? The same research team led by Peter Sokol-Hessner also employed fMRI scans to investigate the brain areas involved when taking the trader's perspective. They confirmed that loss aversion behavior is linked to increased amygdala activity. Further, they found that the amygdala responds to the threat of loss as an outcome by signaling an emotionally salient message to prefrontal cortex areas responsible for assessing value and processing emotion. These signals from the amygdala influence the prefrontal cortex, override normal rational responses, and trigger loss aversion behavior. When study participants assumed the perspective of the trader and considered each trade's outcome as only one of many trade outcomes, however, several positive things happened. It reduced loss aversion in the actual choices made, as we have already discussed: study participants were more willing to hold gains and less willing to hold losses. Taking on the trader's perspective also significantly reduced the arousal response in the amygdala relative to losses. Further, the trader's perspective increased baseline activity in the prefrontal cortex areas associated with both computing value and regulating emotions. Perspective-taking altered how the participants thought about the salience of loss and this was reflected in their functional brain images. Thinking differently about something that normally involves emotion can lead to internal regulation of emotional signals. The decision pathway seen in the brain scan imagery indicates that decisions that require assessing value (as all trading decisions require) involve emotional components. This study suggests that adopting a different perspective can favorably shift those components.

To summarize, these studies show that the amygdala and areas of the prefrontal cortex are two regions of the brain of special concern to the trader. The amygdala is involved in fear, stress, and also our strong tendency to seek to avoid loss. The prefrontal cortex is involved in assessing value, decision making, and also in interpreting and regulating neural activity from the amygdala. Mindfulness meditation can have a significant impact on both of these brain structures.

Mindfulness Meditation and Physical Changes in the Brain

At the Brain and Cognition Center in Toulouse, France, cognitive neuroscientists Claire Braboszcz, Stephanie Hahusseau, and Arnaud Delorme reviewed the scientific research on meditation and its impact on brain regions and emotion. They found that the brain circuitry in both the amygdala and the prefrontal cortex were positively affected by mindfulness meditation. Specifically, they noted that, overall, mindfulness practitioners experienced less body arousal and less brain wave activation when experiencing negative emotions. Brain imagery studies reviewed also showed that experienced meditators had decreased amygdala activity in response to negative emotions that were induced in the laboratory compared to novice practitioners. Further, they found that the more time spent meditating, the more pronounced the decrease in amygdala response. Scientists Alberto Chiesa and Alessandro Serritti reached similar conclusions in an independent review of over 50 studies on mindfulness meditation and highlighted the positive effects of mindfulness practice on the prefrontal cortex and amygdala. They further noted that mindfulness meditation appears to offer protections from age-related cognitive decline. Mindfulness meditation is a mental skill that virtually anyone can develop. Like all skills, the more it is practiced, the better honed and more refined the skill becomes, and the better one is able to employ it proficiently and productively in real-time situations.

Braboszcz and colleagues also noted in their review of the research that the brain images indicate that meditation practice results in regulation of emotion and involves what neuroscientists call *brain plasticity* or actual physical and chemical changes in the structures and connections in the brain. Up until about 2000, scientists believed that the brain was unable to substantially change and grow. They thought that after adolescence the brain stopped growing and became largely static and immutable. We now know that this is not true. The brain changes and remains plastic through adulthood. We also now know that mindfulness meditation is one activity that directly changes the brain.

Just 30 Minutes of Mindfulness Meditation Physically Changes the Brain

Britta Hölzel, Research Fellow at Harvard Medical School/Massachusetts General Hospital, and her colleagues studied men and women between the ages of 25 and 55 years old who were involved in a mindfulness-based stress reduction program. During the study, the participants engaged in mindfulness practice for an average of 27 minutes a day over an eight-week period. The researchers took two brain scans of each participant: one at the beginning of the study and the other at the end. They also took brain scans of individuals with characteristics similar to the study group but who were not practicing mindfulness during the period. This latter group served as a control so that scientifically valid conclusions could be made.

The research team found significant increases in the brain's grey matter (brain cells) in various regions of the brain, including those areas involved in memory formation and in allowing or preventing the recall of other memories during stress, as well as areas fundamental to awareness and perception; integrating sensory information, regulation of emotion, cognition and behavior; and areas involved in modulating arousal and stress and allowing for flexible responses to environmental demands as well as attention. This is the first study to show that the brain structure can and does change from active training through mindfulness meditation. The researchers said the study data indicate that the brain's gray matter increases from repeated activation of the brain through mindfulness and that these increases "... represent enduring changes in brain structure that could support improved mental functioning."

Britta Hölzel and her team of scientists conducted another study of interest to traders. This research project involved stressed but otherwise healthy adults who learned mindfulness meditation over an eight-week period. MRI brain images were taken and stress levels were tracked. At the end of the eight weeks, participants reported significantly reduced stress. What is more remarkable, however, is what went on inside their brains. The images—captured at the beginning and again at the end of the eight-week period—showed *significant reduction in gray matter in the amygdala*. Other brain imaging studies in both humans and laboratory animals have shown that repeated activation of a neural area results in increased gray matter and cessation of activation leads to a decrease in gray matter. Here, Hölzel showed that reductions in stress reported by participants due to mindfulness meditation are also reflected in structural changes in the amygdala. Amygdalas activate less in meditators. The more participants' stress decreased, the more the density of their amygdalas' gray matter thinned. As pointed out earlier, the amygdala is a key neural region involved in stress, fear, the fight-flight response, and loss aversion. This research is highly significant for traders showing brain plasticity in the amygdala associated with stress reduction as a result of mindfulness practice.

As technology improves, scientists will be able to see into the brain more clearly and more definitively. Do-Hyung Kang from the Seoul National University College of Medicine along with colleagues employed sophisticated diffusion tensor imaging (which assesses anatomical connectivity between different brain regions) and cortical thickness mapping (which assesses brain structure) to study both the brain's structure and its communication linkages in 46 long-term meditators matched against an equal number of individuals with no meditation experience. The scientists found significant structural differences between the meditators and the nonmeditators across numerous brain areas that are responsible for decision making, developing adaptive responses involving emotion, and coordinating thoughts and actions with internal goals. In these brain areas, meditators also had greater white matter integrity, indicating more rapid and efficient information processing. Other brain regions in which there were differences between the two groups included areas involved in processing of sensory perception, emotional processing, and long-term memory. All of these mental functions are highly relevant for trading and are enhanced with mindfulness meditation.

Executive Control

Many of the mental functions enumerated above and in which meditators have thicker and more conductive brain structure are collectively known as *executive brain function*. Executive functions involve a number of related cognitive processes, all of which are relevant to trading. These include: attending to relevant information and discarding irrelevant data, evaluating, planning, decision making, overriding impulses and patterned behaviors, and adaptively responding to environmental cues while pursuing goals. Most of these functions are also involved in what we called deliberative mind in Chapter 1. Recall that deliberative mind is difficult to engage and involves careful, effortful thinking and an ability to prevail over impulsive and automatic decision making.

Maintaining the engagement of deliberative mind involves the same processes as maintaining executive control: monitoring the mind and mental processes and overriding automatic impulses. This requires maintaining attention on the present, moment by moment, noticing when we veer off the present by drifting into a future concern or a past memory, and bringing ourselves back to a present moment focus when we have noticed we have drifted from it. This, in essence, is the process of mindfulness meditation.

Mindfully Accepting Emotions Enhances Executive Functioning

According to University of Toronto psychologists Rimma Teper and Michal Inzlicht, mindfulness meditation is the ideal mental tool to cultivate executive control. Teper and Inzlicht looked at two key aspects of mindfulness and how they relate to and affect executive control: present moment awareness and acceptance of emotions. They studied meditators with one year of meditation experience along with nonmeditators to clarify differences between the two. The researchers found a distinct relationship between emotional acceptance and executive control. Meditators and nonmeditators were similar in their abilities for keeping their minds in the moment during study tasks, so that wasn't the defining factor. It was the accepting of emotions where the meditators excelled. *Those who accepted rather than fought their emotions had greater executive control.* Emotional acceptance came with mindfulness practice, indicating mindfulness enhances executive control. The researchers found this ability in the anterior cingulate cortex (recall that this is the brain area connected to the amygdala and the prefrontal cortex and is involved in processing information, decision making, and, especially, assessing the importance of emotional information).

Mindfulness meditation develops an enhanced ability to accept emotions. As the results from this research indicate, it is also a key reason why meditation improves executive functioning. Meditators are highly aware of their emotional states. They are able to identify emotions correctly, and understand them as temporary feeling states—key factors of emotional intelligence. Most importantly, meditators do not struggle with their emotions. They understand emotions as temporary internal events that need not dictate actions. Experienced meditators are able to let emotions go rather than become entangled with them. According to this research, executive control—the engagement of deliberative mind—is clearly related to the ability to deal with feelings in an emotionally intelligent way.

The Wandering Mind

One final line of research concerns mind wandering and mindfulness meditation. As any human being who has taken a few moments to observe their thoughts knows, attention varies. Our minds wander from thought to thought, associating with something that catches our eye, which brings up another thought that then leads us into daydreaming, fantasies, and other meandering thought patterns. Virtually anyone who has read a book has had the experience of reading a few pages and then realizing they have no idea what they just read. This is a good example of mind wandering. Instead of maintaining attention on something specific such as a task or other goal-directed focus, our minds become active with a different, aimless character of thought, which often occurs outside of our awareness. Typically, our thoughts turn inward when our minds wander. Information becomes processed with a self-referential focus, and we tend to think about past events, project ourselves into the future, as well as think more about ourselves vis-à-vis the perspectives and judgments of others. When our attention is not focused on an immediate task or something outside of ourselves, our minds naturally and very actively jump from one fleeting thought to the next with a spotlight on the self in the past and in the future. It is so common, in fact, that neuroscientists view this as our dominant way of thinking and call this our *default mode network*.

And it does seem to be our default way of thinking. A psychology graduate student, Matthew Killingsworth and his advisor, Harvard psychologist Daniel Gilbert, developed a smartphone app to assess mind wandering and happiness. Randomly throughout the day, thousands of participants were asked three questions over their smartphone: (1) to identify what they were doing at that moment; (2) whether they were thinking about something different from what they were doing (mind wandering); and (3) to rate their level of happiness at that moment. Killingsworth collected a large amount of real-time data and the results are a bit stunning. Regardless of what they were doing, peoples' minds were aimlessly wandering 47 percent of the time. Much of the mind wandering involved pleasant thoughts, but that did not make people happier. In fact, people were less happy when their minds were wandering regardless of the activity. Mind wandering took up at least 30 percent of the time during every activity studied (resting, relaxing, working, commuting, traveling, grooming, listening to the radio, watching TV, reading, caring for children, shopping, running errands, eating, praying, listening to music, playing, talking, exercising, walking, sex) with the exception of making love. As the researchers conclude, ". . . a human mind is a wandering mind, and a wandering mind is an unhappy mind."

Kalina Christoff, University of British Columbia cognitive scientist, and her research team at the Cognitive Neuroscience of Thought Laboratory have shown that mind wandering occurs spontaneously—it doesn't need to be prompted, and can be observed in specific regions of the brain as soon as the mind roams off task. Some of the regions that the brain recruits when the mind wanders are the default mode network areas, but Christoff found that mind wandering also recruits brain areas used in executive functioning. Mind wandering is an active mental process and it engages some of the brain's areas associated with executive functioning. Taking up parts of the brain's real estate normally involved with problem solving and decision making helps explain why mind wandering affects performance. Mind wandering competes with our rational thinking center and can interfere with cognitively demanding tasks such as trading. Further, Christoff found that mind wandering's disruption of task performance is greatest when we are unaware that it is happening.

Perhaps this is why intuitive mind tends to dominate deliberative mind. It is our default mode of operating and it is occupying brain areas that are also used by deliberative mind. Perhaps deliberative mind isn't actually lazy, just underresourced.

As an everyday example, think about times you have driven a car and arrive at your destination and have little recollection of the trip. Your mind had obviously wandered. More importantly, during the time you were driving and your mind was roaming, you were unaware of its meanderings—so little aware that you have difficulty recalling the details of the trip once your destination was reached.

In trading, we can easily see how mind wandering can distract us from normal trading performance. A fund manager's experience provides a good example. While on vacation, she decided to take a look at the markets. She noticed a trade setting up in one of the foreign currency futures markets. She never traded while on vacation and wasn't going to take this trade. A few minutes later, however, she found herself in the trade and put on substantially more futures contracts than her normal position size. She broke personal performance rules of not trading while out of the office and money management rules regarding trade size. Later, she said, "I noticed the trade, but wasn't really thinking about trading it. Now, in retrospect, I can see my mind drifted off to my last month's trading (a self-referential focus), though I wasn't really aware of this at the time. I was thinking it had been below par. I wanted to make up for my poor performance. Suddenly, I thought, all I need to do is make this trade with xx contracts and I would change my monthly figures."

Mind wandering can impact everyday trading, as well. Once in a trade, our mind can wander to thoughts of a loss and, taking on the usual self-referential course, the mind reflects on how bad that will be for us. This may (and often does) happen unconsciously, even for just a few seconds. Suddenly we find ourselves tense, uncomfortable, and frightened about a loss. It seems to come on abruptly, but that's just like setting down the book and not knowing what we've just read. Our mind has gone a-wandering, and on its walk-about the mind has concocted a story complete with emotional aspects and physical sensations, so it feels like the truth. Although we have no research directly linking our intuitive mind-to-mind wandering, mind wandering seems like the perfect mental environment for intuitive mind to operate.

A team of researchers led by Judson Brewer, assistant professor of psychiatry at Yale University Medical School, studied mind wandering brain activity in experienced meditators and nonmeditators. In the brain scans, meditators had relatively little activity in the areas associated with the mind wandering default mode network. In contrast, the same brain areas in non-meditators were active during mind wandering. Brewer's team also found stronger linkage between brain areas that are associated with self-monitoring and cognitive control, both while meditating and also while not. The research shows a strong correlation between meditation, less mind wandering, and differing activation and connections within the brain's default mode network compared to those who don't practice meditation. They further found that experienced meditators had better overall brain connectivity within the self-control regions of the brain. Meditators notice when they have a thought unrelated to the task they are engaged in (i.e., a mental conflict), and they are better able to actively return their attention back on task (cognitive control). Such mental skills are of obvious benefit to traders.

Mindfulness practice is a form of training that helps to disentangle us from our normal mind wandering and self-focused cognitions. Emory University neuroscientist and scientific officer at the Mind and Life Institute, Wendy Hasenkamp, developed a model of mindfulness attention that mapped the fluctuations between our default state of mind wandering and sustained mindful attention. She found that different components of the brain related to attentional control are actively recruited for each of the states in this dynamic thinking model. When our mind wanders, our attention has become unfocused. Distinct brain areas activate as we become aware that our mind has wandered and we begin to shift attention back to task. When focused, other brain areas, including the prefrontal cortex, become engaged. Hasenkamp also found that more experienced meditators were faster in reorienting attention after recognizing that their mind had wandered, indicating that the more one practiced mindfulness, the better one becomes at not only maintaining focus, but in reengaging focus once it has been lost.

Like Brewer's research, Hazenkamp's study found meditators have more cognitive control. Her research also suggests that more experience in mindfulness better enables identifying and ending mind wandering as well as disengaging from self-evaluation and negative self-judgment. Recall from Chapter 1 that our intuitive mind dominates our thinking and that the more logical, deliberative mind, crucial to trading, is difficult to engage. Although we do not have direct research connecting mindfulness to deliberative mind and the avoidance of cognitive biases and errors, Hasenkamp's research suggests that mindfulness should help the trader in that regard. To the extent that a trader has practiced mindfulness, she would be expected to be more capable of being able to identify when she is off-task and better able to return to task and reengage her deliberative mind.

People who have never meditated were studied by UCLA psychology researcher Janna Dickenson. Ethnically diverse individuals who ranged in age from 28 to 69 years old were given a brief training in mindfulness meditation. Despite being novices, these individuals recruited the key brain areas related to attention and awareness as seen in more experienced meditators. They were compared to a control group who were asked to pay attention to their thoughts as they normally would. The control group was found to engage the same brain areas as in the default mode network or mind wandering. *Those just taught mindfulness, however, were able to suppress their mind-wandering mode* as seen in brain images taken during the mindfulness exercise. The research suggests that mindfulness is capable of controlling mind wandering immediately, with only minimal training. This is very good news for traders.

Changing Our Genetic Expression

In some of the most recent research on mindfulness, Perla Kaliman, researcher at the Institute of Biomedical Research in Barcelona along with her associates, including John Davidson, neuroscientist, founder and chair of the Center for Investigating Healthy Minds at the University of Wisconsin, have reported some truly remarkable results. After a day of mindfulness meditation practice, experienced meditators showed evidence of altered gene expression. Researchers conducted molecular analysis and could identify epigenetic changes following mindfulness practice in experienced meditators that were not seen in a control group of nonmeditators. Genetic changes included reduced levels of genes involved in inflammation and changes in the levels of genes that regulate the activities of other genes. These differences resulted in a boost of cortisol recovery after a stressful experience, indicating on a molecular, genetic level that mindfulness helps practitioners better deal with stress by directly influencing genetic expression.

As you can see from the research, mindfulness can address many aspects of trading psychology. Traders interested in improving performance and developing a personal trading psychology edge should consider building the practice of mindfulness meditation into their daily routines. In short, the development of mindfulness skills helps the trader:

- Reduce stress

- Tame the fear response

- Counter the strong tendency toward loss aversion

- Strengthen decision making

- Strengthen internal emotional regulation

- Improve and develop emotional intelligence

- Reduce the dominance of intuitive decision making and cognitive error

- Increase deliberative attention

- Better see the market and its trading opportunities

- Stay on task

- Overcome the negative-reinforcing properties of ineffective trading

- Enhance overall psychological well-being.

In the next chapter, we introduce the mechanics of mindfulness and show you how to do it. We detail several alternative mindfulness procedures. To become a mindful trader, start practicing mindfulness and building your mindfulness muscles by following these procedures.

■ Note

1. Jon Kabat-Zinn. *Wherever You Go, There You Are: Mindfulness Meditation in Everyday Life* (New York: Hyperion, 1994), 92.

CHAPTER 6

Practice Mindfulness, Trade Mindfully

As you have learned in Chapter 5, mindfulness offers substantial benefits to traders. We discussed what mindfulness can do for you and some of the mental and psychological difficulties traders confront along with the robust research pertinent to trading. We next talk about what mindfulness is and how to do it. We explain different ways to practice mindfulness and introduce several guided mindfulness scripts for you to use to develop your personal practice. To help you with your practice, audio downloads of many of these scripts are available at the author's website, www .tradingpsychologyedge.com. We also discuss how traders can apply the critical mental skill of mindfulness in trading.

Mindfulness is synonymous with present moment awareness. When we are mindful, our attention is placed on the present moment. Most people can be mindful for a short duration, but we rarely stay focused on the present moment for long. Our mind often travels from something we remember from the past to some projected desire or worry about the future. Once we slide into thinking about the past or the future, we have taken ourselves out of the present moment. We are no longer mindful. We are no longer fully aware of what is happening here and now; instead, our mind is preoccupied with a past remembrance or a future projection. In trading, when our mind has shifted away from the here and now, in other words, the market and our trade, our performance suffers.

If we were to objectively sample our thoughts throughout the day, we would find that much of the time our minds are on something different from what we are doing (recall the research on mind wandering from Chapter 5). Unless we practice, mindfulness for most of us is a random, fleeting event. Because we are rarely in the present moment for long, we are not always aware of what is happening now. Instead, we are living a version of reality constructed by our mind, which is not the same as actual reality. In trading, this has profound implications. If we are about to take a trade or are in the middle of managing a trade, the odds that our mind is fully focused on what we are doing is about 50-50. That's equivalent to chance, and that's not good. For example, if we are about to take a trade, we are just as likely to be thinking about the last loss we had that we "have to make up" (or some other irrelevant thought) as thinking about whether this trade meets all of our criteria. If we are managing a trade our mind might be worried about the consequences of getting stopped out rather than how the market is presently acting relative to our position. If our attention is tied up with the worry about having a loss, how can we be focused on the trade we are in or about to place? How can we trade well? Our mind isn't fully available to us when we need it most. Perhaps the greatest poignancy is that we don't even realize it! We are so conditioned to believe what our mind tells us that the errors it causes us to make aren't even recognized. Here's a detailed example of this incongruous mental phenomenon:

Sunil is a skilled commodities trader. He was looking for soybean oil to break the previous day's low to resume a longer-term, multiweek downtrend. As Figure 6.1 shows, he sold the market short as it broke down below support. The market fell and Sunil was in profit. Despite knowing that a decisive break from a large trading range has very strong odds of continuation, Sunil became concerned that the market didn't fall harder than it did. He compared the down move at C with the previous down moves at A and B. He thought the down move at C did not meet the same standards of A and B. He began to worry price might return to the trading range in the near future. If it did, he thought, he would surely have a loss. He decided to tighten his stop, moving it from S-1 to S-2, a tick above his entry. He was soon stopped out as soybean oil tested the break before heading much lower.

Sunil's mind was so focused on perceived future price action because the downdraft had not been the same as A or B, he ignored the facts that: (a) the soybean oil market was in a larger downtrend and odds favored this would resume, (b) price had failed to reach yesterday's high and then failed to hold yesterday's low, signifying supply dominating this market, (c) the down moves today were larger than the one very weak rally at yesterday's low, and (d) the market broke decisively from the trading range (i.e., it was not a bear trap).

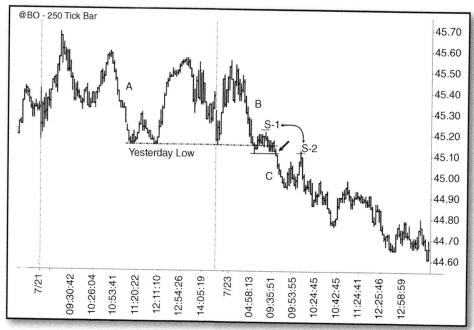

FIGURE 6.1 Mindless Moving of Stops
Source: TradeStation Technologies, Inc.

Sunil was unable to assess the market in the present moment because his mind was in the future. Part of this was caused by his focusing on only one small aspect of market action (his perception of the down move at C). It was salient to his intuitive mind. Seizing the perception that the market has lost its downward push, Sunil began thinking about the future and a loss. Because his mind went to future projections about how the trade would now turn into a loss, his present focus was lost. His mind was lost to worry and he was unable to access his deliberative mind.

Because his future projections made him feel uncomfortable, he moved his stop lower. Sunil didn't even realize that he was making a significant trading error because his projections seemed correct, and to him they were, but only in the future his mind had constructed, not in the present reality of the market.

We typically don't realize it when we have departed the present because we strongly identify with each thought, feeling, and bodily sensation that we have. We believe everything the mind is telling us. In Sunil's case, it told a story that the market was about to rally. It seemed true; and there was a rationale, though a very tenuous one. Because he uncritically believed what his mind was telling him, he made himself feel unnecessarily uncomfortable and acted without ever questioning the soundness or the validity of his mind's story. Sunil's intuitive mind was focused only on one aspect of the price action and ignored all other market input. His future projection about the risk of loss made him feel uneasy and he started to worry. Mindlessly, Sunil believed the story his mind constructed about the future and he acted upon it as if that story were a true reflection of reality.

The greatest value of mindfulness lies in the fact that it helps us step back from our thoughts and cease identifying with them. In performance situations such as trading, mindfulness helps us maintain our attention and focus on the market action relevant to our trade. When we are not mindful, we have a tendency to slip into a focus on an internal process that involves projections, judgments, and a direct effort to control feelings and thoughts, as pointed out by human performance/sport psychologists Frank Gardner and Zella Moore. Instead of sliding into mindlessly constructed projections, mindfulness can help us stay committed to choices and trading actions that support rather than undermine our trading goals.

Mindfulness is being aware of what is happening now, in the present, with an open, unbiased, and accepting attitude to whatever comes up. It doesn't mean that we have a totally laid-back, "I don't care what happens" attitude toward events. Mindfulness means that we don't prejudge and become ensnared in what our minds are telling us. There is a big difference.

Table 6.1 provides several additional examples illustrating mind*lessness* and mind*fulness* in trading. See if you can identify with any of these actions. Most readers will resonate with more than one.

Whether it is strong emotions taking over, a cognitive bias or heuristic that is influencing our actions, or intuitive mind looking at incomplete data, jumping to conclusions, and advocating that certain steps be taken, behind it all is a mind that is telling a story and that story is believed as true. The blind acceptance of whatever the mind tells us as truth is a distinct form of mindlessness that impairs many traders and interferes with effective trading. Because our mind works so well in so many different situations, we trust it too much. But this easily leads to mindless reacting, which is a reflexive response to both the external and our internal environments in an unaware fashion. We don't realize we are doing it, but we do recognize the poor results it causes. We don't quite make the connection that it is the unquestioning trust in what our mind tells us that is causing our difficulties. Ironically, attempts we make to try and resolve it do not help improve performance. Mindfulness is just the opposite.

Mindfulness is a skill and, like any skill, it must be developed through practice. The more it is practiced, the stronger the mindfulness. We saw this in the research. Long-term meditators had better self-control and showed greater changes in the structure of the brain associated with self-control. Mindfulness is also straightforward. Here is a basic and common mindfulness practice. It is one of the best. Read through the instructions once or twice, and then find a quiet place where you won't be disturbed for 10 to 15 minutes and try it.

TABLE 6.1 Example of Mindless and Mindful Choices in Trading

Mindlessness	Comments	Mindfulness	Comments
Holding onto a market bias despite how the market is trading. Trading against market action. This includes trying to pick tops or bottoms against a prevailing trend.	Attention on how the market should be acting. Reality of market action not accepted. Belief in the mind's assertion that the market is about to turn (and market is now at a top or bottom).	Market is trading differently than anticipated from analysis. Key indications are double checked. Trend change is confirmed. Trade opportunities in the direction of the new trend sought.	Attention focused on market in nonjudgmental way. Acceptance of market's action. Focus on the present and on the appropriate trading task.
Seeing a valid trade setup and then trading much larger than normal size for unrelated reasons, for example, to make up for prior losses.	Focus is on prior losses. Trader believes mind's story that increasing size will "easily" make up losses.	A valid trade setup is identified and treated as any other trade with proper sizing in accord with money management parameters.	Focus is on trading the trading plan. Trader may think about earlier losses and sizing up, but accepts those losses along with money management constraints.
Rushing to place a trade and failing to check higher time period trend / support and resistance.	Focus on avoiding the pain of missing out. Trader buys into the mind's story that the market is about to move and there are profits to be made.	Market begins to move but instead of jumping in, analysis is rechecked, including the higher time frame levels. Analysis shows this is not a choice trade and trader stands aside.	Attention placed on market structure and whether or not this is a sound trade location. Feelings of missing out are noticed but mindfully set aside as trader focuses on high-value trading actions rather than emotions.
A live trade is in loss. Trader decides to exit the trade. Instead of closing the trade, the position is mistakenly doubled.	Attention is on the loss and trader is emotionally hijacked. Because of the misplaced attention, an order execution error is made doubling the losing position.	Needing to exit a losing position, a closing trade is entered on the trading platform and double checked before executing the order.	Attention mindfully focused on the task of exiting the trade.
Placing a trade and then shortly thereafter, it is cut short.	Focus goes internal to fears of loss. This drives trading actions. Attention narrows to minute moves in price, which are judged to be a threat. Potential profits forfeited.	A trade is placed but market moves slightly against it. Analysis is rechecked, noted to be sound. The valid trade is held.	Attention placed on price action for a significant sign against the trade. Acceptance that market may move slightly against the position and even stop it out.

(continued)

125

PRACTICE MINDFULNESS, TRADE MINDFULLY

TABLE 6.1   (Continued)

Mindlessness	Comments	Mindfulness	Comments
Failing to notice subtle shifts in the supply/demand relationship as the trend matures. Trader has been sitting on the sidelines and missed the large move. A trade is placed late in the trend which fails.	Focus is on the money missed as the market trended. Trader believes the mind's story that the current pullback is the place to make up for standing aside. The pullback is the beginning of a trend change.	After a large trend, trader notices that the supply/demand relationship is changing and begins to look for a countertrend trade against the prevailing trend.	Attention placed on market action. Acceptance that trend is now likely over.
A winning day trade is closed at the end of the day even though the market has broken from congestion and closes firm. Trader feels uncomfortable holding the trade overnight.	Focus is on discomfort of giving back profits by holding trade overnight. The mind's fear of threatening overnight price action is believed.	Trader has captured a trend day. Because the market is closing firm, trader holds the trade overnight anticipating additional price follow-through the next day.	Trader does have thoughts that the market can pull back and lose some profit, but position held. Trader recognizes that the probability of follow-through the next morning is very strong.
Although the market has reached weekly resistance, a day trade is held. Trader thinks, "This market is really strong. There is more money to be made from this trade."	Focus is on the salience of the recent move. Trader believes the mind's tale that this will continue because it looks so strong.	Trader is keenly aware of higher time frame resistance, which is the trade's objective. When the market reaches that resistance, trade is closed.	Trader notes that the move up has been strong and does have thoughts it may continue higher, but trader also knows the probabilities favor closing the trade at resistance.
A trade has gone bad. Instead of taking the loss, the stop is cancelled. Trader looks to exit on a rally to avoid a loss.	Focus is on avoiding a loss. Trader feels that a loss is unacceptable. Trader believes the mind's story that a rally will bail out the trade. Trader now locked into a bad trade with emotions erupting and all energy channeled to make break-even.	The market has proven your analysis wrong. Trade is closed at its stop for a loss. Trader turns attention toward reevaluating the market.	Trader doesn't like losses and feels the sting of this one. Nonetheless, it is accepted as a part of the probability profile for the trade setup. Because the loss is dealt with quickly, attention is free to return to the market and new trade opportunities.

Begin by sitting in a chair (you don't have to assume any special yoga position, but can if you like). Sit comfortably and maintain a relaxed and straight alignment, as if a string attached to the top of your head pulls gently up. Have your legs uncrossed, feet on the floor. Arms can rest in your lap or along the arms of the chair, whichever is most comfortable for you. Make sure you are comfortable.

Take in a deep breath, hold it for a moment or two, and then gently exhale. As you do, gently close your eyes. Take another deep breath, hold momentarily, and slowly exhale. One more deep breath and then let your breathing go. Just let it flow naturally, there is no need to control it in any way.

Bring your attention to your breath. Simply follow it with your mind. Focus on how your breath travels across your nostrils at the tip of your nose. Try to notice the sensations created by your breathing. You might notice, for example, that your breath feels cooler coming in and warmer going out. The idea is to simply watch your breath. Nothing more, nothing less. Try to keep your attention on your breath for as long as you can.

You will notice that your mind will wander off your breath. Suddenly, you become aware that instead of being on the breath, your mind is thinking about something else. Maybe it is what you will be having for dinner or a new indicator you want to try out. Whatever it is, it's not the breath. Notice this. Notice, too, that the mind did this on its own. You didn't invite other thoughts to come in. You were focused on your breath, but you mind wandered on its own. Gently bring your attention back to the breath. Try and remain with your breath.

You will notice over and over that your mind will wander off the breath. It might tell you that this is boring, or that it will be more pleasant to think about other things than to follow your breath. Just accept these wandering thoughts with a nonjudgmental attitude. Notice that these are only thoughts you are having. There is no need to get upset or become alarmed that the mind wanders as much as it does. It's natural. It is what our minds do. Just bring your attention gently back to your breath. You may need to do this repeatedly. That's Okay. Just bring your attention back to your breath. This is mindfulness: watching your breath and when you notice that the mind has wandered, gently bringing your attention back to your breath.

After about 10 minutes, begin to reorient to the room you are in. Take a few deeper breaths. Wiggle your hands and feet and then stretch your body gently as you open your eyes.

That's mindfulness in a nutshell. We place our attention onto something constant like the breath and when the mind wanders off, which it definitely will, our task is to notice it and return our attention gently back to the focal point (e.g., the breath). Through this process, we become an observer of our thoughts and feelings, rather than treating our thoughts and feelings as inseparable from ourselves. We are not our thoughts; we just have them. Until we learn the skill of observing thoughts and feelings, we will be a slave to them. This is the whole goal of this form of mindfulness practice: to notice when our minds wander by observing our thoughts rather than being enmeshed in them, and then to refocus our attention. When we are enmeshed in our thoughts and feelings, we lose contact with reality. This occurs over and over. When our mind wanders, we completely lose contact with the present moment reality of the breath. The mind traps us in the story it tells us whether it be a benign one like reliving a pleasant memory or more a more distressing one like fearing a trading loss. Both mental events take us out of the present moment. They remove us from what is actually happening. If what we are experiencing and responding to is coming from within our heads, we are that much removed from what is actually happening and we will be unable to trade well.

Because we have lived our entire lives emeshed in our thoughts, it takes dedicated practice to teach ourselves to mindfully observe them. With practice, mindfulness teaches us to separate ourselves from our thoughts and feelings. In doing so, we can place our full attention on the market and allow our trading skills and abilities to emerge without interference. This gives us the best potential to maximize our trading performance.

As you practice mindfulness, you will begin to notice that the thoughts, feelings, and sensations that we have are very temporary. They come and they go. One moment you will feel the mind pulling you down some path with the story it is telling you. Another moment, your mind is thinking about something else. It has dropped what was so important just moments ago and now is onto something new, and something it says is even more important for your attention. This goes on and on. It's a never ending game in which the mind will fully occupy us. Mindfulness takes us out of that futile game and allows us to be more fully present to what is actually happening, not what the mind is projecting.

Through mindfulness practice, we begin to see what our thoughts are all about—often just random, unimportant things. We also begin to see through mindfulness practice that many times, our mind is telling us a version of reality that is simply untrue. Further, we learn that we really aren't in control of our thoughts. They seem to come and go on their own accord. The same is true for emotions. What we are in control of, however, is how we respond to them. This is what mindfulness practice helps us develop: *a much more useful relationship with our thoughts and feelings from which we can better govern our behavior.* This is what helps us reclaim control over our actions.

So how does watching the breath help in trading? They may not seem connected, but watching the breath and trading are not as far removed from one another as they might first appear. Think of watching the breath as an analogy for the trading task at hand. Let's say the trading task is to manage a trade you have on. The trading task involves watching price action and perhaps your indicators for clear signs the market is about to reverse. This trade management task is the same as watching the breath. It has a present focus. When you find your mind wandering and telling you a scary story that the market could turn on you and produce a loss, so you better take your profits, your mindfulness practice will help you see that these thoughts and the emotions that accompany them are simply thoughts and feelings. They do not necessarily reflect the reality of the present market action and they do not have to be responded to as if they were reality. Instead, in mindful trade management, we bring our attention back to the trading task at hand. It's just like returning our attention back to the breath. We might recheck the premise of the trade and deliberatively make sure that nothing has changed. If so, we stay with the trade, despite what the mind may be saying. The point is that because of the mindfulness practice, we have built up the mental skill of seeing our thoughts for what they are—just thoughts—and we can return our attention back to the trade rather than getting locked into believing our thoughts as if they were the truth, causing us to step out of reality, and allowing the fabrication our mind creates to dictate our trading actions.

By practicing mindfulness, you will build the mental muscle that will enable you to keep your attention on the trade. Simply reading about it and understanding it intellectually, however, will not be enough. Mindfulness is a real skill that requires practice to develop. You need to regularly and consistently practice mindfulness to build the mindfulness muscle. Keep in mind, too, that practice will alter your brain structure in positive ways, reflecting new internal capacity for maintaining attention on what is important and also reduce the negative effects of stress. Mindfulness practice gives you a real trading psychology edge.

◼ Starting Your Mindfulness Practice

So how do we practice mindfulness? Start small and let it grow. Find a time and place where you won't be disturbed. If necessary, let others know this is a time you don't want interruptions. Your space need not be elaborate. Although you can buy meditation cushions and other trappings, a simple chair will suffice. Start with sitting for 10 minutes. If that seems too long, then just do 5 minutes. You might find that sometime early in the morning before trading is a good time to practice mindfulness. Others might find it best at the end of the day or sometime in the middle, helping break up the day. Many people like to practice twice a day. You may, too. Go with your own experience and find what works best for you. As you progress, gradually increase the time. Remember, the research showed that about 30 minutes a day was very beneficial. That's a good target. Some may get to 45 minutes or an hour. Again, look to your experience to guide you. You will know what is best for you.

Although watching the breath is a classic method of concentration meditation, there are many other formal and informal ways to develop mindfulness skills. Christopher Germer, psychologist and mindfulness expert, categorizes mindfulness into three main types: focused concentration, mindful awareness, and compassion meditation. Each is useful. We run through several additional mindfulness exercises that cover the first two main types here. Try each one and see what you like. Susan Pollak, psychologist, clinical instructor at Cambridge Health Alliance/Harvard Medical School, and president of the Institute for Meditation and Psychotherapy, notes that different individuals will have different preferences in their approach to mindfulness meditation. Some may like watching the breath; others may prefer one of the other practices outlined in this chapter. Because developing your mindfulness skills requires a level of motivation and commitment similar to learning a musical instrument, becoming physically fit, or learning to trade, it helps to select a mindfulness exercise you like. Therefore, do the one or ones that suit you. All will help you develop the essential skill of mindfulness.

Pollack also notes that people with asthma, respiratory illness, and difficulties with anxiety may find it uncomfortable to focus on their breath. In this case, she recommends substituting watching the breath with listening to ambient sounds. The first mindfulness training, Mindful Listening, is an adaptation based on an exercise developed by Pollack. It is useful not only for those who find it difficult to watch their breath but also a good introduction for anyone first trying mindfulness meditation.[1]

■ Mindfulness Exercises

Mindful Listening

Begin by sitting comfortably with your limbs uncrossed, feet on the floor, hands gently resting on your sides. Eyes may be closed or you can leave them open, with your gaze gently directed a few feet in front of you and toward the floor.

As you settle into your sitting position, allow yourself to become present. Center yourself in your chair and feel yourself sitting in your chair. You might notice the pressure where the backs of your legs make contact with the seat of the chair and where your back makes contact with the back of the chair. Notice these sensations for a moment or two.

Turn your attention gently to the sounds in the room. You might hear sounds coming from outside the room you are in or within your immediate environment. As your mind begins to quiet, you will hear sounds that normally go unnoticed. Allow your full attention to be placed on each sound you hear. Just listen.

Listen with your entire being. There is no need to label the sounds you hear or judge them in any way. Just notice them.

As you notice the sounds, also notice that you need do nothing with these sounds. You don't have to make them louder or softer, change their tone, or alter them in any way. Notice, too, that they come and go on their own and they have a life of their own. There is nothing you need to do with them. Just notice them.

Allow yourself to hear all the sounds that are present. Some may come from above you, others from below. Some may be in front of you, behind you, or off to one side or the other. The task is to simply notice them for what they are— sounds that arise, come into your awareness, and then pass away.

If your mind wanders and begins to think about something else, just notice this and when you do, gently return your attention to mindfully listening to whatever sounds are occurring in the room you are in. If there are no sounds that you can hear, then listen to the silence.

If you are doing this as a first exercise, it is best to keep it short. Set a timer for 5 minutes. Most smartphones have a timer, and mindful meditation phone apps are available with gentle sounds such as soft bells or gongs to let you know when the time is up. This is better than a harsh buzzer. As you gain experience in this you can extend the time. This is true for all the exercises in this chapter.

You can also extend this exercise beyond the formal sitting practice. If you are riding as a passenger in car, sitting on a park bench, or walking along a street or trail, you can bring your attention to the sounds in the environment. Just as in the formal exercise, you can notice and listen to the sounds in a mindful way as you go about your day. Try this while standing in line at a checkout, when eating a meal in a restaurant, or even loading the dishwasher with dishes. You can do this just about anywhere.

Mindfully noticing and listening to sounds may be substituted for the breath in any of the exercises that follow. Also, if you are using your breath as a focal point and find yourself having difficulty concentrating, you can shift to listening to sounds instead of watching the breath. This can often be helpful if you find your mind wandering to be more active than normal and you can't seem to focus on the breath. In this situation, remember that struggling with mindfulness and trying to force yourself to concentrate on the breath is not mindfulness; it's struggle. If you find yourself slipping into a struggle with your mind, shifting to observational hearing of sounds can be a welcomed respite.

A Serene Saying

Here is an exercise that is a variation on watching the breath. As you watch your breath, you can repeat a few simple words as described below. It's known as a *mantra*, and can help keep you focused while practicing mindfulness. If you are tired or feeling sluggish, or are feeling uneasy and anxious this kind of exercise can help keep you attentive and also calm you down. The words of the mantra that you say silently to yourself can provide a little extra boost to help you in focusing the mind. It is in the spirit of Buddhist monk, Thich Nhat Hanh, who uses similar phrases in mindfulness meditation.

Again, your attention is placed on the breath. You might notice it at the tip of your nostrils as in the first exercise, or you might prefer following your abdomen's rise and fall with each breath. Let your experience be your guide. You can also place your hand on your belly to help in connecting to your breath from this part in your body. Also, it helps to breathe in from the lower abdomen, but don't overdo it. Just breathe into the lower part of your lungs, allowing your diaphragm to expand, then fill the middle of your lungs, and lastly the top of the lungs. Be gentle with this. There is no need to breathe hard or force the breath. Also keep in mind that we don't want to control the breath, just feel it.

As you take your first few breaths, notice how the breath is calming. Thich Nhat Hanh emphasizes that the body must be calm when practicing mindfulness meditation as a relaxed body helps create a calm mind. Conscious breathing calms the body, and is the basis of this simple but effective exercise. Depending on whether you are watching your breath flow across the tips of your nostrils or tracking your breath via the belly, repeat the appropriate phrase silently to yourself coordinating the phase with your in- and out-breaths. This exercise is similar to many mindfulness exercises developed by Thich Nhat Hanh (see, for example, his book, *Blooming of a Lotus*). After a while and if you like, you can simply say the single word shown on the right silently to yourself rather than the phrase:

Breathing in, my breath is cool,	In
Breathing out, my breath is warm.	Out
Breathing in, I relax my body,	Relax
Breathing out, I calm my mind.	Calm
Breathing in, my belly rises,	Rise
Breathing out, my belly falls.	Fall
Breathing in, my breath nourishes my body,	Nourish
Breathing out, my mind is calm.	Calm

When your mind wanders and begins to think of other things, simply notice it and gently bring your attention back to the task at hand, which is watching the breath and saying the statements silently. You want to be conscious of your breath and also conscious of the statements. Rote recitation will not be helpful. Focus on what you are saying. If you like this style of mindfulness meditation, you can be creative and make up your own phrases or check out the referenced work of Thich Nhat Hahn.

Leaves On a Stream

The next example is a favorite of many traders I have worked with. It helps you make the shift from looking from your thoughts to observing your thoughts. I first learned it from a description by psychologists John Forsyth and Georg Eifert.[2] It is a standard mindfulness exercise in mindfulness-acceptance-commitment approaches to psychology. Below is my adaptation of *Leaves on a Stream*.

> Start by getting centered and focus on the breath as in the previous exercises. Simply notice the rising and falling of your breath in your belly or just notice the breath coming in through your nostrils, and then going out again. Cool coming in; warmer going out. There is no need to control your breathing in any way. When you are ready, allow your eyes to close gently.
>
> Imagine you are sitting next to a small stream in the woods on a warm autumn day. As you gaze at the stream, you notice a number of leaves of all colors, shapes, and sizes drifting along, each at its own pace, one by one, in the slowly moving current. Allow yourself to simply be in this setting, warmed by the autumn sun and watching the leaves float by on the stream.
>
> Gradually bring your awareness to your mind and your body. Notice and label each mental and bodily experience that shows up—thoughts, feelings, sensations, images, desires, memories, and impulses. Pay attention to what is happening in your mind and in your body, and then label it. You might notice you are feeling excited. Label it by silently saying to yourself, "feeling." Perhaps you are thinking, "I don't have time for this." Notice that thought and label it: "Thinking."
>
> As each thought, feeling, memory, and sensation comes into your awareness, notice them and, in your mind's eye, gently place them onto one of the leaves floating by. Take your time with this. There is no need to rush. Observe each leaf as it floats toward you. As it comes near, mentally place your thought, feeling, or memory on the leaf. Let the leaf serve as a small boat for your thoughts, feelings, and sensations. Then watch as the leaf slowly moves away, drifting along in the current as it carries the contents of your mind and body downstream and out of sight.

If your mind gets stuck in a thought or feeling, notice this as if it were merely a leaf caught in an eddy. Eventually, the leaf carrying your persistent thought or feeling will leave the eddy and float downstream.

Continue placing each thought, feeling, memory, or impulse on its own leaf. Watch each one as you let them float away.

When ready, widen your attention to the room you are in, the sounds around you, and your body within the room. Open your eyes and make the intention to be aware of and accepting of your thoughts and feelings throughout the rest of your day.

Who Is Noticing Your Noticing?

The following exercise incorporates focused concentration with a broader awareness of your current experience. It is based on the work of Russ Harris, an MD and therapist in Australia.[3] Not only does it help you develop mindful awareness on a broadened basis, it also helps you develop the role of the mindful observer. Below is my adaptation of Dr. Harris's Who Is Noticing exercise.

Once again, we start by getting centered. This is most easily done by focusing on your breath as described in the earlier exercises. Once centered, turn your attention to your feet on the floor. Notice your feet and how the soles gently touch the floor. Notice the pressure at the backs of your legs where they contact the seat of the chair. Notice the sensations in your back where it makes contact with the back of the chair. Notice your hands resting on your lap. Now become aware of your noticing. Notice who is doing the noticing.

Now turn your attention to any sounds you can hear. What can you hear? As you listen mindfully, also notice that you need not do anything with these sounds—they just come and go on their own accord. Some sounds may be very quiet and subtle, almost imperceptible, others may be louder. Notice all of the sounds. Now become aware of your noticing. Notice who is noticing these sounds.

Next, turn your attention to any scents you can detect. Is there any scent you can notice? Notice, too, any tastes you can detect in your mouth. What flavor is there? Become aware of your noticing smells and tastes. Notice who is doing this noticing.

Gently turn your attention to your thoughts. What is your mind saying to you? What story is it telling you? Just notice whatever the mind is saying. There is no need to try and control or change your thoughts in any way. Allow them to occur as they are and just notice them. Become aware of your noticing your thoughts. Notice who is noticing your thoughts.

Now notice what you're feeling right now. What emotions are you experiencing? Are they strong or are they more subtle? Just notice and then become aware that you are noticing your feelings. Notice who is doing the noticing.

Take a deeper breath and be aware that there is a you there. This you is aware of everything within your experience. It notices what you can touch, hear, smell, taste, think, and feel. This you that notices is the observing you. It is always present. It always has been. It can always be called upon to help you step outside your thoughts and feelings so that you can move toward what is really important to you.

Walk Mindfully

This next exercise is a walking meditation. You don't have to always sit to be mindful. We can do it anytime and anywhere, standing, sitting, or walking. Walking meditation is another broader awareness exercise that many people enjoy.

Begin by defining an area within which you can walk comfortably and not be disturbed. Although meditation gardens are constructed specifically for walking meditation, any space where you can walk unencumbered for 10 to 15 feet or so will work. Walking from one side of a room to the other, turning, and walking back again is perfectly workable for walking mindfulness.

Start by standing still, breathing, and centering yourself. You want to keep your eyes open for this meditation, but they can be lowered with your gaze focused softly a few feet in front of you. Begin by walking slowly, noticing your foot lift off the ground, traveling slowly forward, and then noticing your heal, then mid-foot, then toes touching and pressing into the ground. Notice the same things as your other foot lifts, travels forward, and touches down.

Your attention will be centered mainly on your feet and movement, but also keep your attention on your breathing. You may find yourself shifting back and forth from your feet to your breath. That's fine. When you notice that your mind has wandered, bring your attention back to the feet and the breath. You can even stop and stand for a moment or two while you re-center yourself. This is known as standing meditation and is a perfectly fine way to practice mindfulness meditation. Remember, you don't want to fight your mind or struggle in any way with it. It doesn't help you to get angry or frustrated when you once again notice your mind is wandering. This is what minds do; it's natural. As with all mindfulness meditation exercises, just notice the mental wandering and gently bring your attention back to the mindfulness task at hand—here it's paying attention to your walking and breathing.

Generally, it is best to move slowly in walking meditation, but as always, see what works best for you. I have seen some speedy walking meditators. Go at a pace in which you can maintain concentration. Also, if your space is limited, when you reach a wall or obstruction, simply mindfully turn around and begin walking in the opposite direction. Walk back and forth in mindfulness; you may look a little odd to others, but that's okay, too. You are developing crucial mental skills—that's what's important.

I first tried walking meditation at the Kripalu Center for Yoga and Health located in Stockbridge, Massachusetts. On the grounds, Kripalu has a large meditation garden situated in a field. It is built in the shape of a spiral, where you begin your walking meditation at the outside and follow a circular path into the center where there is a small garden with benches where you can sit. You then leave the center of the garden by following a circular path that goes in the reverse direction from the entrance path. It is a peaceful and beautiful setting. As you slowly and mindfully walk in, you see people slowly walking out. And, as you walk out, you see other people walking in. I was frustrated by this as my attention kept wandering to the people walking opposite me. I found it hard not to notice them, what they were wearing, how they were walking, and so forth. My mind began to think, "What a terrible meditation garden. These people are so distracting." It was only later that I realized whoever designed this garden was a genius. The people walking opposite to me were exactly like my thoughts. I noticed them as they appeared from around the corner, they dominated my awareness as they approached, and then receded into the background as they passed. Then another person appeared repeating this cycle. Thoughts are exactly the same. They come and go on their own and have a beginning, middle, and end. When I looked in frustration at the other meditators in that garden I was looking at them through my thoughts. I wasn't mindful. I bought into my thoughts that the presence of other people was a negative. My attention was dominated by thoughts like, "Ugh! Another person is walking toward me. How distracting!" I was living in my head and had completely lost my focus on the task at hand, which was noticing my steps and breath. I totally lost touch with being in the present moment with a purposeful, nonjudgmental focus. Isn't this what we do in our trades? Our minds turn to our thinking, which might include fears of loss or fears of missing out or how we are going to make up for recent losses by trading big on this trade. Whatever the thoughts we may have, when we are living in those thoughts we are taking ourselves out of the present moment. We completely lose focus on the trade and the relevant trading task at hand. Buying into such irrelevant thoughts is what causes so many trading errors and why mindfulness is such a vital mental skill for trading.

Informal Mindfulness Opportunities

Informal mindfulness practice can be done anytime in any situation. You can be mindful while taking a shower, brushing your teeth, or washing the dishes, as examples. In each, your mindfulness task is to notice things like the sensations of the water on your body and the feel of the soap in your hand and being rubbed on your body (shower); or the taste of the toothpaste and the feel of the bristles on your teeth (brushing teeth); and the feel of a dish in your hand, the sensation of the water and its temperature, and the slipperiness of the dish soap (washing dishes). These are more mundane activities in which we are often not conscious of the present but instead living in our heads. So these are good activities with which to practice mindfulness. Any time your mind begins to think of something else while brushing your teeth or soaping your body, notice this and gently bring your attention back to the task at hand.

You can be mindful in all everyday activities. For example, when you drink your coffee you can mindfully notice your empty hand moving toward and grasping the cup, note the sensations you feel as you hold the cup—its weight, texture, and temperature, note the sensations of drinking the coffee—taste, texture, and temperature; and then notice as you return the coffee cup to the table and the sensations of releasing the cup. Virtually every activity is an opportunity to be mindful: eating, dressing, dialing the phone, searching the internet, typing on the computer, driving a car, talking with another person, studying charts, taking a trade, managing a trade, and exiting a trade.

It is the formal practice of watching the breath, saying a mantra, or walking mindfully that will help you train yourself to notice when you get off task and to notice when you are looking through your thoughts and buying into them outside of formal practice, including during trading. It is the ability to (a) notice your mind telling you an off-task story, (b) bring your attention back to the trading task, and (c) execute the appropriate high-value trading action (to be discussed in Part III) that formal meditation practice will help you develop for your trading. Keep in mind that mindfulness skills take practice to develop. You may read this and think, "Oh that makes sense, I'll just be aware of my mind wandering when it happens," but that is a story your mind is telling you (probably your intuitive mind making a quick, unstudied, and inaccurate judgment). It requires repeated practice to develop the needed changes in attentional skill and brain structure we've been discussing. Understanding it intellectually is only scratching the surface. This alone will do little for your trading. Mindfulness is a skill and, like any skill worth developing, it requires practice. It's like the tennis player who wants to hit an overhead smash. She will practice the smash many, many times before she brings it into competitive play. You can think of formal mindfulness practice as a mental workout. Do this routinely and you can build strong mental muscle. Otherwise, you are at the mercy of an untrained and ill-equipped mind.

■ Applying Mindfulness to Your Trading

Mindfulness is simple, though it is not easy to do consistently. Because it is so uncomplicated, it can be easy to discount. Some may wonder, "How can something so basic as mindfulness actually work?" Things don't have to be complex to create significant benefit. And although simple on the surface, there is a lot going on underneath the surface that will be helpful for traders to understand. There are several interrelated processes at work in mindfulness. Frank Gardner and Zella Moore review these processes in terms of human performance and Britta Hölzel, Sara Lazar, and their research team look at them from the scientific lenses of psychology and neural imagery. So that you will have a thorough understanding of mindfulness and appreciate that although it is a simple practice, it is nonetheless a powerful one that can change your trading and you as a trader, we briefly discuss these processes and relate them to trading as we conclude this chapter. Table 6.2 provides a summary of these processes and how they enhance trading performance.

TABLE 6.2 **How Mindfulness Works and Enhances Trading Performance**

Mindfulness Process	Description	Trading Performance
Attention Regulation	Returning attention to the focal point (e.g., the breath) whenever the mind wanders enhances the mental skill of conflict monitoring.	Increased performance by maintaining attention on trading related cues; reduced distractibility from both internal and external distractors
Greater awareness of body sensations and emotions; reduced effort to control private experiences	Focused attention on body sensations and awareness of emotions enhances emotional intelligence.	Sensations and emotions seen as temporary events leading to reduced efforts to try to control them and freeing attentional resources for trading tasks
Greater emotional regulation	Nonjudgemental openness to emotions promotes new ways of understanding and responding to emotions. Old, emotionally charged memories become altered.	Experience of emotion changes leading to more flexible trader actions related to market cues and trading tasks rather than actions designed to escape or control the trader's internal state
Perspective Change	Enhanced identification with an observing self that is more than the sum of its experiences.	Metacognitive awareness leads to less rule-governed behavior and promotes sensitivity to trading cues and more flexible response to trading demands

Attention Regulation

As taught in the mindfulness exercises in this chapter, attention is placed on a single point (e.g., the breath) and, when the mind wanders, as it most certainly will, to return attention to the object of focus. Hölzel and Lazar note that this practice increases the brain's capabilities of *conflict monitoring*, that is, the executive brain function of maintaining attention while at the same time recognizing and disregarding distractions (both internal and external distractions). Improved attentional focus and conflict monitoring capacity directly results in increased performance enhancement. Gardner and Moore note that performance rapidly becomes derailed when attention drifts away from the performance task and goes inward to private thoughts and feelings. Although computers can multitask effectively, humans cannot. Attention is really an all-or-nothing asset. When attention shifts away from the trading task to deal with internal feelings, thoughts, and sensations, attention is literally removed from the trade. Actions are then made in the service of one's internal state rather than in the service of the trade because that's where the focus is placed. Unless you get lucky, performance must therefore suffer because the trade is not being attended to. Trading performance and trading results deteriorate. Mindfulness meditation increases attentional regulation and the important mental skill of conflict monitoring so that we can recognize and disregard irrelevant thoughts and feelings while continuing to maintain our attention and present focus on the kinds of actions and behaviors that support our trading.

Greater Awareness of Body and Emotions; Reduced Effort to Control Private Experience

Mindfulness is scientifically shown to promote the ability to notice body sensations and physiological states. Because bodily sensations and emotions are closely interconnected, body awareness helps us become more consciously aware of our emotional life. Bodily sensations (e.g., muscle tension, minor pain, pressure of the body against the chair, sensations of the breath) are common points of focus during mindfulness practice (some of the exercises described in this chapter focus on body sensations). Emotional intelligence is promoted through mindfulness training as we begin to connect our sensations to emotions. Mindfulness helps us to identify emotions as they arise and what they mean, a key aspect of emotional intelligence. Body sensations for many are the first thing noticed when emotions arise. Just as important, we become conscious that both sensations and emotions are merely temporary internal events through mindfulness practice. As this awareness is developed, we begin to reduce our effort to control our inner experiences naturally. Reducing effort to control body sensations, emotions, and thoughts helps keep us focused on performance tasks. All else being equal, this will naturally result in improved performance. This includes the experience of intense emotions during performance situations. Although we may experience strong emotions, mindfulness elevates our abilities to keep focused on what's really important and to keep committed to the high-value trading actions that support our trading and not get sucked into fighting our emotional state and becoming derailed from our trading.

Greater Emotional Regulation

It is important to recognize that although mindfulness practice does result in improved emotional control, this is not accomplished by trying to control your emotions with mindfulness. In fact, it is just the opposite. By learning to accept and be open to your emotions in a nonjudgmental manner through mindfulness practice, you can develop *internal* emotional regulation. Here, internal refers to the brain and psychological structures that foster and promote emotional governance. It is paradoxical: *you can't directly control your emotions and attempting to do so defeats mindfulness; by mindfully being open to your emotions and accepting them for what they are—just temporary, passing events, you develop emotional control.*

The science shows that experienced meditators develop stronger prefrontal cortex control over the amygdala and mindfulness activates the brain regions responsible for emotional regulation. The science is also beginning to show that emotional benefits from mindfulness practice most likely result from *cognitive reappraisal* where we assign new meaning to stressful events and experiences. Recall from Chapter 2 that the brain is not able to alter memories through subtraction; it works only by addition. Instead of reacting to stressful situations as we always have, which continues to reinforce patterned responses, mindfulness offers a different response. We train the mind and the brain through mindfulness that stress can be responded to in a more open and accepting manner without having to control or eliminate it. We thereby *add* different responses, experiences, and results to stress. If we actively fight it and try to remove the stress, we remain stuck in an unproductive cycle. Steven Hayes often says, "If you don't want it, you've got it." Rather than avoid the unpleasant internal experience, we can learn through mindfulness to "lean into it." Mindfully leaning into and being open to what we don't want changes the response patterns in the brain. This naturally takes more attentional effort in beginning stages. As practitioners gain experience, they develop their abilities and draw on less mental resources in maintaining emotional regulation. In this regard, mindfulness is a powerful technique as no other mental procedure is known to be able to do this.

Practitioners soon realize that just as the mind is always wandering, their thoughts and feelings, though sometimes strong and seemingly overwhelming, do recede. All thoughts and feelings—even very intense ones—are only transitory mental events. Mindful traders quickly learn that unwanted internal experiences are soon replaced by more pleasant thoughts and feelings. The more one practices mindfulness, the more one learns that difficult emotions are like a paper tiger. They really have no teeth.

To help illustrate this process, we often use a metaphor I first learned from psychologists and anxiety experts George Eifert and John Forsyth.[4] It's called "Feeding the Baby Tiger," and below is my adaptation.

> Imagine a baby tiger lives in your home. Although the tiger is small, he is still scary and you fear it will bite you. When it growls, you give him some food, hoping that will satisfy him. It does. He is preoccupied when eating and he lets you alone for a while. But he also grows bigger. The next time he is hungry and growls, he's just a little bigger and so you go and get more food for him. Well, this same drama plays out over and over, again and again. Every time the tiger growls, you feed him more and more. The bigger he gets, the more you are afraid of him. So you keep feeding him more and more food, hoping he'll leave you alone for good. But of course, he doesn't, because you keep feeding him.

In this metaphor, the tiger represents an unpleasant internal state. Like the tiger growling, you don't want it and you act to try and control it. With the tiger, control is achieved by feeding it—a negative reinforcement. But the control is only temporary; as long as you feed it, it will never go away. Why should it? You are supporting it. The more you feed it, the bigger and scarier the tiger gets. The more you feed your negative internal state by treating it as if it were accurate and real and something that must be responded to (and trying to control it, suppress it, reduce it, or change it in any way is treating it as if it were substantive, important, and must be responded to) the more it will seem real to you and the bigger and scarier it gets.

Mindfulness helps you to stop feeding the tiger. Mindfulness helps you be open to it and see it for what it is—just a paper tiger, a temporary feeling evoked by a few scary words or images that soon go away, nothing more. By not engaging in actions that are designed to get rid of or avoid the unwanted experience, you expose yourself to the tiger and see that it isn't really what it says it is. It has no teeth. Mindfulness also promotes calmness and a relaxed state. When you expose yourself to the tiger and your body is calm and relaxed, it sends a different message to your brain, indicating it need not become alarmed. Practiced enough, we begin to add onto our memory of similar experiences and we begin to change them. This is known as *reconsolidation* of existing memories. In other words, through mindful exposure we break the habit of feeding the tiger and in the process learn there is nothing really to fear or avoid. Thus, when we hear the tiger growl in the future, we simply acknowledge it, "Oh yes, there's that paper tiger," and turn our attention to what's important to us, in other words, the trading task at hand. We no longer respond rigidly to our internal state, but instead we can act in a flexible manner and do whatever is best for our trading at that time.

Perspective Change

Rather than looking at the world through our thoughts, mindfulness helps enhance our internal awareness such that we can develop clarity in our mental processes. We begin to decenter from thoughts, including thoughts about ourselves. We begin to recognize that the content of consciousness is transient and ever changing. This includes our conscious reflections on our own identity. Instead of seeing ourselves as static and immutable, we begin to learn that, in fact, we are changing all the time, and that what we call self is another construct of the mind. The "I" is not quite as solid or permanent as we tend to believe. Instead of habitually placing ourselves in the center of our worlds, we begin to adopt the "Observing I," or a sense of self that has ever-changing experiences and can stand apart and separate from its experiences. It is a sense of self that is not defined by any one experience, or any set of experiences, or any one label such as "I am good," or "I am bad," or I'm a trader," or "I'm a psychologist." We are more than our experiences, roles, labels, and titles—much more. Mindfulness practice helps us understand all this.

The science is limited in this area, but early studies reported by Hölzel and Lazar indicate that mindfulness brings greater acceptance of oneself and greater self-esteem. We also saw in the previous chapter that our default mode of mind wandering has a large self-referential component, which is usually experienced negatively. Mindfulness helps to take ourselves out of excessive self-referencing, allowing us to experience life in a fuller, less egocentric manner. It helps us develop an overall *metacognitive awareness*, which is a fancy word for seeing thoughts and feelings as mental events that are separate from ourselves. When thoughts and feelings are viewed in a self-referential manner as absolutes, we tend to think and act in a rule-governed manner. We typically set up unspoken rules for ourselves such as, "If X happens, then Y will occur." These are generally hardened and lead to rigidity in behavior. For example, "If I have another losing trade, it will be terrible" easily leads to self-referential thinking (e.g., "It will be bad for me if I have a loss" or "I'll never be a good trader if I have another loss") and further leads to inflexible actions such as jamming stops, holding losers beyond the stop point, and cutting winners short to avoid experiencing the negativity of our unspoken rules. Rule-governed thinking and rigid behavior reduces the trader's ability to interact with the market effectively.

When the mindful trader has the thought, "If I have another losing trade, it will be terrible," she will notice the thought simply as a thought. This metacognitive awareness helps to shift the trader's perspective and allows for more flexibility in her response to the market. She is not buying into "If X, then Y," and therefore isn't adamantly locked into preventing X. Thus, rather than believing her thought and jamming her stop or cutting the trade short, she can place her attention back onto the price action. In doing this, she becomes more sensitive to the cues the market is giving her and she is in a mental state that will allow her to flexibly respond to the market rather than rigidly respond to her internal state. Flexibility in this example might mean: letting the trade run; scaling out of (taking off) a portion of the position; adjusting (but not jamming) stops; hedging the position; adding to the position—whatever the trade objectively calls for.

■ Bring Mindfulness into Your Important Trading Activities

Now that you have learned the benefits of mindfulness and have practiced one or more of the techniques listed earlier in this chapter, it is time to start bringing mindfulness into your trading. You will find that mindfulness will begin to change the mental side of your trading in positive ways. Over time and with practice, you can expect to see the market more clearly, begin to become aware of market cues you hadn't seen before, and have a much more relaxed and focused mental state while trading. The latter will allow you to be more flexible in how you interact with the market. Instead of rigidly acting in limited ways and becoming distressed over an inability to act more skillfully, you will likely find that your repertoire of trading actions becomes more adaptable and that you choose more high-value actions. With mindfulness, your mind becomes suited for the demands of trading.

It is best, however, not to begin trying to apply mindfulness on significantly challenging situations. If you have had difficulty holding onto winning trades, for example, attempting to be mindful after putting on a trade is likely to have limited benefit, at least at first. You will need to practice mindfulness for a period of time before you can expect to see good results on trading situations that seriously challenge you. It is best to start applying mindfulness in more modest situations. Later, in Chapter 8, we detail an effective procedure for the more consequential difficulties. For now, let's stick with less psychologically taxing matters and ease our way into applying mindfulness in trading. Even major league baseball players have to spend some time in the minor leagues perfecting their skills before they are ready to use them on a professional level. Trading is really no different.

To begin using mindfulness in your trading, select one or two things you do either before you start the trading day or after trading is over. There are a wide range of activities in both periods where you can derive significant benefit by being mindful. At the end of the day, many traders review their trades and how the market traded during the day. We can just go through the motions of the activity or we can choose to do it mindfully. As you study your trades, notice any thoughts that draw your attention from the activity. These can be virtually any thoughts—from wanting to avoid reviewing a particular trade because your performance wasn't what you wanted it to be to thinking about what you will have for dinner. Notice any thought that takes you away from reviewing your trades. Observe it and any associated feelings like tension, embarrassment, sadness, or anger. Notice also that these thoughts and feelings take you out of the present moment. They pull you back into the past or push you forward into the future. You can make a mental note by putting a label on the thought such as "thinking about dinner" and on the feeling, for example, "hungry." Then, remind yourself what really matters to you at this moment and turn your attention back to your trade review. If the errant thoughts and feelings persist, notice this. You might even make the mental note of "persistence." Take a few breaths and mindfully watch your breath for a few cycles to center yourself before bringing your attention back to what matters—your trade review.

You will be well-served by first applying mindfulness to important trading-related activities that occur outside actual trading such as when you are preparing your game plan for the next day, when making your notes in your trading journal, and when reviewing the overnight data and making any revisions to your daily game plan due to overnight changes.

After applying and experiencing the benefits of applying mindfulness in these less challenging situations, you can take the next step and begin to practice being mindful when going through your checklist before you take a trade. Some traders become a bit over-aroused with excitement before taking a trade. Slow yourself down and center yourself. Take a few breaths and mindfully go over the current market and how it meets the criteria for your trade setup. If your mind wanders into the future or the past, notice this and bring it back to what's important—the present moment task of qualifying a trade by mindfully checking the current situation against your trade criteria. Applying mindfulness to qualify a potential trade setup begins to bring mindfulness into your actual trading.

When applying mindfulness to these various, less demanding trading activities, be sure to also notice what mindfulness does for you. See if distracting thoughts and feelings recede into the background. See if you are more attentive and aware of the task you are performing. See if you start seeing things you might normally miss. See if you are engaging your deliberative mind, rather than jumping to quick and easy conclusions. Keep in mind, too, that being mindful when performing these activities will build mindfulness skills for more challenging situations later. Remember, mindfulness is a mental skill and, like any skill, the more we practice it, the more proficient and effective we become in using it. You will also likely find that you will be more efficient and more observant as you mindfully perform these important trading tasks.

■ Notes

1. Susan M. Pollack, "Teaching Mindfulness in Therapy," in *Mindfulness and Psychotherapy*, ed. Christopher K. Germer et al. (New York: Guilford Press, 2013), 140.

2. John P. Forsyth and Georg H. Eifert, *The Mindfulness and Acceptance Workbook for Anxiety: A Guide to Breaking Free from Anxiety, Phobias and Worry Using Acceptance and Commitment Therapy* (Oakland, CA: New Harbinger, 2007), 242.

3. Russ Harris, *ACT made Simple: An Easy-to-Read Primer on Acceptance and Commitment Therapy* (Oakland, CA: New Harbinger, 2009), 177–180.

4. Georg H. Eifert and John P. Forsyth, *Acceptance and Commitment Therapy for Anxiety Disorders: A Practitioner's Guide to Using Mindfulness, Acceptance and Values-Based Behavior Change Strategies* (Oakland, CA: New Harbinger, 2005), 138–139.

CHAPTER 7

Defusion: An Advanced Mindfulness Skill

L et's start with the following scenario:

> You are driving along a deserted road late at night. You are several miles from the nearest town and no other cars are traveling this road. Suddenly, you car loses power, the engine dies, and the car rolls quietly to a stop. You note that your gas tank is half full; so you realize there must be something wrong with the engine. You take the flashlight from the glove compartment and open the hood. Your inspection reveals that the fuel line has a small hole leaking gasoline. This has caused the engine to die. You try to call emergency road service, but your mobile phone has no battery life, so you look in your car for tools to repair the leak. All you can find is a ballpoint pen and a drinking glass. How can you use what you have to fix the problem so you can get to the next town? Try to solve this in the next few minutes before reading on.

If, after a minute or two, you haven't solved the problem, consider that broken glass can cut a plastic fuel line and removing the ink cartridge from a pen leaves you with a hollow plastic tube. Think for another minute or two with this information and try to solve the problem before reading on.

Most people will solve this late-night automobile challenge by breaking the glass on the road, carefully using a shard from the glass to cut out the section of the fuel line with the offending hole, and then inserting the hollow pen tube into each end of the cut fuel line as a makeshift splice so that gasoline can again freely flow into the carburetor and fuel the engine.

Psychologists Steven Hayes and Chad Shenk described a similar mental challenge to help illustrate the concept of *fusion* and the essential, contrasting mental skill of *defusion*. Fusion refers to our responding to thoughts and mental images as if they were real. Solving the fuel line problem is an illustration of fusion. When we read the scenario above, we can visualize the dark, deserted road, and the car stopped by a blown fuel line. But they do not exist in reality; they come to life only in our mind. In our present reality, there also is no flashlight, drinking glass, or ballpoint pen. These items were created in our mind through the printed words on the page. Yet most of us could imagine the scene along with the specific items. In working through this problem, we experienced the highly valuable abilities of our mind. We could—in our mind—freely manipulate these items. We could "see" ourselves breaking the glass, cutting the fuel line, and splicing the fuel line by inserting the hollow pen tube, despite the fact that none of these things existed in reality. As we progressed through the problem, we evaluated our plans and actions against the goal of repairing the car. If our mind initially created a solution that didn't quite work, most of us would attempt an alternate approach. As we conceived, planned, and evaluated mental solutions, we could determine with reasonable certainty whether we actually could cut the fuel line with the glass and make a temporary splice with the pen tube. All this was done as if we were directly maneuvering an actual glass shard and ballpoint pen, but we were not. This is what Hayes and colleagues call fusion: treating the thoughts, images, and feelings generated within the mind *as if they were real*. Fusion is sometimes described as two pieces of heated plastic coming together and fusing into one. Mentally, we "join" thoughts and images to reality. This is what allows us to effectively solve the car problem. We can manipulate all the pieces of the puzzle (glass, fuel line, pen) in our mind as if they are real in order to develop a solution.

Our mind is a wonderful tool in this regard. It is precisely these mental abilities that have helped us figure out how to travel through the skies and successfully land on the moon, how to open up the body and repair and even replace diseased organs, and how to create and operate a worldwide Internet that can send information across the globe instantaneously. These and many other amazing wonders came about because of the unique and valuable abilities of our mind. It is the gift of evolution that has enabled our species to thrive.

But, as Hayes and Shenk point out, there is a dark side to the mind as well. It simply doesn't know when to stop. As you have learned from your mindfulness exercises, the mind is very difficult to quiet. It generates thoughts constantly throughout the day, and even during sleep through dreams. It is also constantly solving problems. As you watch your mind closely, you will find it is continuously comparing, contrasting, evaluating, planning, and trying to figure things out. Virtually everything becomes a problem to solve. In a very real sense, because our minds have evolved into outstanding problem-solving machines, problem solving has become our preferred way of thinking. In the process, we fuse with the content of the mind and take what the mind tells us literally as if it were the truth. Fusion is not useful in all situations. You can think of it as the carpenter whose only tool is a hammer. Although the carpenter's hammer is finely made and marvelous, not all problems should be seen as a nail to be pounded. As you might have already guessed, fusion and unregulated problem solving often become problematic in trading.

When you take a trade and you have the thought, "I could have a loss on this trade," what do you think your mind will do with that? It will try to problem-solve it, of course. But this is unlikely to be workable as it will encourage our mind to treat our internal experience of thoughts and feelings the same as a blown fuel line and act as if our normal private events (thoughts and feelings) are a real problem to be solved. We can be fruitlessly pounding nails every time we enter a trade. Hayes and Shenk tell us that problem solving should produce positive results, not add to our woes. The exercises in Chapter 3 highlight that applying problem solving to eliminate fear and other unwanted internal experiences typically accomplishes unsatisfactory results. These exercises serve to demonstrate that we often create more harm to our trading and to ourselves when we fuse with thoughts and feelings and try to solve them as if they were real problems.

In fact, the greatest psychological difficulty in trading is that our minds treat our unwanted internal events—our thoughts, feelings, and sensations—as problems to be solved. Unfortunately, the usual problem-solving approaches that work in everyday situations not only fail miserably when applied to what occurs internally— "between the ears," so to speak—but as many traders discover, they can cause harm and suffering in many instances. This is vital to understand. To help illustrate the difficulties created when we allow the mind to run full rein in problem solving our internal events, let's look at a psychologically induced event with which every trader is familiar: cutting a winning trade short. Steph, an experienced day trader, provides a typical example of cutting a winning trade short.

> I did it again, and I don't know why. I mean, here I was trading the yen. I saw on the hourly chart that a multiday uptrend was dying out as it approached longer-term resistance. I saw supply come in as the market started to fall below the high from yesterday. I was very patient—I give myself credit for that—and I waited for the low volume pullback and test of yesterday's high. This occurred, and I knew that the market was now in a position to turn. The uptrend was over; I expected a sizable reaction. I had a great entry a few pips from the top of the retracement. I was really proud of myself at that moment. I knew I had the potential for a great trade.

Figure 7.1 shows a combination of the 60-minute and 5-minute Japanese yen market as Steph had viewed it. She had seen that the 60-minute uptrend was mature and showing signs of weakness as it came into resistance. On the 5-minute chart (right-hand side), yesterday's high is marked, along with the location Steph entered her short sale trade as the market tested that key level.

Steph continues,

> So everything was looking good. I actually felt pretty calm, knowing that I was trading my plan. I felt really good. The market started to fall, just as I anticipated. But then it started. I think I noticed tension first. My body became tight, muscles tense. My leg started twitching like a sewing machine, you know, moving up and down on its own. I felt very uncomfortable. I was scared, really. I didn't want to have another loss. My trade was in profit, and I started thinking, "What if this goes against me? I mean, how many times have I been wrong and lost money? Here I'm in profit, why not book it and take it to the bank?" This is what I was telling myself. I can still hear the words my mind was telling me, "Steph, you are going to have a loss if you aren't careful. Do the right thing, take your profits. Don't be a fool and let them slip away." That's what I was thinking.
>
> Then it got worse, really bad. The yen started to rally a bit. All I could see was price going against me. My stomach felt queasy. I really felt the fear. It was pretty strong. My mind was screaming at me by this point. "Take the trade off! Take the profits you've got! Hurry up, before it's too late!" So I closed the trade.
>
> The yen moved up a few pips higher and I started to feel good. In fact, I was relieved to have saved my profits. My mind was telling me, "Nice job!" All the tension was draining away. My legs stopped twitching, my stomach felt better, and the fear was gone. I felt good. But then it happened. The market started falling, and it fell with a vengeance. My trade was unfolding as I had planned, but I was no longer in it. The market fell, and fell, and fell. It closed on the low for the day and continued falling the next day. I was depressed; I mean now I felt really bad. I became very self-critical. My mind now told me that "I'll never be a good trader," that I was "stupid for taking the trade off; this is what I had planned for. Why did I do that?" it said. "Can't I ever learn to trade my plan? I'm a failure when it comes to trading, I ought to just give it up and go back to my old job." That's what my mind was telling me.

Figure 7.2 shows how the yen trade unfolded after Steph covered her short position.

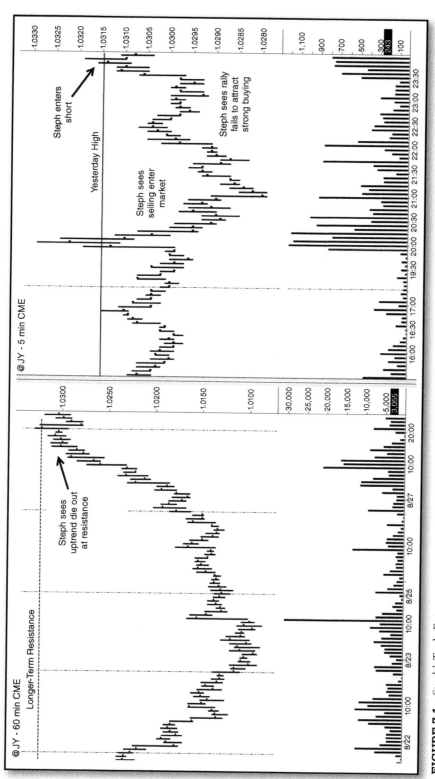

FIGURE 7.1 Steph's Trade Entry

Source: TradeStation Technologies, Inc.

DEFUSION: AN ADVANCED MINDFULNESS SKILL

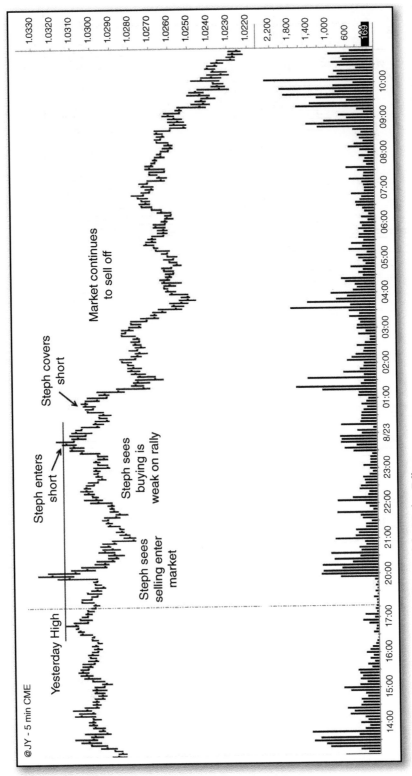

FIGURE 7.2 Steph Covers Her Short and the Market Falls

Source: TradeStation Technologies, Inc.

As Steph's mind automatically generated thoughts about loss and she fused with them, she completely abandoned her plan to trade for a larger reaction. Like Nathan in Chapter 1, Steph's mind only focused on the immediate market context. Lacking any distance from her thoughts, her intuitive mind was given free rein to operate. As we have seen earlier, the intuitive mind is highly impulsive, vulnerable to being influenced by emotion, ignores the probabilities of a situation, and is quick to come to a judgment on limited information. All of these characteristics of the intuitive mind were evident in Steph's case. In addition, Steph treated the content her mind was generating about how the market was moving against her and how this would result in a loss as if it were real. She fused with what her mind was telling her. Her fusion exacerbated her emotional reaction and she lost all semblance of emotional intelligence. Because she completely bought into what her mind was telling her, Steph became hijacked by her own mind. *Fusion with her thoughts and feelings of loss caused her to act in the service of her mind and her emotions, that is, to solve the problem of her fear of loss, rather than in the service of a well-conceived and well-executed trade.*

Like many traders in similar trading situations, Steph's mind rapidly came to the obvious solution: close the trade. On the surface, the decision to bank the profit seemed to be reasonable. But the real motivation was to escape the distress. This is precisely where the harm of fusion in trading occurs. Fusion typically results in actions that address our internal state rather than what the trade calls for. Fusion leads to unskilled trading behaviors and poor trading outcomes. As we saw in the Vicious Cycle of Ineffective Trading in Chapter 5, our focus on the trade will evaporate when attention shifts inward as we become fused with our mind's story about loss. Relief occurs as we act on the mind's intuitive, problem-solving solution to close the trade. This negatively reinforces the escape behavior and virtually guarantees it will be the preferred action in future similar situations. This is why trusting the mind unconditionally poses the greatest danger to successful trading.

You can work out the idea of fusion for other common trading problems. Jumping into unplanned trades are typically caused by fusion with the mind telling you how the market is about to take off, you shouldn't miss this move, you can make up for past losses with this trade, blah, blah, blah. If you hesitate about pulling the trigger on trades, your mind is likely telling you stories replete with loss and doubt about the quality of this trade setup. And, if you press a trade beyond its life expectancy, see if you aren't buying into your mind telling you that this trade is going to the moon, don't leave money on the table, it will push through the resistance, the market is exceptionally strong. . . . We are not saying the mind is your enemy, as in many circumstances it is extremely helpful, but we need to know that the mind is not always our friend. We need to learn to defuse and gain some distance on what the mind is saying so as to differentiate between when the mind is being helpful and when it is likely to cause us and our trading to suffer.

Let's discuss a few important things from Steph's experience further. The elements discussed next both create the context for fusion and are characteristic of fusion as initially described by Hayes and Schenk. Reviewing them will help us step back and begin to defuse from our thoughts and feelings. This mental skill allows us to treat them as temporary mental events—when appropriate—that we need not lock into and believe as authoritatively representing reality or as something that demands our immediate response.

1. **Thoughts and feelings are generated automatically by the mind and we don't have much say over what thoughts and feelings occur.** You have likely experienced this first hand through your mindfulness exercises. Thoughts, feelings, and sensations simply arise on their own. This is natural. We have little control over them. Review Steph's experience to see how many times her thoughts and feeling changed. She began her trade feeling calm and relatively confident. Then, unprompted by her, her mind began thinking about a loss and her body became tense. After closing the trade, she said to herself, "Nice job!" The congratulations didn't last long, however; she soon felt down and her thoughts became toxically self-critical. We see Steph's mind automatically generated widely varying thoughts and emotions within a brief period of time. Because she was fused to her thoughts, Steph was whipsawed back and forth by her own mind.

2. **The environment and the situations we are in highly influence what the mind tells us.** You may have also noticed this from mindfulness practice. What we see, hear, smell, taste, and feel can trigger memories, images, thoughts, and emotions. One thought will lead to the next as the mind tries to make sense of things by connecting a stimulus from the environment with a memory, perhaps an image, and, then, other thoughts follow. Soon, a mental story emerges. Again, it is important to note that we are not really in control of this. It is just what our minds do. If we are fused with what the mind is telling us, we become lost in that story. Here's an everyday example: Walking along a downtown sidewalk you pass a bakery and smell the aroma of freshly baked buns. This scent triggers memories of your mother's baking. Almost immediately, you see in your mind's eye your mother in her kitchen, baking cookies. Ah, the cookies she baked! You remember that your brother loved her cookies, too. You now see your brother in your childhood kitchen having a cookie. In your reverie, you notice he is wearing your favorite childhood baseball cap. Suddenly, you feel angry and a little guilty over the unkind words you recall you once said to him about wearing your hat without your permission. Although this happened over 20 years ago, you feel it now. You have fused with your mind, treating the thoughts and images as if they were real, so real that you had an actual emotional response even though the event existing within the memory was not reality, but experienced only internally, entirely

within your mind. Can you see how this readily applies to trading? In Steph's example, she—like virtually all traders—had had prior losses and some of the losses were painful. Her mind would automatically begin thinking of a loss when she puts on a trade. It's the same as the scent of a bakery triggering memories from childhood. When the price action ticked against her, it stimulated even more strident and more insistent thoughts. Her mind said she would have a loss and demanded she exit the trade *as a solution to the problem it created, which was stimulated by the environment and trading situation.*

3. **When fused, we uncritically believe the mind and become entangled in its story. This causes us to lose contact with the present.** This occurred with the bakery story. Even though we were walking on a city street, our mind had us living in the past so persuasively it caused strong emotions. Our mind created an "alternate universe," as Hayes and Shenk describe it. Think back to when you were working on the fuel line problem at the beginning of this chapter. Because we were fused while solving the problem, it took us out of the present moment. When you were engaged in solving this problem, did you also notice how your feet touched the floor, the temperature of the air, or the ambient sounds that were occurring in the room you were in as you worked through the problem? Probably not. Your mind was fused with repairing the fuel line, taking you out of the present moment. When Steph was fused to the story her mind was telling her that she was about to have a loss, she was not present for her trade but living a projection of the future. When we are fused, we accept the mind's story literally and become enmeshed in and live through the mind's story as if it were true, missing the present and all its opportunities. Steph was unable to see that the market was having a normal pullback on light volume before heading lower because she was fused with the story her mind was telling her. She was unable to read the market as it unfolded. She was not in the present but in some future mental space her mind had constructed projecting a loss. In a similar vein, a trader, anxious and fearful over the loss from her last trade, may fail to notice that the trade opportunity now setting up is of high quality and high odds. Instead, what is most likely noticed are the uncomfortable feelings and thoughts associated with anxiety and fear that were discussed in Chapter 2. Lacking contact with the present and fused to internal mental content and the effort to solve that content as a problem, the trader is likely to make poor trading decisions and miss a sound trading opportunity just like Steph.

4. **When fused with our thoughts and feelings, we lose focus with the trading task at hand.** When our focus is on our internal experience, it dramatically diminishes our performance capabilities because it diverts attention from the trade. Attention is a limited mental resource. It is virtually impossible to manage a trade when fused with a compelling story the mind is telling us. This is the real crime of fusion in trading. We get mentally sidetracked

from what really matters: the trade! Instead, our attention shifts to what isn't even true. In trading, we want to have a task-focus, not a self-focus. For Steph, that meant a focus on the tasks of trade management including reading the strength of the unfolding supply and demand. Instead, like many traders, she was fused to her thoughts and feelings and the story they were telling her. It was as if her mind was like a sleight-of-hand artist misdirecting her attention. Unfortunately, this isn't about being entertained by a magic trick but a serious trading performance concern. If you want to trade well, you must keep your attention on the trading tasks at hand and not be misdirected by the chatter of your mind.

5. **The mind can be remarkably shameless in the stories it will tell. When we are fused, we can't tell the difference between what is truly useful and what is not.** Steph's mind insisted she exit the trade. It told her how she could not tolerate another loss. Fused with her mind she covered her short trade. Then, a few moments later, the market fell. Did her mind say to her, "Gee, Steph, I made a mistake; I am really sorry for persuading you to exit that trade?" No. Instead, it shamelessly told her how bad she was, that she couldn't follow her trading plan, and that she will never become a competent trader. Because she was fused, Steph believed what her mind told her: first to exit a sound trade because she believed her mind when it told her she would have a loss and then to feel down because she believed her mind when it told her that she is incompetent for exiting the trade it told her to exit only moments before. Obviously, neither mind was right, but when we are fused we are unable to tell. We can be highly vulnerable to mental and emotional whipsawing when fused. Virtually all traders have had this experience. The mental skill of defusion we discuss next in this chapter will help you begin to deal much more effectively with your mind. Defusion will help protect you from this kind of mental abuse, and help you to begin to produce the kind of trading performance you desire.

Before we get to that mental skill, however, you might be thinking, okay, I get this idea of fusion. We can be overidentified with our thoughts. But maybe the problem lies in the thoughts themselves. If they were more accurate, we wouldn't be making so many mistakes and trading psychology would be easier. For example, you might now be thinking that Steph thought she was about to have a loss and that didn't turn out to be the case. If instead, she thought something different, something that was more accurate, all would be well. After all, if Steph was thinking more clearly and more accurately, she wouldn't have taken her trade off and would have walked away from the trade with a large profit. Maybe the feelings of having a loss and the fear that this generates are due to faulty thinking. So, you might try to challenge your thought that you are about to have a loss with some rational, logical counterargument that disputes the thought of loss and this would take care of the problem. It may sound like a good idea (another example of problem-solving?), but our experience and the psychological research clearly tells us differently.

Pioneering psychologist Kelly Wilson says it is very tempting to construe the mental difficulties we have been discussing as resulting from inaccurate thinking. Because what we think and what we do are definitely linked, it is appealing to believe that if we sharpen our thinking, our trading performance will improve. All we need to do is figure out which thoughts are inaccurate and then change them into accurate ones. If you are thinking along these lines, you are not alone. This is the standard approach in western culture and this has been how psychology has approached, and, in many respects, continues to approach distressing thoughts and feelings.

Permanently modifying thoughts is definitely not easy to do. Kelly Wilson points out that we have all had thoughts and feelings that we were convinced were true, only to find later that they failed to hold up to our predictions. Steph's foretelling of a loss from a rally against her short trade is a good example. Jumping into an unplanned trade, averaging down, and failing to enter a trade are all examples of actions traders take because they are convinced that at that moment what their mind is telling them is true. And, it's not only traders who experience this. Everyone, including nontraders, experience it, too. Being late to an important meeting, making a public presentation, and asking someone for a date are some common, nontrading situations that people can make a big deal of in their minds and which then usually occur without the anticipated problems. We can try to fight these thoughts and feelings with more accurate thoughts, telling ourselves "the presentation is really no big deal," for example, but these rarely alter our underlying concerns or change how we act.

Keep in mind that you already know from the exercise in Chapter 3 (see Exercise 3.2: The Short- and Long-Term Costs and Benefits of My Control Strategies) that trying to suppress or eliminate your thoughts and feelings isn't workable. Changing your thoughts in the attempt to make them more accurate is merely a variation on this theme. Many readers will have also documented their efforts to change their thoughts by trying to make them more precise, correct, and truthful in that exercise and found that this didn't remedy their problems.

Sound psychological research verifies your experience that trying to change, make more accurate, and otherwise control thoughts and feelings just isn't effective. A research team co-led by University of Washington psychologist Neil Jacobson and Keith Dobson from the University of Calgary developed enlightening research on this question. Jacobson (now deceased) and Dobson taught skills to modify thoughts that arise automatically—just like thoughts of loss—to counter negative thinking in people who were clinically depressed. To fairly assess the effectiveness and value of changing thoughts, they compared this with another group who simply engaged in activities that were personally meaningful, challenging, and/or pleasurable. The challenging of holding on to a trade instead of cutting it short is an activity that would fit into this category. Jacobson and Dobson were completely surprised by the study results. Because the key feature of the type of therapy they practiced and were testing focused on changing dysfunctional thoughts, they fully expected that modifying negative thoughts would be far superior to mere activity engagement. That wasn't the case. Much to their credit, Jacobson and Dobson published their results in one of the premier psychological journals concluding "it may be possible that engaging in meaningful activities may be more effective in changing the way people think than directly attempting to alter thinking."

A decade later, UK psychologists Richard Longmore and Michael Worrell reviewed all studies that assessed differences between changing thinking and getting people involved in activities they found meaningful. They found no differences in effectiveness between changing cognitions and activity engagement. Interestingly, Longmore and Worrell also reviewed studies that applied both changing thoughts and meaningful activity engagement at the same time to see if there was any "added value" in developing skills in reframing and modifying thoughts. In other words, given that participating in meaningful activities was effective, was there any additional benefit to also changing thoughts? There was none. Longmore and Worrell concluded that putting effort into changing thoughts is simply not necessary.

Although the research cited above involved clinical populations, the findings also pertain to the broader population. In the sport world, for example, Zella Moore reviewed the research on traditional psychological skill strategies designed to alter and control negative thoughts, emotional states, and physiological sensations. These traditional strategies included many that traders report trying: goal setting, arousal control, imagery, and positive self-talk. Moore failed to find research sufficiently adequate to classify these approaches as evidence-based interventions of choice in enhancing athletes' performance. Like the research on altering thoughts, these strategies have not been found to be effective in controlling or changing one's inner state. Forward-thinking sport psychologists, like Yuri Hanin at Finland's Research Institute for Olympic Sports in Jyväskylä, understand this. Hanin incorporates negative feeling states and negative cognitions in his model that profiles the psychological components of peak athletic performance for individuals. His Individual Zones of Optimal Performance model, for example, allows for such negative states as anxiety and anger to coexist alongside joy and confidence. Our internal state need not be skewed toward a positive, one-sided polarity in order to trade well. Just like Captain Sullenberger landing his jet in the Hudson River, success lies in maintaining a focus on the tasks at hand and acting on them; it does not lie in a self-focus on internal thoughts and feelings and the distracting struggle to try and correct them.

Before we leave this topic, there is an important note regarding positive self-talk with which traders should be aware. Repeating positive affirmations such as, "every day, I'm becoming a better and better trader," are widely believed to change one's negative thinking, boost mood, and promote enhanced self-esteem. This is not true. Joanne Wood, psychologist from the University of Waterloo in Ontario, Canada, led a research effort to study positive self statements in relation to self-esteem. She and her team found that those with low self-esteem actually felt worse when they repeated positive self statements or considered the truth of the statements. Those for whom positive self-talk is aimed to help were found to do worse. People with higher self-esteem did feel a little better after repeating their affirmations, but not by much. The bottom line message here is that positive self statements are contraindicated; they should not be used. This is especially so for those whose sense of self-worth runs low.

Kelly Wilson points out that aside from the research showing that trying to change thoughts doesn't work, there is also a practical aspect to keep in mind. Consider the trader who has a history of becoming fearful of losses whenever he puts on a trade. Like Steph, he becomes overwhelmed by the idea that he is in danger when in the market. This causes him to experience all the symptoms of the flight-fight response we discussed earlier. While he may see the need to rid himself of his anxious thoughts and feelings as a solution to his problem, he—like every trader who places a trade—actually is at risk. He has had losses in the past and, because his trade setup has a probability of loss on any given trade, there are many times he will experience a losing trade. So his thoughts are at least partially accurate. He could, and at times, will experience loss. It doesn't make sense to try and alter thoughts that are already accurate. Whether or not his thoughts about a loss are accurate in any given trading situation, they will nevertheless provoke fear and cause poor trading behavior if he is fused with them. Thus, for the most part, we don't really care whether thoughts are accurate or not. What we care about is having some mental distance from them.

To be clear, problem-solving skills are highly valuable in everyday life and essential in developing new products, managing projects, and negotiating the daily challenges we all confront *when the issue is located outside the skin*, as Steven Hayes and colleagues often describe. In trading, problem-solving skills are highly valuable and needed for many trading activities, such as developing, testing, and refining new trade setups, creating trading plans, evaluating our trading performance, setting trading goals we can work toward, and other similar activities. But they are not useful for dealing with thoughts, feelings, and sensations.

We've been discussing fusion and how it affects our trading. When we buy into and imprudently believe what the mind tells us is a true and accurate reflection of reality, we are fused. This is when the trouble starts. Sport psychologists understand this. A tennis player in practice executes a backhand drive perfectly. It's a lovely shot. On the very next ball, however, she tries the exact same shot and misses. Why? When queried, the player will say, "Well, I thought I could hit it better." How can a perfectly executed shot be improved on? It can't, but her mind told her differently *and she believed it*. She was fused.

We can't stop our mind from thinking and we can't control the things the mind tells us. Sport psychologists Zella Moore and Frank Gardner explain that when we struggle with trying to control the mind or listen too closely and buy into what the mind is saying while trying to play tennis or any other sport, we take our head out of the game. Whether you are performing as a trial lawyer arguing a case, a musician giving a concert, or a trader managing a trade, the same principle applies. When you fuse with what the mind is telling you, it takes you out of your game. If a lawyer was overly worried about the outcome of a case and focused on the jurors, their reactions, and what his mind told him about how the jurors were thinking (e.g., "this juror doesn't like me; that one is against the plaintiff;" etc.) her closing argument won't be very effective. If the musician is focused on how the audience is responding to her music, she's not putting her attention into the music and her performance will suffer. It's exactly the same in trading. When the trader is concerned about the trade's outcome, her focus is not on the market. How can we expect to be strong performers when our center of attention is not on the market or the trade but swallowing whatever random commentary the mind is conjuring up? To perform well in trading—as in any other performance-based activity, the key psychological task is to gain some distance on your thoughts and feelings. The key skill for this is mindful defusion. Defusion is the ability to accept thoughts exactly as they are for what they are (just words and feelings), not what they represent themselves to be (e.g., the truth). Defusion keeps us from buying into thoughts and feelings and acting from them. We don't try to change them or get rid of them, we simply let them go. Letting thoughts go is possible by developing the skill of defusion. The following defusion methods and techniques will help you develop this critical trading psychology skill. Put the effort in to learn and practice these techniques, and they will become your high-value mental skills you can rely on.

■ Defusion Strategies and Techniques

Keep Track of Your Feelings

A useful exercise is to track your feelings over the course of a week or two—see Exercise 7.1. You need not make this overly complicated, simply note your mood three times during the course of your day: morning, afternoon, and evening. In addition to your mood, note any prevalent thoughts at the time you take your reading. See if you can identify anything in the environment that might have stimulated your feelings and your thoughts. Note, too, whether you chose to have these thoughts or if they just arose on their own.

Exercise 7.1 Tracking My Thoughts and Feelings

Use this form to track your feelings and thoughts over the course of a week or two. We want to begin to develop better awareness of our thoughts and feelings, and especially how they show up and change. Three times a day, simply note your mood, sensations, any prevalent thoughts, anything specific that might have stimulated your feelings and your thoughts, and whether you chose to have these thoughts or if they just showed up on their own.

Time	What I Was Feeling/ Mood	Body Sensations I Noticed	What My Mind Was Telling Me	Situation/ Event	Did I Choose to Have These Thoughts and Feelings or Did They Just Show Up?
Sample: 8:00 A.M.	Upbeat and excited. I was also feeling confident.	Warmth; tingling in arms and hands	"Today is going to be a good day. I can't wait to trade"	Pre-open reviewing my game plan for the day.	Even though these were positive, they showed up on their own. In truth, I didn't choose them.
3:00 P.M.	Tired and bored.	Shoulders tense. Body felt heavy.	"Markets are dull." I noticed my mind encouraged me to surf the 'net and call friends.	Narrow trading range. Nothing happening in the markets.	Arose on own. I believe they were stimulated by the dullness of the market. I certainly didn't want to feel bored.
7:30 P.M.	Feeling positive and energized.	Body felt light. Ready to get going.	"A breakout tomorrow will lead to a big move. I can make good money tomorrow."	Reviewing markets and making game plan for tomorrow.	Again, they show up on their own. Funny how I'm not really in control of what I think or feel!

The form above has one day completed as an example. Note that the trader who filled in this example felt upbeat and excited in the morning. He noticed pleasant body sensations and had positive thoughts about how the day would unfold. He felt confident. His mental state changed in the afternoon. At three o'clock, he records feeling lethargic, heavy, and bored. His thoughts were on things other than trading. In the evening, he felt excited once again about the prospects for the next day. He felt lighter as he thought about where he would likely take trades if his game plan for tomorrow developed as he anticipated.

The example shows a fairly typical day in the life of a trader. Mood, feelings, and thoughts change frequently. Your days, of course, are likely to be different from the example but will still show wide variability. Some periods may be calm and relaxed; others may be filled with emotion. You might experience apprehension and fear, anger, sadness, joy, excitement, and a range of other feeling states. Likewise, your thoughts will likely vary from one period to the next, never staying the same. What thoughts and feelings you have really doesn't matter for this exercise. It's the variability that should be noted.

If you are like most people, you will find your feeling states and thoughts change from period to period. They may or may not change dramatically. You might not go from joy to sadness back to elation again all in one day. In fact, it is unlikely that you will. But your states will nevertheless change, even if they don't change dramatically from period to period. The point is to notice the changes, even when subtle. As you become more aware of your thoughts and feelings, you will begin to notice that they never stay the same and they come and go quickly. Thoughts and feelings are fleeting. Very often, we do not choose to have the thoughts we have, they just show up on their own, usually triggered by the situation we find ourselves in or something in our environment.

The fact that they change frequently, last only a little while, and come and go on their own with little choice on our part is often a revelation for many people. Unless we are paying attention, we really don't notice how our thoughts and feelings change, how quickly they pass, and how little control we have over them. It's not even us who cause them in the first place. And yet we buy into them, believe them completely, and allow these temporary, sometimes random mental events to control our trading lives. That is fusion. Beginning to notice that our thoughts and feelings do change and change frequently throughout the day is a part of defusion. We begin to see our thoughts and feelings for exactly what they are: temporary mental and emotional events that arise on their own and come and go. We can also begin to understand that thoughts and feelings are not always reflecting reality. When we recognize their transient nature and that they do not always tell us the truth, we start to become defused from our thoughts and feelings. If we are mindful and pay attention to our thoughts—observe them, rather than becoming enmeshed in them—we begin to see that they are often just temporary mental and emotional chatter—background noise, really. Although at times they may be uncomfortable or they may be demanding we take some action, they never last for long. We always have a choice. We can learn to take on a different perspective from what we normally have by developing the mindfulness skills to observe our thoughts and feelings for exactly what they are: temporary internal events that will soon pass and nothing we need become ensnared in when more important things like managing a trade require our attention. This and the exercises that follow can help us develop the ability to step back from our thoughts and see them as just thoughts, nothing more.

Hold Your Thoughts at a Distance

Try this quick exercise. It's a very good one developed by Steven Hayes and Russ Harris. Hold the palms of your hands in front of you, palms facing in toward your eyes. Lightly interlock your fingers so that although your fingers are loosely knitted together, there is still some space between your fingers that you can see through. Now imagine that your fingers represent your thoughts. Your fingers might represent thoughts of loss or the worries, anxieties, and concerns you have—all the unwanted and unhelpful thoughts you have. Slowly bring your interlocked hands up to your face, until they get only an inch or two from the tip of your nose and you have to look through the spaces between your fingers to see out. Notice what this is like. The closer your fingers get to your face, the more caught up you get in your thoughts. This is what it is like to be fused.

Look around to the left with your hands like this, and then to the right. Now look down and then up, and then return your head to a level position. Notice how difficult it is to see things. Notice how much you are missing. Because your view is blocked by your fingers, you are missing out on large amounts of information. This is what it is like being fused to your thoughts. They truly block out large pieces of reality. Imagine trying to trade like this. How difficult would it be to effectively execute a trade when fused like this? What would it be like to put on and manage a trade when your thoughts are so in your face? When we become so caught up in our thoughts, we can miss out on much of what the market has to offer and we will find it extremely difficult to trade effectively.

Now slowly lower your hands away from your face and notice what happens. Notice that the space between you and your thoughts increases as you lower your hands. We can now see what's around us much more clearly. It is now much easier to engage in things that are important to us because we aren't engulfed by our thoughts being right up there in our face. This is defusion. Notice that we still have our hands and fingers. We haven't cut them off to get rid of them. Hands and fingers and thoughts are still useful, so we don't want to get rid of them. We've just gained some distance on them. Having some distance on our thoughts frees us from them. They aren't in command of what you see or take in from the environment and how you respond to it.

Now take your dominant hand, spread the fingers wide and hold your hand out at arm's length. Your fingers still represent your thoughts, and they can be scary, troublesome thoughts, but held out at arm's length like this allows us to see them as they are and for what they are—just thoughts that we don't have to buy into. We can examine them, wave them around, or just set them back down on our lap and do whatever it is that is meaningful and important to us.

Notice that when our hands are up close and in our face, we have one perspective. It is a fused perspective in which we are experiencing the world by looking through our thoughts. When we hold our hands away from our face at arm's length or down at our lap, notice that we haven't gotten rid of those uncomfortable thoughts but we have created for ourselves a completely different perspective. This is a defused perspective. *We are changing our relationship to our thoughts by changing our perspective.* Our hands and thoughts are still there, but by treating them as just temporary mental events we have gained some distance from them and changed our perspective. Through defusion, we can have a different perspective on both our world and on our thoughts. This change in perspective is key because our relationship to our thoughts has changed. We are no longer slaves to them, but instead are liberated to see the world more accurately and to act in harmony with what we value. We now can act consistently with what is most important to us as a trader and, if we have a trade on, we have the mental flexibility to now act in congruence with what is important to the trade.

Practice holding your thoughts at a distance. Defusion is a skill and, like all skills, we get better at them and can use them effectively when it really counts if we have practiced them. You can't just read about the techniques, or try it once or twice and expect to be able to apply them effectively. You want to own them and ownership means practicing them. Here are two ways to practice this exercise. The first one is informal. Make it a goal for the next week to mentally put your thoughts out at arm's length whenever you notice them. Whatever activity you may be engaged in, when you notice your mind talking to you or notice a feeling, pause and observe it. You might, for example, be brushing your teeth and notice you are thinking about what you will be doing later that day. Pause and observe that thought. The second way is formal. Set aside time each day to specifically notice your thoughts and hold them at a distance. Simply sit quietly for a few minutes and observe your thoughts. See if you can notice a thought and also hold it out at arm's length. Try the same with feelings.

When you practice defusion either formally or informally, be sure to notice the effect it has on your thoughts and especially your reaction to them. As you practice and get better at this, you will begin to notice that any mildly emotionally-charged thought will begin to lose its emotional charge as you hold it away and observe it. Don't turn this into an objective, though. In other words, don't hold your thoughts at a distance expecting them to lose their emotionality. That won't work. Just hold your thoughts at a distance and observe them. Paradoxically, when you don't try to change them and just observe them, they do loosen their grip on you. When we try to force the issue, however, we are not observing but struggling, enmeshed in our thoughts and feelings. We are then fused and stuck.

Mindfulness

Mindfulness is itself a powerful method of defusion. Mindfulness promotes awareness of the actions of your mind. Through practice, it teaches us that thoughts come and go on their own. It helps us to develop a calm space between a stimulus such as the market ticking against our position and how we respond. That calm space allows us to notice the thought as simply a momentary mental event. When we can defuse from our thoughts, we are free to choose to do what matters to our trade. Defusion requires that we be mindful of our thoughts and feelings. Defusion is a form of mindfulness. The Leaves on a Stream mindfulness exercise found in Chapter 6 is a particularly good defusion exercise in this regard as it has you noticing your thoughts and then, rather than buying into them, mentally placing them onto a leaf and watching that thought atop the leave float on its own down the stream.

Notice that in all defusion techniques we are not trying to change our thoughts and feelings, make them more accurate, make them less intense, or make them go away. We are simply noticing them. As soon as we try to alter them or remove them, we are caught in the web of self-focus. Mindfulness and defusion should not be used to get rid of unwanted thoughts. In a very real sense, we want to invite them in, not do battle with them. As soon as we engage that battle, we take ourselves out of the present moment, enter an alternate, self-focused universe and become distracted from trading. Because this is a skill, it takes practice. The research on mindfulness reviewed in Chapter 5 and the changes that can occur both psychologically and anatomically should provide strong incentive for serious readers to practice mindfulness and the defusion techniques explained here. Let's look at a few more defusion methods you can use to strengthen your ability to avoid becoming hijacked by your thoughts and feelings.

Label Thoughts, Feelings, and Sensations

This next defusion technique comes from Steven Hayes and colleagues who have developed many of the methods found in this chapter. Find a quiet space where you won't be disturbed for the next 10 to 15 minutes. Now just watch your thoughts, images, memories, emotions, urges, and any bodily sensations you may have. When a thought arises, simply label it quietly, "Ah, a thought," and let it pass. Do the same thing with feelings—both emotions and sensations. For example, if you are feeling a bit sad, just mentally note "Sadness." If you notice an itch somewhere on your body, give it the silent label "Itch."

Your mind may tell you that this seems silly and not worth your while, but what you are doing is training yourself to hold your thoughts, feelings, and sensations lightly. By noticing and labeling your thoughts, you are keeping a distance from them. You are keeping yourself from becoming fused to them. Normally, when we have a thought, not only does it often go unnoticed, it also gets automatically accepted by us as true. If we have an itch, for example, we automatically scratch it. Here, we are observing it and learning that not only can minor discomforts be tolerated, they eventually go away on their own. When practicing this skill, notice any bodily discomfort that may arise. You might notice a little tension in your feet, a cramp in your leg, or maybe a facial itch. Normally, we act to remove the minor discomfort. In this exercise, try just noticing it. Label it and then sit quietly and observe it. If you have never done this before, you may be surprised that the minor discomfort does quickly go away on its own. The same occurs with thoughts and feeling states. Doing this not only helps you to defuse from your internal state, but it also helps build your tolerance. We learn that we don't have to act on every little itch, minor discomfort, thought, or feeling. They will leave on their own and we are perfectly fine having them.

This skill becomes useful and applicable when you are in a trading situation. You might, for example, notice a nice trade setting up. Your mind might tell you to double up on your position size to make up for a loss you had earlier that day. If you remain fused to this thought and trade outside the parameters of your money management and risk principles, you are trading poorly and that will have consequences for you. Being able to notice this thought and label it as just a passing thought allows you to defuse from it, disregard it, and maintain a task-oriented focus, which in this case involves correctly sizing the position. Being defused from this thought places you in the advantageous position of trading your trade setup rather than trading your mind. Had you remained fused to the thought of increasing your position size, you would have likely committed to an oversized trade. If that is the case, your risk for this trade is now beyond your personal money management considerations, and you now are likely to become tense and nervous. With the extra size, you certainly don't want to have a loss. If you now fuse with the tension and thoughts about not being able to tolerate a loss on an oversized position, you would take yourself out of managing the trade and start to work to manage your internal state. This can end up in a trade cut short, or, ironically, a very large loss—both occurring because you took action from a fused state of mind (remember, you were going to make up for a previous loss—whatever happened to that great idea?) and have subsequently become fused with other thoughts and feelings about now avoiding a loss. So even though labeling your thoughts may seem simple and not worth the practice, don't get fused to that thought! Thought labeling is a very valuable defusion skill to develop. Have fun with it!

I Am Having the Thought That …

Here's another technique developed by Hayes and colleagues. It's an extension of the Labeling exercise. As you notice any arising thoughts, feelings, and sensations as in the exercise above, add these words to what you notice: "I am having the thought that. …" For example, you notice that your mind tells you the thought, "I'm bored." Rather than say to yourself, "I'm bored," say, "I am having the thought that I am bored." Do you notice the difference between the two? Saying to yourself, "I'm bored," is fusion. We are buying into that thought. It's right up in front of our face. Saying, "I am having the thought that I am bored" is defusion. It gives you a little distance on that thought. It has changed our perspective on the thought. It is no longer "I am X," it is "I am having a thought that I am X." Can you also see that when you are fused and simply buy into the thought "I am X" that your actions are going to be limited? You are going to act however X makes you act. If you defuse with the idea and are having a thought of X, well, you now have choices in how you act.

If you notice that you feel sad, rather than say to yourself, "I'm sad," try "I am having a feeling of sadness." Again, you gain a different perspective. In the first instance, you are sadness. It's a fused state. In the second instance, you are not sadness at all. You are having a feeling of sadness, but the "you" is the observer of that sadness. It is very different.

Try this. Say to yourself, "I am going to have a loss." Let yourself experience what that feels like for you. Once you have taken a moment or two to experience the "I'm going to have a loss" thought, say the defused alternative: "I am having the thought that I am going to have a loss." How does this change the experience for you? In a trade, your mind might say, "I am going to have a loss." Staying fused with this thought will influence your behavior and dramatically increase the likelihood you will act erratically. Practicing this exercise will help you step back a bit, pull your thought back away from being in your face, and be able to observe that thought and note that "I am having the thought that I am going to have a loss." Being defused increases the likelihood that you will take actions that better match the needs of the trade rather than erratic actions that serve to address your fused internal state.

Follow the Bouncing Ball

Older movies sometimes used the "bouncing ball" device to involve audiences in the film. Karaoke uses the same method. Lyrics of the song being played are seen across the screen and a ball bounces to the rhythm of the music, landing on each syllable as an aide for singing the song.

In this exercise developed by Russ Harris, set aside 5 minutes or so and take thoughts that have distressed you and especially ones that have interfered with your trading and jot them down. Then, in your mind's eye, imagine them to be displayed across a TV, computer, or karaoke screen, word for word. Add the bouncing ball, seeing the upsetting thoughts as words that run across the screen with the ball bouncing along as each syllable is considered.

Notice that in this and all defusion exercises we are not trying to get rid of these thoughts, but simply to learn how to step back and see them for what they are—just words passing across the mind's screen—not truth, not reality, and not commands to which we must respond or spoken by a commander to whom we must answer. Defusion exercises are important because, when we are fused with what the mind is telling us and the mind is telling us things like "I am going to have a loss," "I need to get a trade on; I don't want to miss this move," or "I can make up for that loss by doubling my position," we will behave contrary to what is important to us and our trading. If what really matters to us is being a competent and skillful trader, we will need to act in skilled and competent ways. When fused, we move ourselves away from what we want. This should be readily understood. Buying into the thought "This trade will turn into a loss" will have us acting in a particular way. Being defused from that thought frees us from acting unskillfully and allows us to trade consistent with what is important to us both as a trader and for the trade.

Sing a Joyful Song

This defusion technique comes from the clever mind of Joel Guarna, a clinical psychologist in Maine. This is especially good for times when you get down on yourself and have self-critical thoughts. Take a moment and jot down the kinds of negative, critical things you might typically say to yourself. The things I might hear myself say when I am frustrated over a mistake or bone-headed trade I made would include things like, "You're an idiot," sometimes "stupid," and, even, "loser." All are pretty harsh. When we fuse with these kinds of toxic labels we can really drag ourselves down. It is never helpful or even remotely useful to be so self-condemning, though we all tend to do it to one degree or another. So here is a very effective way to defuse. Sing the song *For He's a Jolly Good Fellow*, but replace the word fellow with whatever label stings you the most. Let's use "loser."

> For he's a jolly good loser,
> For he's a jolly good loser,
> For he's a jolly good loser, which nobody can deny!

Again, it is important to do this, not just read about it. How does it make you feel to sing your toxic self-criticism in this way? It takes the sting out of it. Singing it affords some mental distance. We certainly hold the idea, "loser," much more lightly. Suddenly, we have defused from a self-label that normally takes us down. Do this any time you notice your mind becoming critical. Just like Steph, our minds can turn on us and condemn us in the worst way. Trying to fight it, correct it, reframe it, or change it in any way isn't going to be helpful, as we have already discussed. Singing about it, however, does change the perspective. To deepen the defusion experience, you can add the Bouncing Ball technique described above and see "For he's a jolly good ..." passing across a screen in your mind's eye and a ball bouncing along the words. And, if for whatever reason you don't like the song *For He's a Jolly Good Fellow*, pick another tune. Be creative.

Say It from Someone Else

What if you don't like to sing? No worries, there are other ways. Here is a defusion exercise from psychologist Kelly Wilson. In this exercise, we take a thought we feel fused with and imagine it comes from someone else—someone other than you. You can do this with any thought you get caught up in. Here are some typical thoughts with which traders fuse:

- "Having a loss would be terrible";

- "I'm not a good enough trader";

- "I'll never be a competent trader";

- "If I don't get into the market now, it will take off without me";

- "I can put on XX contracts and make up for all my losses";

- "If I enter this trade now, it will go against me";

- "I can press this trade, I know it has more profit to give."

Pick a thought that you find yourself getting caught up in frequently. It is helpful to keep notes in your trading journal of thoughts that you believe and cause you to act in ways that are contrary to skillful trading.

Once you have a thought that frequently ensnares you, take 5 to 10 minutes and play this exercise game. Let's say you find yourself getting caught in the thought, "I can't have a loss, it would be terrible." Now imagine someone else or something else telling you this. For example, you can imagine some pompous boot camp sergeant telling you, "You can't have a loss, it'll be terrible." What if a comedic actor or a rock musician you don't like said this to you? The point is not to ridicule yourself or condemn yourself with the thought, or to make fun of the thought or even what it has to say. Rather, the key is to imagine someone other than you tell you the thought you get stuck on. Again, we are shifting perspectives from automatically coming from within yourself to deliberately and consciously evoking them in a novel context. When we can shift the perspective, we change our relationship to the thought. When it is said from the perspective of another person, it gives us distance on the thought and it loses its power. We become diffused.

This is a particularly useful exercise if you tend to ruminate. For example, after a loss, you might have a tendency to spend the rest of the day thinking, "I'll never be a successful trader." Fusing with such a thought will be totally unworkable if you have the goal of developing yourself as a trader. Not only does it disturb your trading, it will bring you down and put you into a negative space which does you no good. What if a French poodle was telling you that thought, complete with a French accent? See what I mean? We want to give ourselves some distance on such disruptive thoughts and *change our relationship to them.* Again, we are not trying to get rid of them, just hold them more lightly, at a distance, and thereby change our perspective and how we view them. You can go a little further with this. You can have Donald Duck in his unique voice tell you, "You'll never be a successful trader." Again, you can be creative if you like, but don't try to change or eliminate the thoughts in any way other than how they are presented.

The point is to experience what the mind tells us as mere words, this includes thoughts that are emotionally charged and demand we do something like size up into a trade or take it off prematurely. When we are fused with what the mind is telling us, it interferes with skillful trading because our responses become limited. If we are in a trade and we have the thought, "I can't have a loss," and we are fused with it, the odds are good that the only action we take is to cut it prematurely. If, however, we are in a trade and we have the thought "I can't have a loss" told to us by a chipmunk, it just might let us hold that thought more lightly and hold that profitable trade a little longer. Keep this paramount in your mind: we are not trying to change what the mind tells us because that continues to keep us fused with the thought and have us experiencing it as more substantive than it is. Trying to change it puts us into a struggle with the mind and that will disrupt our trading. Trying to avoid or eliminate the unwanted thoughts and the internal state they generate takes us away from the trading life we want. Defusion offers a more workable option. We continue to have the thought, "I can't have a loss," but because we defuse from it we can experience a shift in our perspective. We still have the thought, but it doesn't command our attention. It's like a radio playing in the background or our hands (representing our thoughts) away from our face in our lap. We know the thought is there, but it's not dominating our attention. With defusion, our perspective opens up and our attention can be put to more important things such as reading the unfolding market and managing our trade. We are no longer digging ourselves into a psychological hole that keeps us stuck in unworkable actions.

Am I Digging?

Here is a story created by Stephen Hayes and associates used here to help you to remember to step back, hold your thoughts and feelings lightly, and observe.[1] Below is my adaptation of the "Man in the Hole."

> This is a story about a blindfolded man. He was taken up blindfolded in a helicopter and then dropped off in a large field, still blindfolded. Before he stepped out of the helicopter and onto the field, he was given a sack and told, "You might need this."

After stepping safely onto the field, the helicopter flew up and away. Still blindfolded, the man walked about the field. Unbeknownst to him, the field was full of deep holes. Being blindfolded and unable to see, he naturally fell into one of the deep holes.

At the bottom, unhurt, he removed his blindfold and looked around. He saw he was in a deep hole and was unable to reach the top to get out. He then remembered the sack, opened it, and looked inside. There he found a shovel. He thought, "Ah, this will be helpful, I can dig stairs and walk out." But soil conditions were sandy and the walls of the hole just fell away as he tried to dig steps. Seeing that didn't work, he thought he could dig a tunnel from the side of the hole, angle it up to the surface and get out that way. But again, the sandy soil collapsed filling in his tunnel.

He tried other things, as well, like piling up the sand to create a mound he could climb onto to get out, but once again the sands shifted as he tried to climb up causing him to slip back down to the bottom of the hole. Whatever he tried failed, but he kept digging and digging.

A little while later, I came walking along and stopped at the edge of the hole. I could see the man way down at the bottom, sweaty, dirty, and vigorously digging away. I called down to him and said, "Hey, it looks like you are stuck down there. Do you need any help?" Startled, he looked up and saw me. He yelled back, "Oh yes, I do. Do you have a better shovel?"

Take a few moments and let this story sink in. It has more than one meaning. Whatever you personally pull in terms of meaning from this story will be most relevant and useful for you, so take the time and let the story percolate a little before reading on.

One of the meanings this metaphorical story prompts is how difficult we find it to give up the struggle of trying to control our mind and emotions. The digging here represents all the different ways we try and stop unwanted and uncomfortable thoughts and feelings. Nothing we have tried works, yet we keep digging anyway. This connotation is reflected in the exercises in Chapter 3—all that was tried failed. Despite these failures we still try to fruitlessly control and change what is unwanted, discounting our experience that this really doesn't work, and clinging to the belief that there must be a better shovel out there somewhere. We are fused with the idea that we have to get rid of or control what's unwanted, even though that's impossible. We're digging. When this is deeply understood and accepted, traders can make the decision that shovels aren't at all helpful when stuck in a hole. They begin taking steps to become more mindful and accepting of their internal experiences as just momentary, paper tiger–like events that really have no teeth. We begin to drop the illusion that we need to control.

Another meaning, somewhat related to the first, is that the digging represents being fused with what our mind is telling us. We can be so caught up in the digging that we miss the opportunities and richness of the present moment, such as the offer of help from somebody at the top of the hole. Fused, we live in that alternate universe constructed by our mind. Who in their right mind would dig themselves deeper into a hole unless they were fused with their thoughts? Crazy, isn't it? Yet that's what we do. The implication here is to drop the shovel and wake up to the present moment by defusing from what our mind tells us. That is when we begin to part the veils our mind drapes over us and see reality more clearly. When we are able to see more clearly our actions will be more consistent with what is of real value to us. When defused, the digging man will naturally ask for a rope to be thrown down from the top of the hole.

We can use this story effectively by asking ourselves, am I digging? Am I still struggling with my internal state, trying to control it and escape what I don't particularly like, which I know doesn't work and which I know hurts my trading? Am I digging? Am I so caught up and fused with what my mind is telling me that I am living out of past memories and projections of the future missing the richness of the present and all the opportunities it offers? Am I digging?

Because of the way in which the mind works, most readers will find it difficult to remember to ask themselves, "Am I digging?" We need a little help. There are a number of ways we can remind ourselves. Write down, "Am I digging?" on an index card and keep it near your trading desk. Use a post-it note and post alongside your monitor where you will see it frequently during the day, "Am I digging?" Have a section in your daily journal and call it, "What did I dig today?" Write a sentence or two each night about your digs as you review the day. Buy a sheet of dots or squares that have adhesive on the backside from a stationary store and stick these in different places you frequent to remind you about digging. Good places to stick these are on your coffee mug, on the bathroom mirror, on your computer screen, and on anything you are likely to see during the course of your day. If you work with others in a trading firm, this is a way to maintain your privacy while still having reminders available. However you do it, get into the habit of asking yourself, "Am I digging?" After a while, you will begin to catch yourself when struggling or when fused and you will hear yourself say, "Whoops, I'm digging." This will serve as an automatic, personal signal to step back and hold your thoughts and feelings at more of a distance, and to refocus your attention back to the present and onto the trading task at hand.

■ Note

1. Steven C. Hayes, Kirk D. Strosahl, and Kelly G. Wilson, *Acceptance and Commitment Therapy: An Experiential Approach to Behavior Change* (New York: Guilford Press, 1999), 101–104.

CHAPTER 8

Acceptance and Committed Trading

It is universal truth that all traders experience stress along with unwanted emotions and thoughts sometimes in their trading life. No one is completely free from this. Trading will always have moments of pain. There will always be mistakes made, missed opportunities, losing trades, down days, and even slumps for protracted periods. There will always be adversity in trading because trading is a game of probabilities. Any given trade has a probability of a win and also a probability of a loss. Losses are, therefore, a certainty in trading.

No one likes losses. There are obvious financial consequences when we suffer losses, and there are also psychological consequences associated with losses, that is, pain and stress. Hence it is only natural that we do not like losses. But interesting enough, it is not the pain and stress themselves but the struggle we have with the pain and stress that actually causes trading problems. This is of vital importance for traders to understand. Let's be very clear: *It is not stress itself that causes trading difficulties, but our rejection of stress and fighting it that creates trading problems.* As we have seen earlier, working to escape, control, manage, or get rid of unwanted emotions and thoughts takes our focus and attention away from our trading tasks, thus causing trading problems. And, it is not just trading problems, but problems in life as well. Psychologist Steven Hayes and his colleagues assert that psychological disturbances are primarily brought about by the struggle with unwanted thoughts and emotions.

Stress is often maligned as a scapegoat. It is viewed as a force that impacts negatively our life, health, work, and relationships. "If I didn't have such stress, I would trade better"; "If I didn't have stress, I would be healthier." Such beliefs naturally lead to the efforts of struggling with stress and trying to get rid of it.

However, as we all know, stress is a natural part of life. Stress serves as a motivator. When faced with a challenge, we can become excited about our potential to meet that challenge. Stress can help push us to achieve things we wouldn't be able to achieve without it. Stress definitely is a normal and necessary part of trading life. When we put on a trade, we are putting our money at risk. Of course we will feel some stress. That's a natural response that warns us to be on guard. Trying to get rid of that stress is fighting our natural response. If you didn't feel a little stress when putting on a trade, something would be wrong. You would be like Phineas Gage. This is not to say that we need to be happy and cavalier when we feel stress or be resigned to it. Stress also has its dark side. Unchecked stress can lead to poor health-related behaviors like smoking cigarettes, drinking too much alcohol, overeating, and skipping exercise. As we have seen, it can also lead us into taking unplanned trades and managing trades poorly. Notice that in each of these instances, we are trying to get rid of unwanted, stressful feelings. A few drinks after the market closes relieves the tension of the day. Deciding not to place a hard stop eases the anxiety felt over a perceived potential loss. The principal idea is that we act contrary to our best interests—whether it be drinking too much or erratic trading actions—to avoid uncomfortable feelings. When we fight our stress, we are going against our natural response, and that, in turn, is what creates difficulties. Let's look at some ground-breaking recent research to shed a little more light on this.

Health sciences researcher Abiola Keller and her team of researchers at the University of Wisconsin examined the relationships among the amount of stress, the perception that stress affects health, and the death rates of 28,000 adults in the United States over an eight-year period. The study asked the respondents about the level of stress experienced in the previous 12 months, how much stress affected their health, and whether or not any steps were taken to control or reduce stress. The results were astonishing and noteworthy. Keller found that people who experienced high levels of stress and *who also believed that their stress affected their health* had a 43 percent increased chance of premature death. In contrast, people who experienced high levels of stress and *did not perceive that their stress was harmful to their heath* were no more likely to die. In fact, this group (high stress and low belief) had the lowest risk of dying, lower than people with low stress. This is a significant departure from what almost everyone believes—that stress is bad for you. The study shows that stress itself is not the problem. What turns stress into a culprit is *the perception* that stress is bad for you—in other words, when we are fused to the idea that our stress is harmful. The researchers estimate that having high stress and believing it is bad for you results in about 20,000 premature deaths a year, putting the perception that stress is bad for your health as one of the top causes of premature death in the United States.

Harvard psychologist Jeremy Jamieson studied stress directly in an interesting way that adds to the idea that how we perceive stress has important consequences. Jamieson and his research group put study participants through a very stressful situation. He had them give public speeches and added a stressful twist. Most people already feel stress when they have to give a speech.[1] Imagine that you had to give a five-minute videotaped speech in front of two evaluators and the topic of the speech was your personal weaknesses. That would be pretty stressful for most of us, and that is what these study participants did. To make the task even more stressful, the evaluators gave clear negative nonverbal feedback (e.g., crossed arms, furrowed-brow glances, rolled eyes, and similar disheartening body language) as the speeches were given. After concluding their speech, participants next performed a math test by counting backward by 7 from 996 (i.e., 989, 982, 975, . . .). While they were doing this, the evaluators provided more negative feedback. For just about anyone, this would be a stressful experience.

Before the speeches and math tests began, some of the participants were instructed on stress and how to view it. They were specifically told that increased arousal during stressful situations is not harmful. Further, it was explained that our natural response to stressful situations has evolved as a protective way to meet challenges. In fact, the stress symptoms we feel in the body (racing heart, quick breathing, etc.), they were told, prepare you for action, help address the challenges faced, and actually support your performance. In other words, they were instructed to view the stress symptoms as beneficial and as helpful—exactly the opposite of how most people view stress. As a result, these participants were less stressed and more confident as they went through their stressful performance while being badgered by evaluators. More importantly, the researchers measured blood flow and vascular dilation/constriction during the speech and math performance. Those instructed to view their stress reaction as a natural and helpful response had less constricted arteries and greater blood flow. This is highly significant because in our typical stress response, blood vessels constrict. This is one of the main reasons why stress is associated with cardiovascular disease and why chronic stress can be so unhealthy. We don't want to be in a constant state in which our blood vessels are constricted. By simply accepting our stress symptoms as positive and viewing them as an aid in preparing to meet a challenge, blood vessels remained dilated and relaxed providing not only a better physiological response when confronting a challenge, but also a much healthier overall cardiovascular profile.

In another study involving public speaking, Erica England (at the time, a psychology graduate student at Drexel University) and her research team recruited people with severe fear of speaking publicly for treatment. These study participants were clinically diagnosed with public speaking anxiety.[2] When faced with having to speak publicly, these individuals—some even just speaking up in a meeting of familiar colleagues in business settings or classrooms—experienced significant anxiety and even panic attacks (feeling acute anxiety which is often mistaken as a heart attack). The phobia is so severe that their normal occupational, relationship, and social activities are adversely affected. While many people find speaking in a public setting uncomfortable, these individuals had a significant fear of it and it seriously affects their lives.

The first line psychological treatment for persons with public speaking and other anxiety-based difficulties is known as *exposure therapy*. Common sense tells you that when an uncomfortable or frightening situation is constantly avoided, you will never learn to handle it. Exposure has you encounter the fearsome situation therapeutically so that you are not simply becoming alarmed and afraid once again at the experience, but instead are learning through the therapy that you can overcome the fear and respond differently. Although there is a rich variety of techniques that are used in this effective form of clinical treatment, the basic idea is to bring the patient into contact with the feared object or situation, usually gradually, and without any harm resulting from the contact. Thus, situations that involve greater levels of speaking in front of others—for example, from greeting a stranger, to making a comment in a meeting, to giving a prepared speech—would be practiced. Through the guided exposure, the patient learns that what is feared is not as fearful as initially assumed. Coping skills are also developed and practiced, and within a short period of time, successful therapy results in the patient being able to handle what had earlier been fearful and debilitating.

Erica England and her research team employed exposure with the adults suffering from public speaking anxiety in her study. Treatment was brief and ran for six sessions. In addition to standard exposure treatment, one-half of the study participants were also instructed to accept their distressing thoughts and feelings while they engaged in public speaking activities. Similar to the preceeding study in which some of the participants were instructed on how to view and accept stress symptoms as beneficial, participants in this study were taught how to accept distressing thoughts and feelings associated with public speaking. The other half of the participants also engaged in public speaking exposure exercises, but they were not instructed in acceptance procedures. Instead, they were encouraged to stay in the feared speaking situation until their feelings of distress abated.

Results were positive for both groups (and you would expect this from exposure therapy, as it is a very effective therapy for anxiety). But those trained in acceptance of unwanted thoughts and feelings did better. All of the individuals (100 percent) in the acceptance group improved over the six treatment sessions such that they no longer met the criteria for the diagnosis. They all achieved remission. In the standard exposure group, 17 percent continued to meet diagnostic criteria. What is already a robust anxiety treatment was made better by adding acceptance practices. These are the same kinds of mindfulness and defusion procedures taught in the preceding chapters.

So what do these studies mean to the trader? First, trading can be a stressful occupation. Many traders find that even after years of trading, they can still feel stress. Most traders will acknowledge that they feel increased levels of stress while trading, especially when a trade is going bad or when market volatility picks up. But stress doesn't occur only during adverse events. Even when in a profitable trade and a stop is set to ensure some profit, many traders will continue to feel wary and on alert for a market reversal. They describe this as stress. Stress is a part of trading and we want to do what we can to minimize its negative effects. One clear takeaway from this research for trading is that it is a bad combination to both have stress—especially frequently—and perceive that stress as harmful.

Most people believe that stress is harmful, but the research shows that belief determines the level of harm, not the stress itself. Stress is only harmful when we are fused to the idea that it is harmful. Remember, those with high stress who believed that stress was not a problem had low death rates. One positive thing you can do is to change your perception of stress. Make some room for it. Defuse from the negative ideas we may have associated with it. Having stress is both natural and functional; it helps you remain alert and on guard when you expose yourself to a potential loss. That's all it is. It isn't some dreaded, awful, and frightening thing that takes over a trader unless you allow it. It's just a natural response. View the stress you feel in this way rather than as something detrimental. Hopefully, this research will help you change your mind about it.

Note, too, that when people face their fear, drop the struggle with it, and let it come and go as it will while, at the same time, do what is important to them, they can do well. We see this in the clinical research on fear of public speaking. Everyone was afraid of speaking in public. Nevertheless, they gave speeches and felt fearful while giving those speeches. The key is that they allowed themselves to have their fear, not struggle with it, while speaking in public. It is more effective to do what we need to do, even if we are afraid of doing it, without fighting our unwanted thoughts and unpleasant feelings. Accepting our thoughts and feelings—even though this can be uncomfortable—can play a significant role in this process. Rather than cutting a profitable trade prematurely because your mind and feelings are pressing you to avoid a loss, traders can overcome the disposition effect by facing their fear, holding the trade—even if just a little longer, and, in the process, being as open to their feelings and thoughts as they can, understanding that they are a natural response to the threat of loss, not something to fight, control, or get rid of.

This last point is an important one. Thoughts and feelings—as uncomfortable and unwanted as they may be—aren't something to try and get rid of or control. While this is definitely counterintuitive, keep in mind that when we aren't open to and accepting our thoughts and feelings—all of them, including the difficult ones—we shift our attention off the trade, channel our focus to our internal state, and this, above all else, wreaks havoc with our trading.

■ Acceptance

We can't get rid of stress by giving into what it demands. Psychologists Georg Eifert and John Forsyth, experts in anxiety, refer to this as "feeding the baby tiger." We told the story of the baby tiger in Chapter 7, but it is an important metaphor we will refer to several times in this chapter, so a brief review will refresh your memory. You have been given a baby tiger that is cute and playful, just like any baby animal. When hungry, it lets out a growl. The growl is tiny at first, but as you feed it and the tiger grows, the growl grows into a roar. You begin to think that if you don't feed it, the young tiger might now attack you. So you give in to what it wants. Every time it growls, you give it food. The tiger grows, it's no longer cute. It's now a threat.

Isn't this what happens when we give into our fear and stress and hesitate to take a perfectly good trade setup or cut a winner short? Each time we do this, we are feeding the tiger. This is the consequence of fusion. Stress and fear demand that we avoid a loss, so we fail to pull the trigger or exit a trade too early and the tiger gets fed. We are not open to what goes on internally as just thoughts and feelings that will dissipate on their own. They are only paper tigers, but we treat them as if they were real tigers about to attack us unless we feed them. Feeding them is giving into their demands not because it is in the best interest of the trade, but because we seek to appease our fleeting and impulsive feelings. We become stuck in the vicious and ineffective cycle of erratic trading caused by trying to control our feelings through constantly feeding them. We are caught in a struggle with our transitory internal state, and this isn't trading. We touched on controlling unpleasant feelings in Chapter 3 (see *The Price I Pay for Controlling Emotions*). It would be a good idea to review that section.

Here is another way to think about this. If feeding our tigers (i.e., struggling to control unwanted feelings and thoughts) were so effective, virtually every person entering the trading game would be a winning trader. We know this isn't the case. In fact, it's far from it. Common estimates suggest that more than 80 percent of all aspiring traders lose and drop out of the game within a relatively short period of time (see, for example, Ann Logue's *Day Trading for Dummies*). We know that these traders put a lot of effort into trying to control and eliminate their emotions. Their lack of success is not due to the effort expended at trying to solve the emotional side of trading or to any personal limitations. Controlling emotions is simply not possible. Control, in fact, *is* the problem. As we discussed earlier, if you don't want it and work to try and control and suppress it, you'll have it.

It is important that readers not misunderstand the idea of acceptance. Acceptance, as used here and in the studies cited above, does not mean giving in to difficult or painful experiences. It does not mean passively tolerating them, putting up with them, liking them, or approving them. It also does not mean that we necessarily have to blithely accept adverse circumstances or be passively resigned to them. Far from it. Acceptance as used here refers to a conscious action on your part that makes room for uncomfortable thoughts and feelings without fighting or struggling with them. It is a conscious decision to experience and not fight challenging thoughts and feelings in order to carry out the kinds of high-value trading actions that match your trading aspirations. A useful way to think about acceptance and unpleasant internal experiences is to hold these thoughts and feelings lightly, by viewing them as mere thoughts and feelings that come and go on their own accord. This is a more expansive mental view that helps you drop the struggle with unwanted thoughts and feelings. Mindfulness and the defusion techniques we discussed in Chapter 7 are of great help in learning to accept our thoughts and feelings.

If we step back a bit and notice how we react to disagreeable feelings and thoughts, we see we are in a tug-of-war with them. Psychologists Steven Hayes, John Forsyth, and Georg Eifert describe it as being in a tug-of-war with a monster. You stand on one side of a deep crevasse, the monster on the other, each pulling fiercely on the tug-of-war rope. Every time you get a little purchase and pull yourself away from the crevasse, the monster redoubles its effort and pulls you back. Back and forth you go in constant battle. This is struggle. It is what most of us do with distressing thoughts and feelings. What would happen, however, if we refused to struggle? What would happen if you just dropped the rope? The monster may jump up and down and scream, "Pick up the rope!" But you don't have to. And if you don't, what power does the monster have over you? None. You are now free to engage in activities that matter to you, rather than to spend your time and energy playing tug-of-war. This is what acceptance means.

Try this exercise to understand what we mean by acceptance: Hold your hand about two feet in front of your face and extend your index finger. You should be holding your hand up as if it is pointing to the sky. Look directly at your finger and focus on it. You can see all the details of your finger clearly—the skin tone and color, the fingernail, small creases and wrinkles in the skin, and its other details. Now shift your gaze to another object farther away from you somewhere in the distance, but still keep your extended finger in sight. As you focus on the distant object, notice that the object is clear but what happens to your finger? It becomes fuzzy and less distinct. You have simply changed your focus. Your finger is still there. It wasn't taken away, and yet you can focus on something else. This is acceptance. We don't have to get rid of our finger to see another object. If we wanted to, we could walk around all day with our finger held in front of our face. We might look a little silly, but it wouldn't hamper our sight much. We can still see what we want to see and do pretty much any activity throughout our day. It's the same thing with unwanted thoughts. We can hold them lightly and carry them wherever we go and, especially, while doing whatever is important to us. We can drop the rope, stop feeding the tiger, and get on with what's important to us: our trading.

Mindfulness plays a key role in our being able to hold our thoughts and feelings lightly and allow them to appear, hang around for a while, and then depart—all on their own, while at the same time we pursue what's important to us in our trading. Mindfulness teaches us that thoughts and feelings are ephemeral. They come and go on their own. When we practice mindfulness, we learn that it is easy to get caught up in our thoughts and feelings, and we can also disentangle ourselves from them and pursue higher value actions rather than remain entangled by struggling with them. Mindfulness helps us decenter from our inner thoughts and feelings and see them as simply passing mental events.

Mindfulness also helps us shift our attention from outside events to internal experiences and back to external observations without getting stuck in thoughts and feelings. Trading requires this ability. We see a market event, we go inside to process it, and then return to our screens to take appropriate action. Much of the time this happens outside of our awareness. Mindfulness brings it more into our consciousness. With mindfulness practice—both sitting in formal practice and while being mindful during trading activities—you can develop a capacity to experience emotions and thoughts differently from how you have experienced them in the past. You can learn to become less reactive and recognize when you are about to act out of emotion because you want to avoid something unpleasant and mindfully assess whether or not this action would be congruent with an action that would be of real trading value. And you make your decisions accordingly.

Sport and human performance psychologists Frank Gardner and Zella Moore make a clear distinction between acceptance and avoidance. Avoidance is nearly always emotion-driven behavior done to escape or sidestep something unpleasant. The trader who has just had a loss and is feeling gun-shy, decides not to take a trade that sets up perfectly. Her actions are driven by emotions, specifically to avoid feeling the threat of loss. She fed the tiger, giving in to her emotions in the hope that they might go away. This is an unskilled response. Although it helps us avoid uncomfortable feelings, it also keeps us from doing what is important in our trading and gets in the way of developing needed trading skills. Acceptance, on the other hand, is a skillful response. It lays the ground for value-driven behavior, which, at times, feels uncomfortable to do, but we know it is what the situation demands. The same trader acting with acceptance feels the pain of the previous loss and also feels the threat of another loss if the trade setting up is taken. These don't magically go away. She mindfully sees that the trade setup meets all her criteria and also knows that being a competent trader sometimes requires that she act with courage. Because she has practiced mindfulness, she is able to defuse from her thoughts of danger and loss. Her attention goes to the high-value actions that serve her trade, not her emotions. These high-value actions include looking for an entry trigger, setting her stop, and then managing her trade, despite her internal discomfort. She sees the tiger for what it is—a paper tiger—which is not something she wishes to continue to feed. Rather than giving in to her emotions or fighting them, she drops the rope and focuses on what is important to do in the context of a qualified trade setup. Acceptance is the skillful alternative to challenging emotions. It is a deliberate stance we take toward trading to do what is needed for the trade and not feeding and struggling with our thoughts and feelings.

■ Commitment

As you practice mindfulness, you will begin to realize that not only difficult trading situations promote unpleasant feelings and thoughts that we reflexively seek to avoid, but that minor situations produce minor mental obstacles and discomforts that can easily derail our trading. Mindfulness practice helps us become more aware of these. Mindfulness, defusion, and acceptance help us overcome them.

A useful analogy that many of us have confronted is the challenge of becoming physically fit. Psychologists Gardner and Moore describe this as a series of ongoing decisions where mindfulness and acceptance can be employed to support the initial goal. We determine that physical fitness is important for our appearance and well-being. After doing a little research and maybe joining a gym or purchasing exercise equipment, we develop a plan and schedule to work out and revise our diets. All this is very good and commendable, but now the real work begins. Not only will we feel some discomfort in exercising, but there will be daily choices that must be made in order to follow our plan. On days that we are very tired and just don't feel like going to the gym, will we feed the tiger, giving into our feelings, or will we say to ourselves that there is a greater goal and choose to prevail over feelings of fatigue? Mindful acceptance plays a huge role here. Can we make some space for our fatigue and for the things our mind is telling us like how nice it would be to skip the gym, that you've had a hard day and "deserve a break," and "you can go tomorrow." If we can't make room for them and defuse from them, but instead give in to them, we won't be able to pursue what's important. We end up feeding the tiger and, before we know it, skipping the workout becomes the routine and the goal of fitness is lost. Many choices over many days, weeks, and months are necessary for fitness to be achieved. Mindful perseverance is required, otherwise the many obstacles that always seem to be present can get in our way. As we reflect on what it takes to achieve a goal of improved fitness, it becomes easy to see that immediate comfort can and for many, often will trump future benefits, causing us to act inconsistently with our goals.

It is no different when it comes to trading. To achieve a level of success in trading, many decisions must be made over many days, weeks, months, and even years. It really never ends. It isn't just the difficult trading situations that need to be overcome. It's the everyday situations, too. At the end of the day, we should be assessing the day's charts, identifying how we could have improved our trades, making notes in our journal, setting up a game plan for tomorrow, and similar activities. It's easy to feed the tiger when our mind says, Hey, it's been a long day. Let's go have a drink with a friend, watch a little TV, or engage in some other activity irrelevant to our trading. It is little decisions like these where our immediate comfort is chosen over what we know will be of benefit over the long term, but the longer-term benefits seem far off, take effort, and somehow become less critical than how we feel now. These can easily add up and begin to interfere with our trading by encouraging us to avoid the high-value activities we know are important to do. Like the physical fitness example, short-term comfort can readily win out over long-term benefits unless we are mindful and willing to make room for such thoughts and feelings, all the while keeping in mind what's really important to our trading and to us in our development as a trader. What's really happening is something we've discussed before: we are avoiding the unpleasantness associated with the harder work of reviewing our charts for the pleasantness associated with the ease of doing something different, such as having a drink with a friend. If you reflect a little deeper on this, the same thing happens when we cut a winning trade short, fail to pull the trigger on a trade, jump into an unplanned trade, and other unconstructive trading actions many traders make. We allow ourselves to be fused with what the mind is telling us. Short-term comfort is chosen over long-term objectives. These also quickly add up and traders can easily become stuck in the unproductive, vicious cycle described earlier in Chapter 5. Learning to deal with less emotionally charged situations like mindfully maintaining your trading journal after each trading day builds the mental muscle to help you mindfully act constructively when confronted with much more challenging situations such as overcoming trading fears.

As we discussed with the goal of becoming fit, large goals like trading require numerous decisions to engage in actions that affirm and support what's really important to your trading and to you in your development as a trader. This requires a serious and enduring dedication not only to do the work, but to do the work when you don't feel like it, or when other, unrelated activities turn up that seem more enticing, or when your emotions are running high, or you are tired or bored. This isn't easy, and many will find it difficult to do. Those without the capacity to make a deep commitment to their trading often look for an easier way. There isn't one. There is no psychological magic wand that can be waved to relieve you of the work required and the tolerance of discomfort that it entails. We all wish it were easier, but in truth, it isn't. The adage that nothing worthwhile is ever gained without effort—and lots of it—truly pertains to trading. This includes the effort needed to develop a psychological edge. You will know you are on the right track, committed to your trading and your development as a trader when you are routinely doing the kinds of activities that are likely to generate sound and effective trading performance. This is what we mean by committed trading.

There are many activities that when practiced mindfully will help enhance and improve your trading. You can apply mindful engagement in studying charts, assessing trades you took, analyzing the trading day, maintaining your journal, simulation or practice trading, preparing for the next trading day, researching a trade setup, and so on. Part III of this book details additional important trading tasks and actions all of which can be undertaken mindfully.

Take a few moments now and use Exercise 8.1 to identify common situations—not difficult trading situations, but common, everyday situations related to your trading—that often become decision points where your thoughts and feelings can derail important trading-related activities. In the first column, jot down the situation that occurs; in the second column, note feelings; and in the third, note any prominent things your mind is telling you. Finally, in the last column, note the consequences of allowing important activities to become disrupted because you feed the tiger and give in to your thoughts and feelings. Examples are given for the first two entries.

It will be useful for you to track your tendencies toward avoiding important trading-related activities because of your thoughts and feelings for a couple of weeks. Use the last column on the form in Exercise 8.1 to make a check mark each time

Exercise 8.1 Minor Decisions That Impact My Trading

Situation	Feelings	Thoughts	Consequences	✓
Example 1: *Sleeping later than normal*	*Felt tired*	*"I can sleep a little longer; it won't really matter."*	*Couldn't revise game plan to incorporate overnight data. Missed a great trade. Felt rushed all morning.*	
Example 2: *Skipped simulation/ practice trading. Watched TV instead.*	*Lethargic, bored*	*"Paper trading without real money on the line isn't real trading. I can skip this."*	*Nothing immediately, but long term, I'm not doing my best to develop my skills.*	

this occurs. This will help you develop greater awareness of where you are feeding the tiger on the minor issues so that you can take steps to make the right decisions. Simply putting awareness to your tendencies can have a positive effect. Building the habit of mindful awareness when avoidance situations occur and also the habit of mindful acceptance by making room for these thoughts and feelings without believing them as truth, or giving in to them, or struggling with them will be an important step toward your development as a mentally skilled trader. Skills developed practicing mindful acceptance of minor events will help build the mental muscle to better handle more challenging trading events. Be particularly mindful of the things you say to talk yourself out of doing what's important. It will give you special insight into how we easily and seamlessly believe what our mind is telling us.

There is little difference between fusing with "I had a tough day, I'll skip doing my charts" and "I better take these profits quickly and avoid a loss." Developing excellence in trading requires that we have a clear mind. We don't want to work on autopilot; instead we want to be mindful. We are looking to ferret out instances where we almost unconsciously sabotage our better interests by mindlessly listening to what our minds are telling us. Again, we aren't looking to engage in a tug-of-war with our mind; we simply want to be aware of our self-talk, recall what is most important to us, and make room for whatever disagreeable thoughts and feelings arise as we turn our attention to the tasks we know have high value and are important over the long haul, such as reviewing our trades for the day, keeping our trading journal, or preparing for the next day's trading. Accepting a little privation or facing a little difficulty in the service of your trading is associated with achieving your goals and values. Table 8.1 shows this relationship in a graphic format.

At this point, traders should understand that avoiding these important tasks because it is less effortful and more comfortable to do so is clearly related to immediate personal contentment, but does nothing for their trading. Avoidance derails trading goals and personal development as a trader. A big part of the mental game for traders is developing the ability to do what is necessary for the trade even while experiencing unwanted thoughts and feelings. The most important mental skill to develop in this regard is mindfulness. Keep in mind that mindfulness is not practiced to "fix" or eliminate unwanted thoughts and feelings. That just brings us back to the struggle and playing a fruitless tug-of-war with our mind, a distraction at best. Mindful accepting of unwanted thoughts and feelings is acknowledging them, making room for them without struggling or buying into them, and then putting your attention onto whatever important trading task is at hand. Practicing mindful acceptance of undesired thoughts

TABLE 8.1 Relationships between Mindful Acceptance, Attention, Actions, and Consequences

Mindful Acceptance	Unwanted Thoughts and Feelings	Attention	Actions	Consequences
Yes	Defuse and accept them, realize they are just temporary, make room for them	Remains on the task or the trade	Done in the service of your trading or trade	Long-term goals more likely to be achieved
No	Don't accept them, remain fused and believe they are intolerable and/or enduring, seek to get rid of them	Shifts from task or trade to internal state; trader distracted	Done to reduce or eliminate discomfort	Long-term goals will not be achieved

and feelings outside the trading session on minor trading related tasks will help you develop this skillful mental competence when it counts most—while trading.

By this point in reading this book and putting its information into practice, you likely have been practicing mindfulness on a daily basis and have been using some of the several defusion techniques described in Chapter 7. As you practice being mindful while assessing your charts, simulation trading, keeping your journal and other trading-related activities, you are likely to notice that you are developing better concentration, find you are wasting less time, and putting more energy into important activities. You are also developing the skill of being able to view more and more of your thoughts and feelings as thoughts and feelings that are useful at times, but that do not always have to be blindly followed or responded to as if they were unquestionable commands. It is likely that you are more consistently choosing to do what is most important to you as you have carefully defined it, not what your mind construes on the spur of the moment.

You may have also begun to use mindfulness and defusion in your everyday life outside of trading. For example, rather than allowing yourself to become upset or angry at someone or some situation that wasn't to your liking, you noticed your hot thoughts and feelings arise and made a mental note that these were just thoughts and feelings. And perhaps you acted differently now than you have in the past. Although what is described in this book is trading psychology, it is, at its roots, psychology and useful in day-to-day activities, not just trading. Noticing the mental skills you are learning for trading in nontrading activities indicates that you are assimilating and integrating these skills effectively.

Spend some time practicing with the minor trading-related activities before jumping into more difficult trading difficulties. For example, if you have a tendency to react to fear and cut winning trades short or hesitate on pulling the trigger on trades for fear of loss, it will be harder for you to overcome these significant challenges without first becoming adept and handling more modest challenges. This is just common sense. If you want to develop the ability to hit effective tennis strokes, for example, you spend time practicing and developing your skills with basic forehand and backhand ground strokes before learning to hit much more challenging strokes like approach shots, backhand slices, half-volleys, and the overhead smash. What you learn and the skills you develop from practicing the fundamental strokes will make learning the more difficult ones easier. It's the same with trading psychology. Spend a few weeks being mindful and practicing defusion and acceptance when keeping your trading journal, studying charts, preparing for your trading day, and other less challenging trading-related activities. And, you don't have to limit your practice to your trading routines. Try to apply your developing mental skills in everyday life, as well. When repairing a household item, washing the laundry, mowing the lawn, or preparing a meal, keep your mind in the moment and be mindful of what you are doing. The same goes for conversations you have with others. If we observe ourselves carefully, we will find that we frequently are thinking about what we are going to say next before the other person has finished talking. Be more mindful and really listen to the other person you are talking with before crafting a response. Remember, our mind wanders nearly half the time. Start catching your thoughts when they have gone on a walkabout, and gently bring them back to the here and now. The more you can practice mindful attention in various situations, the better the skill will be honed and the more reliable it will become when you are faced with a more difficult trading challenge that draws out strong emotions such as fear.

■ Developing Commitment

We now turn to more challenging trading situations that, if overcome, can bring about a significant improvement in your performance and, ultimately, your bottom-line results. Commitment, according to sport and human performance psychologists Frank Gardner and Zella Moore, involves routinely engaging in specific actions that increase the odds of sound trading performance. These specific actions are wide ranging and varied. These are actions that enhance trading performance and, therefore, are of high value to the trader. A few examples include holding on to a winning trade, taking only those trades that fall within the scope of your trading plan, practicing sound money management, setting stops, maintaining a trading journal, evaluating trades taken at the end of the trading day, and other similar actions that directly add value to a trader's functioning. In Part III of this book we discuss how you can incorporate high-value trading actions into your trading. For now, we just want to make the distinction that high-value actions add to your trading, and committing to them is necessary if you want to trade effectively and at a high level.

This makes sense. Holding on to a winning trade until it reaches its logical profit object or the market gives clear signs to exit the trade is an obviously valuable action in the service of the trade. Contrast this with cutting the trade short due to fear of losing profits already accrued. Cutting the trade short is an action in the service of your feelings and what they demand. As we have discussed, the action has nothing to do with the trade. Virtually all trading performance difficulties arise from either the inappropriate use of cognitive heuristics, which we covered in Chapter 1, or emotion-driven behavior.

Our emotions need not dictate our behavior. Mindfulness plays a key role in the relationship between what our emotions and mind are telling us to do and doing those things that are high value and in the service of the trade. As we have learned, mindfulness is a skill that helps us to distance ourselves from our emotions. We can decenter from our thoughts and feelings and step away from being entangled in them by practicing mindfulness and becoming an observer of our thoughts and feelings, rather than becoming captured by them. Mindfulness also improves our attention and concentration. When confronted by a challenging trading situation, we always have a choice: listen to what our mind is telling us and give in to our emotion—feeding the tiger, in other words—or apply our mindfulness skills and return our focus to the market, our trade, and the trading task at hand.

So how do we effectively begin to move from emotion-driven trading to mindful, committed trading? The first step is to understand what is personally important to you about trading. What matters to you in your trading? What do you want to stand for and how do you want to act? In other words, what are your values?

■ Mindfully Committed Trading: The First Step

University of Mississippi psychologist Kelly Wilson and Amy Murrell, a psychologist at the University of North Texas, consider our values to be one of the key ingredients in overcoming emotion-driven decisions that limit us: what they call psychological inflexibility. In any important endeavor, it is never the experience of pleasure or pain that causes us to act in concert with what is important. We have all done things we didn't want to do for a greater goal. For example, most of us didn't want to study or write papers in school, but we did it and endured the unpleasantness of the task to pass the course and gain a degree. We valued an education over temporary discomfort. We do this all the time. Many people would rather avoid cutting the grass or cleaning the house. There are many more pleasant activities than yard work and housecleaning we'd rather do, but we do them. We value a well-kept home. Even though we may not like public speaking we will suffer through making a presentation at work because we value having a job and the future promotion that might bring. Granted, yard work, writing a term paper, cleaning the house, and even public speaking feel less aversive than suffering a trading loss. But it is the idea that Wilson and Murray put forth that is important. Comfort and pleasure do not drive our actions; what really drives our actions is what we hold dear.

Wilson and Murrell make this critical point: in things that really matter to us, we are not looking to achieve pleasantness or comfort. These are not important concerns. What is important, in contrast, is that we strive to act consistently with what matters to us. We can take this a step further. It is through what we value in our trading and what is important to us as traders that we can alter our relationship with adversity. There is no question that trading creates aversive experiences. It is just the nature of the game. When we start to shift our attention to what is of value to us in our trading and to what matters most to us, both in our individual trades and to us as traders, we can begin to adopt a different attitude from the one which struggles with our internal state and seeks comfort and pleasantness. In doing so, we begin to open up and act in more flexible ways rather than rigidly trying to avoid anxiety, fear, and discomfort by trading erratically.

In order to maintain our attention to what's of value in our trading, we need to understand what is important to us in our trading. Few traders have taken the time to think about their values. Those who do say that it is some of the most useful time they have spent. Again, traders face adversity in their trading. If you don't know what is important to you trading-wise, you run the real risk of being mentally and emotionally whipsawed with every adverse event. When in the throes of an emotionally challenging situation, we can forget what really matters. You want to stand above this. Without a deep understanding of what is important to you—what you value—you have no compass. You will become easily lost psychologically and continue along a dead end path of inflexible trading.

As a first step, ask yourself, why do I trade? It is a broad question and there is no single right answer. Many traders will immediately say it's for the money. There is nothing wrong with that. Money is why we all trade. But try to go a little deeper. If all that was important was the money, why not choose real estate or corporate management or establishing your own business? Each of these has the potential for generating money. They may even be easier than trading. If it was only about the money, then it would be expected we would strike out on the easiest and least aversive route to making money. That may not be trading. So if money is the answer that comes readily to mind, go a little further and think about what you would do with the money. What is important to you that the money will create, add to, or enable more of?

In a seminar at which I was speaking, we were discussing why we trade and a woman stood up and said:

> For me, trading is really important. I have two young children. When I was working a regular job, I wasn't able to spend time with my kids. I saw other mothers with their children in the park and it pained me terribly because I had to leave my children each day and go to a job I had little interest in. It tore my heart. I saw trading as freedom from the job that took me away from my kids. This is why I trade. Yes, the money is certainly important; I want to provide for my kids and give them what they need financially, but most importantly trading lets me spend time with them. Even when I trade, I am present. I can be there for them.

You can begin to see that with this kind of reason, we can begin to loosen the grip that uncomfortable feelings and unwanted thoughts produce when in a trade. The trader can begin to ask herself, which is more important to me? Is it to feel good or is it to trade well for my kids?

Others will have different reasons for trading. For some, the reason may involve financial independence. For others, there is great value in generating the money to send their children to college. Many traders find that they love the analysis involved in trading and relish being able to anticipate the next move of the market. Some traders have told me they would be analyzing the markets even if they couldn't get paid for their work. Some who have experienced difficulty learning to trade take it as a personal challenge to win at the game. They see it as their personal Mount Everest and find great meaning in surmounting the obstacles. Others like the idea of being able to master a challenging field, especially one that involves not just the ability to read a chart but also developing mastery over oneself, one's psychology and behavior. There are as many reasons to trade as there are traders and no one reason is better than another, as long as it is important to you. It might involve leaving a financial legacy, seed-funding an important business idea, or contributing to a meaningful organization that does community or humanitarian work. For others it might be buying a coveted item or building a dream house. The reasons are limitless, and everyone's will be unique. It's the uniqueness that makes them special and gives them power. Spend some time thinking about why you trade and jot down a few of your ideas.

After thinking through why you trade and jotting down a few of the reasons, consider this question: What is really important to you in your trading? There are many ways to answer this question, and again, each individual trader will have a different answer. Some things you can consider in answering this are:

- How important is your method of trading to you?

- Where does research for your trade setups and about market conditions fit into your trading?

- How about consistency in your trading actions, how important is this to you?

- Is maintaining adherence to your trading plan important?

- How important is planning out your trades or keeping abreast of the markets you trade?

- What about assessing your performance for the day or week and working to improve yourself as a trader?

- Does improving your skills and getting better at something challenging have real meaning to you?

Note that we are not asking about how many points or how much money you strive for each day or week. What within trading is of personal value to you? What is important to you both for your individual trades and for you as a trader? Consider these questions and other things you believe are important and spend a little time thinking about what is really important to you in your trading.

One trader said it this way:

> It used to be that I jumped from one method to another. I would read about an indicator or trade setup and would immediately try to trade it. Those days are now behind me, thankfully. I began to realize I was spinning my wheels and really getting nowhere in my trading. I wasn't grounded. When I began to think about what was important to me as a trader and what gave real value to me, I began to see myself as a trader more clearly. I began to realize that consistency would only come from me; it wasn't coming from outside of myself. When I thought about

how an expert trader would work, I recognized that following a single method that worked for me and that I had researched would keep me grounded. Acting when the market favored my play, and being patient when it didn't, and constantly studying the markets to see how they behaved, and also constantly reviewing my decisions and actions—all of this was of real value because it served as an anchor for me. I always know where I stand. Before, I was all over the place chasing this idea or that idea. It is when I began to think about what is truly of value to me in my trading that I really appreciated that it all comes from me. Being a great trader means acting like one. This is what I know I need to do. More than anything else, this has been my compass.

Here is what another trader who is a member of a proprietary trading firm had to say:

> One of the most meaningful things about trading for me is that I get to interact with a group of really great people. We are all like-minded. We all love the markets and love trading. It is the people I interact with day after day that make it all worthwhile for me. I love sharing my trading ideas. I like helping some of the newer traders and learning from the more experienced traders. The partners are great, too. They have helped me to grow, giving me encouragement and more responsibility in my trading. We really are a team. That sounds funny for traders, because we are all supposed to be fiercely independent and cut-throat, and all that, but that isn't the way it is in my firm. It's like when I played baseball. There's a camaraderie we feel, and also lots of support. I really feel connected to them and that more than anything keeps me going and striving to do better.

Knowing your values is not a minor thing. They inform you about what sort of trader you want to be and can help you set relevant goals and give you a real sense of purpose in your trading. If you are struggling with self-defeating patterns in your trading, knowing your values can be motivating and inspire you to reach beyond where you are right now. When you are guided by what's important to you, it helps you to stay on track. You will be less likely to stray when you have something of greater importance as your signpost pointing the way. You are better able to act in concert with what matters to you, and when you do, you have a real sense of being true to yourself even when it is difficult to do so. This is reinforcing and adds a richness to your trading. You know what you stand for and how you want to behave. Values provide all of this, and potentially more.

Given a little serious thought, this exercise typically brings out our deepest aspirations—what we truly care about and what we want our trading to be about. This may seem inconsequential, but it is not. A University of California research team headed by psychologist J. David Creswell studied personal values and stress. They put study participants through a highly stressful exercise that elevated blood pressure and heart rate in all participants. Those participants who reflected on and affirmed their personal values before the stress test, however, had significantly lower cortisol responses than participants who did not. Cortisol is the stress hormone we discussed in Chapter 2 that becomes triggered in response to stressful situations and helps activate the fight-flight response. Affirming our values helps to buffer us against stress.

Think about what matters most to you and the kind of trader you want to be. What are the qualities and characteristics you want to possess as a trader? Russ Harris, the Australian physician and expert in acceptance and commitment psychology we met earlier, suggests you think about your values by addressing these important questions: If nothing could hold you back from being the trader you really want to be, what would that look like? Remember, nothing can stop you. How do you really want to be and act as a trader? Use Exercise 8.2 to answer these questions.

After thinking about this, consider that you actually have become the kind of trader you want to be and have traded this way over the next ten years. At the end of that ten year period, a journalist writes a story on you as a trader. What would the writer say about you? What would the journalist say are three or four of your greatest qualities? Play the role of the journalist and provide the answers on the form.

The point of these exercises is that you want to know and live what gives your trading meaning. You want to live a valued trading life. At the end of ten years, you don't want the journalist to say, "Well, to sum it all up, this trader was very, very good at avoiding uncomfortable thoughts and feelings."

In a very real way, it comes down to a basic, fundamental, and crucial choice, as outlined by Wilson and Murrell.[3] I paraphrase them and apply their words to trading here:

> On the one hand, you can have the choice of no fear or anxiety. You won't have trading stress or uncomfortable feelings or unwanted trading thoughts. In fact, you can have no further trading losses and never

---

Exercise 8.2 Finding My Trading Values

Part 1: If nothing could hold you back from being the trader you really want to be, what would that look like? How do you really want to be and act as a trader?

Part 2: After a decade of living and trading as you describe in Part 1, write about what sort of trader you have been. Imagine you are a reporter writing an article on yourself. Describe 3 or 4 of your greatest qualities?

Quality #1:

Quality #2:

Quality #3:

Quality #4:

be fearful of the market again. To get this, however, you need to give up something. That something, of course, is trading.

On the other hand, you can have an extraordinarily meaningful trading life. You can make money, become deeply involved in the markets and your method of analyzing them, and enjoy all the benefits that come to successful traders. Again, though, there is a cost. With this choice, you will continue to have losses. At times, you will continue to experience fear and be anxious and you will have unwanted thoughts. But even though you have them, these unpleasant experiences will not stop you from doing the things you need and want to do in your trading.

What is your choice?

■ Using Your Values for Committed Trading

Now that you have identified your values, you want to use them to give guidance and direction in overcoming difficult trading situations where emotions and unwanted thoughts have you acting in ways that are ineffective, undesired, and less than optimal. We will start with two case examples and then turn to ways in which you can face challenging trading situations with more poise, courage, and commitment to your personal values and engage the high-value trading actions that reflect those values.

Case Examples

Case Example 1: Ammar

Ammar had been trading currency futures for the past few years. He was profitable, but often found himself increasing his position size right after a losing trade. He referred to this as 'doubling down,' and a way to quickly make up his loss. Probing deeper, Ammar said that having losses "was not a good thing. I don't like booking a loss. I feel like I have to make it up right away.... Sometimes," he admitted, "I feel like a failure after having a loss."

In reviewing the values exercise, one of things Ammar said the journalist would say about him is that he traded with a calm steadiness over his career. He neither got very excited at large wins, nor very upset at drawdowns. He rode the ups and downs of the market as if he were a boat on the ocean. No matter how stormy the seas, he was always able to ride the waves. This is how Ammar wanted to experience his trading and also how he wanted to be remembered by others: as a steady trader.

In considering his tendency to double down after a loss, Ammar recognized that this behavior reflected neither calmness nor steadiness. "If anything," Ammar noted, "overtrading my position size leads to more ups and downs; my behavior is capricious and unreliable—just the opposite of being a steady trader. It's not how I want my trading to be."

Case Example 2: Priyanka

Priyanka trades equities off the National Stock Exchange in Mumbai. Her most challenging trading situation is holding on to a good trade. Like many traders, she cuts winners short prematurely. She tried numerous times to correct this tendency, but everything she did left her frustrated.

One of the most important things that she wanted to be known for in her trading—a value she held dear—was that she give her trading everything she had. She wasn't afraid of challenges. "I am willing to do whatever it takes," she explained. "I want to succeed." This drive was honed as a college athlete when living abroad. "My team trained hard. Many times I had doubts and thought I couldn't do it, but I did. There was a value to persist and give it your all no matter what. I have the same desire for my trading," she said.

Like Ammar, Priyanka's actions were incongruent with what she wanted her trading to stand for. She wanted to give it her all, but she was giving in to her emotions and feeding the tiger.

Take a moment and identify one or two trading situations where your trading actions are driven by your emotions and cause difficulty for you. For each challenging situation, carefully describe the thoughts that go through your head while in the situation. These are the things your mind tells you about the situation and about what you need to do about it. Also record feelings you have. These include emotions such as fear, anxiety, nervousness, anger, frustration, sadness, and the like. In addition, note the sensations you feel in your body, paying particular attention to any tension in your body such as in your shoulders or legs. Note any nervous ticks or twitching, sour stomach, racing heartbeat, sweatiness, dry mouth, and any other bodily sensation you may feel. Try to be as clear as you can with these, without going into excessive detail. Finally, note the value you identified from Exercise 8.2 that seems most relevant to your challenging situation in Exercise 8.3.

In Exercise 8.4 we will develop a specific plan to overcome a challenging trading situation you have identified in Exercise 8.3. We show exactly how to do this by developing plans for the difficulties experienced by both Ammar and Priyanka, taking you step-by-step through the process of setting workable goals, a specific plan to meet those goals, identifying what is most likely to keep you from reaching our goals, and laying out specific actions to overcome any anticipated barriers. You

Exercise 8.3 Challenging Trading Situations, My Internal State, and Values

Challenging Situation	Thoughts	Feelings	Body Sensations	Relevant Value

will find this to be a practical and an effective approach to overcoming the mental and performance challenges you may experience in your trading. Before turning to Exercise 8.4, however, we first discuss a method for learning to accept unwanted thoughts and feelings.

■ Making Room for Uncomfortable Emotions and Thoughts

Here is a specific mindfulness exercise geared toward acceptance of uncomfortable feelings. Any unwanted emotions or thoughts that cause you difficulty can be addressed in this mindfulness training. A form of this exercise was originally developed by Eifert and Forsyth for persons who suffer from severe anxiety.[4] I've adapted it for traders. Those who have used it have found it beneficial when learning to make room for their difficult thoughts and feelings.

In the mindfulness exercises described in Chapter 6, we picked an object of focus, such as the breath, and returned to it each time the mind wandered. This exercise will be a little different. Here, we want to be fully aware of unwanted thoughts, as well as uncomfortable bodily sensations and emotions. In this exercise, you will "lean into" unwanted thoughts and feelings rather than appease or fight them. This is a form of exposure similar to that which we discussed in one of the earlier research studies on fear and anxiety that you can do on your own. It is designed to help you develop acceptance, which simply means that we make room for unwanted thoughts and feelings and experience them for exactly what they are—just passing thoughts and feelings, not a certainty of doom, danger, or calamity that they want you to believe they are. You will need to set aside 15 to 20 undisturbed minutes to do this exercise. Below is my adaptation of the Acceptance Exercise developed by Eifert and Forsyth.

Acceptance Exercise

Sit in a chair with limbs uncrossed and both feet comfortably on the ground. Rest your hands in your lap or along the arms of the chair, whatever is comfortable for you.

Take in a deep breath down into your belly and slowly exhale. As you exhale, begin to bring your attention to your breath. Take another deep breath in and notice the breath coming across the tip of your nostrils. As you exhale, you might notice that the breath going out is a bit warmer than the breath coming in. Notice this for a few breaths. Breathe in deeply one last time and, as you do, allow your eyes to gently close. Bring all your attention to your exhaling breath, noticing it traveling across your nostrils and also noticing your belly deflate a bit. Now let go of the breath. There is no need to control it in any way, just allow yourself to breath naturally, observing your breath coming in and going out. Observe your breath for 30 to 60 seconds.

It's natural for the mind to wander. You will suddenly notice that your attention is no longer on your breath but on some thought you are having, perhaps about the future or maybe about a memory. Sometimes your mind becomes occupied with a sensation such as an itch or maybe a minor pain. No matter what it is, simply acknowledge that your mind has wandered and gently bring your attention back to your breath observing as best you can your breath coming in and going out. Again, observe your breath for 30 to 60 seconds.

Now bring into your awareness what it is that challenges you in your trading. For many it will be the fear of loss. Some may fear missing out or leaving money on the table. Simply be aware of your fear and notice any unease, qualms, worries, and anxieties that you may have about your fear. Don't try to fix them, change them, or get rid of them in any way; just be with your fear and the qualms and worries. Sit with them—making room for them—for 30 to 60 seconds.

Now bring your attention to what is important to you in your trading. How would you like to be as a trader? What do you want to be remembered for in your trading? What do you want to be able to remember about yourself and your experience as a trader after a career of trading? Consider this for 30 to 60 seconds.

Now bring your attention to a trading situation that has been difficult for you. It might be cutting trades short or jumping into unplanned trades, not taking a trade after a loss or something different. Whatever the difficult situation is, it usually involves a mix of uncomfortable thoughts, worries, images, emotions, and bodily sensations. Gently and with determination, place your attention on the discomfort associated with this trading situation. Notice any strong feelings or hot thoughts and try to hold them lightly, opening up to them and making room for them. Stay with the discomfort as best you can for 30 to 60 seconds.

You may notice yourself resisting the uncomfortable experience. That is natural. Notice how you resist. Are you tugging on the rope or feeding a paper tiger? Remind yourself that to be the trader you want to be it is important to make room for these uncomfortable feelings and thoughts. Do the best you can to allow these into your awareness. It can help to breath into them. As you experience them, take a deeper breath—inhaling and exhaling—all the while keeping your unwanted experience in your awareness. As you do this, note what it really feels like to have these thoughts and feelings. Ask yourself, "Are these really so bad? Do I always have to fight them or can I make some space for them and still take the actions I need to take in my trading?" Stay with the unpleasant experience, making room for it, for 30 to 60 seconds.

Take in a deep breath and let it go. Remind yourself how you want to be and act as a trader. Also remind yourself of your difficult trading situation and the inner experiences that situation brings. As you consider how you want to be as a trader and the discomfort some situations bring, can you see yourself facing a difficult situation and, at the same time, acting as the trader you want to be? What would this be like for you? Hold this idea of trading through your difficult situation in the way you would like to be as a trader for 30 to 60 seconds.

As you are ready, take a deep breath and begin to reorient to the room you are in. Expand your awareness to other sounds you can hear. Notice that you are sitting in your chair. Wiggle your fingers and toes, and as you reconnect with the room you are in, make an intention to make room for unpleasant thoughts and feelings as they arise as best you can. Gently, open your eyes.

This exercise is a powerful one, but it must be practiced. Merely reading it through will give you an intellectual understanding, but that is all. You will want to experience what it is like to hold unwanted thoughts and uncomfortable feelings and practice doing so. This way, you develop important mental skills which will serve you well in your trading. It is best to do this exercise daily for two weeks or longer. A sustained experiential practice over a couple of weeks will help you develop the needed mental skills to face difficult situations in real time. If you experience more than one challenging trading situation, rank them according to the level of difficulty they give you. Then, select the one that presents the least level of difficulty—the one you feel would be easiest to deal with—and start with that. It is smarter to start with the least difficult and build mental skills needed more quickly and more easily that can later be applied to more challenging situations. You will be ahead of the game by taking this route; you will find it harder, and unnecessarily so, to pick the most difficult situation you face to deal with first.

Once you have practiced the acceptance exercise, review how you feel about your challenging situation. Eifert and Forsyth—the creators of this acceptance exercise—recommend that you ask yourself these important questions, taking the time to consider each one carefully:

- After practicing this acceptance exercise as recommended, has the difficulty lessened compared to how it seemed before your practiced the exercise?

- Do you know clearly what to expect when you face the challenging situation in terms of thoughts, emotions, and bodily sensations?

- Are you better able to accept the unwanted thoughts, emotions, and sensations and not struggle with them by feeding them (giving into them) or fighting them?

- Are you clear on what you value in your trading, what you want to stand for? Are you clear on what you need to do to achieve your goals and aspirations as a trader?

- Do you think you can do what is needed even though you are having unwanted thoughts and unpleasant feelings at the same time?

- Do you understand that although symptoms of stress can be uncomfortable, they need not be harmful when viewed as helping prepare you to meet trading challenges?

- Are you clear that attempts to reduce or eliminate the discomfort felt during challenging situations provides no benefit to your trading, and that only committing to high-value actions are of real benefit?

- Are you confident that the unwanted thoughts and feelings are not permanent and will eventually go away on their own accord, even though they may feel intense at the moment?

- Are you ready to commit to your trading and what you want it to stand for by keeping your attention focused on the appropriate high-value action, regardless how you feel?

If you can answer each of these questions affirmatively, you are ready to put your practice to the test. If you still have doubts, use the questions above to pinpoint where you feel you need additional work. Focus on specifically addressing these doubts in additional acceptance exercise practice until you feel ready to use these skills in real-time trading. Exercise 8.4 will help you prepare to confront your difficult trading

Exercise 8.4 Overcoming My Challenging Trading Situation

What I stand for in my trading:	
My challenging situation:	
My Goals: My initial goal:	
My longer-term goal:	
Plan for my initial goal:	
What will present the greatest challenge for me:	
How I will meet that challenge:	

situation in the live market. Its use will be explained through the case examples of Ammar and Priyanka (see Tables 8.2 and 8.3).

At the top of the form, we want to state what's important to us in our trading or what we want our trading to stand for. For Ammar, as he described in Table 8.2, this was a sense of his steadiness in his trading. Regardless what the market did, he valued riding the market's waves as if he were a boat, gliding along the surf. The simple word "steadiness," then, describes what he stands for. Ammar's challenging situation occurs after he has had a losing trade or two. Because he feels pressure to make up for the loss, he disregards money management and increases position size substantially.

His initial goal is to reduce oversizing his trades by 70 percent over the next two weeks. There are two things to note here. The first is that Ammar's goal is stated in specific terms against a schedule. He is looking to reduce his overtrading by 70 percent by the end of two weeks. It is critical that goals be specific. We discuss more about the details of framing goals in Part III. The second thing to note is that Ammar isn't looking to eliminate all oversized trades right away. We are all human and we all have our limitations. By stating his goal as less than 100 percent, he is acknowledging and making room for the fact that he won't get it right all at once. Making an important change like this is a process. We aren't looking for perfection. Reaching a goal of 70 percent will demonstrate solid commitment and a strong trend in overcoming his erratic trading behavior. In addition, it gives Ammar a little 'psychological cover' to come up short. We already know that he can be hard on himself when his trades end in loss. There is no reason to promote self-criticism when falling short of the behavioral change you are envisioning. Give yourself a little room and, above all, don't become harsh and self-critical when you don't get it exactly 100 percent right away. Remember, this is a process. Look for the trend.

The plan for your initial goal is the vital component of this exercise. In Ammar's case, taking a short break to do a brief mindfulness exercise structured on the acceptance exercise will help Ammar keep his mind in the moment and fortify him for changing his behavior. He also reminds himself of the importance of being a

TABLE 8.2	Ammar's Challenging Trading Situation
What I stand for in my trading:	Steadiness
My challenging situation:	Increasing position size after a loss
My Goals: My initial goal:	To notice when I am vulnerable to oversizing my position and to reduce this behavior by 70 percent over the next two weeks of trading
My longer-term goal:	Eliminate placing outsized positions completely within 45 days
Plan for my initial goal:	(1) Immediately after a losing trade leave my trading desk and engage in a 10-minute abbreviated acceptance exercise. (2) Affirm my commitment to being a steady trader and state to myself that increasing position size runs against how I want to trade. (3) Before taking the next trade, reconfirm my commitment to be a steady trader and trade with appropriate size.
What will present the greatest challenge for me:	The tension and agitation I feel for having a loss along with the thoughts and emotions that I failed.
How I will meet that challenge:	Rather than try and fight them, I will notice the tension in my body and also acknowledge the thoughts of failure and the emotional unease that these bring. I will apply mindfulness and recognize that these are only thoughts and feelings that will soon leave me. Taking a few deep breaths, I will make room for my unwanted thoughts and feelings, remind myself that steadiness is more important than making up for losses with unsound trades, and place my attention on the next trade, properly setting my position size.

steady trader and explicitly affirms that oversizing his position runs counter to what matters to him in his trading. The critical thing to note is that the form in Exercise 8.4 is encouraging you to develop a process of high-value actions for changing your unconstructive trading behavior. You are not just toughing it out. That's unlikely to work. By taking what you have learned from this book and creating two or three specific, constructive steps you can do to counter your tendency to commit erratic trading behavior, you are establishing an explicit and unambiguous process for your own self-development as a trader. This is how effective change can occur.

Part of your plan for change is to know what will pose the greatest difficulty for you in carrying out your plan. For Ammar, it is the tension felt and the toxic mental commentary he has when he experiences a loss. Here, mindfulness can play a huge role by helping you see that uncomfortable feelings and critical thoughts are merely feelings and thoughts, nothing more. They don't have to dictate what you do, and they will quickly pass only to be replaced by more thoughts and feelings. Ammar has an "in-flight" routine of taking a few deep breaths, remembering to not fight but defuse and accept his thoughts and feelings as they are (not what they tell him they are), and making the effort to orient his attention on the important, high-value trading—relevant action he needs to execute next. By anticipating what can derail his plan, he fortifies his plan psychologically and is well-prepared to tackle his most challenging trading situation.

In Table 8.3, Priyanka identified cutting winning trades short as the challenge she would like to overcome. This is one of the most common unconstructive trading behaviors. Priyanka noted that persistence and maximal effort were values in her trading. Remember, values indicate direction. In Priyanka's case, persistence and maximal effort leads to success. This was her experience in sport. She would also say that there was joy for her in the effort. Like many, she viewed the journey and meeting the demands of the journey as mattering more to her than the destination because of the rich experiences, learning, and self-development that the journey brings. For Priyanka, the journey involved an initial goal of partially reducing her unconstructive

TABLE 8.3	Priyanka's Challenging Trading Situation
What I stand for in my trading:	Persistence and giving maximum effort
My challenging situation:	Cutting winning traders short
My Goals: My initial goal:	To reduce this unconstructive behavior by holding onto trades for at least two additional points above my average on at least 60 percent of my trades over the next two months of trading
My longer-term goal:	Eliminate cutting winners short completely within five months and gradually increase my winning points per trade average
Plan for my initial goal:	Practice mindfulness prior to trading. State my intention, mission, and commitment for today are to hold my trades for at least two additional points. After entering a trade, set my stop. Move it up to breakeven when appropriate. Exit only after I have achieved two points above my average or the trade gets stopped out.
What will present the greatest challenge for me:	My fears that I will give back profit earned or suffer a loss. Tension in my stomach, strong emotion, and negative thoughts.
How I will meet that challenge:	I will do my best to be mindful and not feed the tiger. This will be hard, but not feeding the tiger means I am being persistent and applying maximum effort, and I will feel good about this. I will remind myself that the stress I feel is helping me meet the challenge of interacting with the market and even though it feels bad, it's worse when the market continues to go in my direction and I've cut the trade. I will strive to see my thoughts and feelings as temporary and only an indication of my fears, not what is actually happening in the market. I will also strive to put more attention on the market and my trade and less on my thoughts and feelings, though I will also let them occur without fighting them or running from them by closing my trade until I reached my goal.

tendency by increasing her average points made per winning trade by two points on at least 60 percent of her trades during the next month. This is a strong goal as it specifically states her intention during a specific time frame. Like Ammar, she is not looking for perfection in her initial efforts. As she gains the needed skills to hold on to her winning trades, she expects to eliminate cutting trades short prematurely as her longer-term goal.

Her plan is also very specific and highlights the high-value actions—both mental actions and trading actions—that support her initial goal. She understands well what the major challenge will be: not giving in to or fighting a strong and fearful emotional response to loss. She has specific ways to not give in to her fears, reframe her stress as helpful and her fears as fleeting, temporary psychological events. Most importantly, she is connecting her value of persistence and maximum effort directly with working hard at meeting her greatest trading challenge.

When you confront your own challenging trading situations, be aware that this will be hard work. It is unlikely to come easy. This is to be expected because making changes from emotion-driven trading actions to values-driven trading actions is difficult. Having a little bit of Priyanka's persistence and giving maximum effort will certainly help. Also be aware that one of the most important considerations in this endeavor is not to get down on yourself. If you fall short of your initial goal, do not let self-criticism set in where you become fused with your mind shamelessly telling you things like "how difficult this is," or "how it can't be done," or worse, "how much a failure you are," and so on. This is merely your mind talking unconstructive and useless trash. Be mindful, make some space for those thoughts that don't reflect reality and will soon go away, and turn your attention to the important task at hand: overcoming your challenging trading situation.

One of the key tasks here is to monitor your efforts and progress. When doing this, focus less on goal achievement and focus more on how well you commit to and execute the actual process of overcoming your challenge. Priyanka's process involved practicing mindfulness before trading, stating her intention for the day, setting her stop, moving the stop to breakeven when appropriate, and then holding her trade for two points. This is her process. She can readily evaluate herself on each of these important components. If she fell short on any of them, she can revise her plan to address this. For example, if she moved her stop beyond breakeven before it was appropriate to avoid giving up profit, she can address that by acknowledging that her mind was telling her to tighten her stop and she was believing it and so she give in to the tiger. To correct this, Priyanka can apply mindfulness to her thoughts and feelings about her stops and perhaps use one of the defusion techniques from Chapter 7, if needed. She can also remind herself that channeling maximal effort to her process is more important to her than avoiding unpleasant thoughts and feelings.

Thoughts and feelings like this can easily creep in and derail our best-laid plans. It is our job to be diligent, make adjustments, and then try again. Monitoring how we are doing—especially how we are doing with our process, not getting down on ourselves when we fall short, and taking corrective actions by modifying our plan and process are the component actions needed to make behavioral change (see Exercise 8.5). It may not be easy, but it is also not impossible. Nothing of value comes right away. Don't give up.

Exercise 8.5, Monitoring My Progress in Overcoming a Challenging Trading Situation, provides the format to a process with which you can monitor your progress in transforming challenging trading situations. You would complete this form each time you encounter a challenging trading situation that you have developed a plan for using the form in Exercise 8.4. The monitoring process involves identify-

---

Exercise 8.5 Monitoring My Progress in Overcoming a Challenging Trading Situation

Challenging Situation: Cutting profitable trades short

Actual Event: *Stock trade on Monday*

What I did well: *I did my mindfulness routine and intention, as planned. I took the trade and set the stop.*

Where I fell short: *Moved stop too quickly and was stopped out.*

What caused me to fall short: *I wanted to start the week with a cushion of profit. I didn't realize at the time that this was just another excuse to cut a profitable trade. Starting the week profitable seemed reasonable at the time.*

What I can do next time: *Be more mindful of my thoughts. When this occurs again, I will remind myself that this is just a thought unrelated to the trade and remember that following this process is more important than the results of any individual trade.*

Actual Event:
What I did well:
Where I fell short:
What caused me to fall short:
What I can do next time:

Actual Event:
What I did well:
Where I fell short:
What caused me to fall short:
What I can do next time:

Actual Event:
What I did well:
Where I fell short:
What caused me to fall short:
What I can do next time:

Actual Event:
What I did well:
Where I fell short:
What caused me to fall short:
What I can do next time:

ing what you did well, where you fell short, and making corrective adjustments. It is important to identify where you performed competently, not just where you fell short. Noting what we did well highlights parts of the process with which you are at least performing satisfactorily and with which you can rely on. As you progress, you will find that the things you are doing well grow or expand. This is an indication that you are improving and moving toward your goal.

Where you fell short are actions in your plan from Exercise 8.4 that you didn't do or you did ineffectively. In the example provided in this Exercise 8.5, the trader was working on overcoming loss aversion and cutting trades short. He noted that he fell short by moving his stop too quickly, causing a good trade to be stopped out prematurely.

The next question asked in this monitoring form is a critical one: What caused me to fall short? It is here that you will normally find that you were either fused to uncomfortable thoughts and feelings or your intuitive mind jumped into your trading and gave poor advice. In the example, the trader was fused with the notion of starting the week with profit. This, of course, had nothing to do with what was best for the trade at hand.

Finally, you can determine if an adjustment to your plan is needed by addressing what can be done next time to address the shortcoming. Think carefully about what would be helpful and be sure to apply what you have learned from this book.

Overcoming difficult trading challenges takes time and effort. Developing a plan that incorporates our values along with mindfulness, defusion, and other techniques is an effective way to achieve our trading goals. Monitoring your progress helps ensure your efforts at transforming your challenges are well-directed at the specific actions you take. We expand on all of this in Part III.

■ Notes

1. Fear of public speaking is very common in the U.S. population. In fact, it is reported as the most common social fear over the lifetime, according to national survey research conducted by University of Pennsylvania psychologist Ayelet Meron Ruscio and her colleagues.

2. Public speaking anxiety is a form of social phobia (often referred to as social anxiety disorder). Individuals afflicted by social phobia would be fearful of most social situations that involve people they are unfamiliar with and can experience acute anxiety when in the company of others. People who experience public speaking anxiety would generally not be fearful in other social situations (e.g., going to a party, playing a team sport, meeting a friend for dinner, attending a lecture or a concert, and other common activities that involve other people) but would experience clinically significant anxiety when speaking in front of others. The majority of persons with social anxiety disorder would also be fearful of public speaking.

3. Kelly G. Wilson and Amy R. Murrell, "Values Work in Acceptance and Commitment Therapy: Setting a Course for Behavioral Treatment." In *Mindfulness and Acceptance: Expanding the Behavioral Tradition*, ed. Steven C. Hayes et al. (New York: Guilford Press, 2004), 139.

4. Georg H. Eifert and John P. Forsyth, *Acceptance and Commitment Therapy for Anxiety Disorders: A Practitioner's Guide to Using Mindfulness, Acceptance and Values-Based Behavior Change Strategies* (Oakland, CA: New Harbinger, 2005), 161–166.

PART III

Maximizing Your Trading Performance

CHAPTER 9

The Trading Psychology Process: High-Quality Preparation

In Part I and Part II of the book, we have looked at how our minds work and what we can do to develop effective mental skills to overcome the psychological challenges we face in trading. If you have made the effort to complete the exercises and have applied some of the methods presented in the book, you may now be able to begin recognizing the mental shortcuts that affect your trading and to engage your deliberative mind better, and you may now see the influence of cognitive heuristics and biases beginning to subside. For traders who have become ensnared in thoughts and feelings of fear or other strong emotions, if you have started practicing mindfulness, you may be able to begin defusing from those thoughts and feelings, maintain better attention on the market, and start to take the actions that support your trades. You are now on the track to greater success. However, overcoming psychological challenges is only one aspect of trading psychology. For traders to maximize their trading performance there is another very important aspect of trading psychology traders need to know and learn: performance psychology.

So far we have dealt only with what seems to be "negative" psychology: the psychology of negative emotions, unwanted thoughts, cognitive biases, and erratic behaviors. But there is a "positive" side of psychology traders can employ in their trading. In fact, it is the positive psychology that can constructively help enhance traders' trading performance and, if pursued and developed, can lead to excellence and optimum performance in trading. We cover "positive" psychology in Part III.

We look at the interconnected aspects of trading competency and excellence: high-value trading actions (HVAs) and high-value mental skills (HVMSs) within the context of a trading psychology process. What do HVAs and HVMSs mean? It is important to emphasize that HVAs and HVMSs do not regulate emotional comfort. They are not aimed at controlling or suppressing the stresses of trading. HVAs and HVMSs are designed specifically to improve competency in trading.

HVAs and HVMSs are specific actions and skills that:

- Are under the trader's control.

- Directly relate to the process of trading.

- Enhance and expand the trader's ability to interact effectively with the markets.

- Maximize the trader's likelihood for improved trading results.

- Indirectly improve a trader's emotional state and confidence when practiced and developed over time.

In his first book on trading psychology, psychologist Brett Steenbarger describes taking stock of his trading to correct some of his trading shortcomings and enhance his overall performance. He used the tried and true method known as the "fearless personal inventory" first described by Bill Wilson and Bob Smith, cofounders of Alcoholics Anonymous. This is described as fearless because confronting one's shortcomings takes fierce honesty and courage. Nothing is held back. Every personal flaw is brought to light. For those suffering from alcohol abuse, this personal housecleaning can mark the beginning of recovery. Steenbarger used this approach and looked sincerely at his personal trading to uncover correctable flaws that eventually led to improved performance. For traders, taking honest stock of their trading can help enhance performance. You can't just sweep under the rug the things you don't like about your trading and expect to become a competent trader.

One day trader, Jane, conducted such an inventory and found much to her surprise that she didn't understand trending conditions very well. In a strong, intraday down move, she frequently looked for a bottom, repeatedly buying into the falling market, and quickly getting stopped out. Such trading often wiped out gains she made over several days. Worse, she missed excellent trending opportunities and the large, quick profits associated with the 'sweet spot' of trading. "It was only by stepping back and honestly assessing my trading that I realized I had a gaping hole in my trading," she said.

How do we conduct a "fearless personal inventory" in trading? An effective way to do that is through looking at our trading process.

The trading process comprises the systematic steps you take or perform in your trading. One's trading process is of great importance in trading. Michael Mauboussin, former Chief Investment Strategist at Legg Mason and currently head of Global Financial Strategies at Credit Suisse, places top value on the process of investing. He notes that performers who maintain success in probabilistic fields are those who pay good attention to their process. This is true in casino operations, sports team management, professional gambling, and investing and trading. Mauboussin maintains that achievers in investing have more in common with achievers in seemingly unrelated probabilistic fields than they do with the typical participant in their own field. In other words, a successful trader will have more in common with a successful sports team manager or successful casino operator than with the average trader. Why is this? Because achievers in those disciplines understand it is by following a proven process that the probabilities will play out and profits will be realized. Failing to follow a clear process leaves the trader vulnerable to mental blind spots and emotion-driven decision making. Having a solid process that you follow is one of the best antidotes to becoming trapped by cognitive biases and heuristics. When a trader follows a trading process consisting of both HVMSs and HVAs, they are better able to avoid the mental blind spots many traders succumb to: ignoring base rates, becoming seduced by saliency and recency effects, or lazily substituting and answering the easy mental question. Having a process helps engage deliberative mind. Following a specific process also helps reduce emotion-based judgments and decisions. A process grounds you and guides your focus to what is important. To their distinct detriment, many traders focus solely on their trade results and pay scant attention to their trading process. This allows emotions and mental blind spots to extract their toll. In contrast, successful performers are focused on their process rather than outcomes. What this means is that *how we make trading decisions is more critical than what we get for results*. Appraising our trading decisions with honest, constructive feedback and an openness to learn from our errors will better prepare us to execute our trades and ultimately improve our trading results. This is one important reason why Steenbarger took a fearless inventory of his trading.

When we think about a trading process it is helpful to think in terms of time frames. Trading process time frames are not the same trading time frames that traders usually think about. We are not talking about the 'triple screen trading system' popularized by Alexander Elder that incorporates longer-term, intermediate-term, and short-term charting time frames to select and manage trades. The time frames used in this trading process framework are simple and direct. They are composed of *Before, During,* and *After*.

The *Before-During-After* time frames specifically relate to what we do *before* trading, what we do *during* trading, and what we do *after* trading. If you think about it, these are the only three areas where we can have a direct impact on our trading performance. In fact, these are the only three areas in which a psychologist can work with a trader to enhance his or her trading performance. A psychologist can only help a trader's performance by working to improve what they do before they trade, what they do while trading, and what they do with their trading results (after trading). This is a broad categorization with multiple aspects. Take an individual trade for an example. We can break it down by focusing on what we do before the trade is entered (e.g., how the trade is identified), what we do during that trade (e.g., trade entry, management, and exit), and then how we handle the trade after it is over (e.g., assessing our performance and the outcome of the trade). We can also think about this not just by individual trade but also the trading day: again, what we do before the trading day (how we prepare), what we do during the trading day (how we manage our attention and concentration), and what we do after the trading day is over (assessing our trading, maintaining our trading journal). We can further extend this to the trading month, quarter, year, or even our trading career.

Before-During-After allows us to break down each of these horizons (a trade, a trading day, a trading week, etc.), separating them logically to give us greater clarity about our trading and greater control over our trading performance and our development as traders. Let's say we are day trading and it is now the middle of the trading day and we are in a profitable short trade. We don't want to now start looking for weekly support levels as a logical exit for the trade. That would be a distraction from our managing the trade we have on. Identifying longer-term support is a *before* activity, to be done when we are preparing for the trading day, not while in the midst of a trade. When in a trade, we want to be focused on high value *during* activities such as managing our trades and carefully attending to the market for signs to continue to hold the trade or, conversely, the signal to close the trade. Likewise, when in the trading day, our job is to find solid trade opportunities. It is not the time to think about what we might have done better on the last trade we took that ended in a loss. That is an *after* activity, to be undertaken calmly and objectively once the market has closed, not during the course of the trading day when we are looking for and making trades. We can't effectively evaluate a trade when our attention is called upon to read the market, identify trades, and manage our trades. *Before-During-After* helps us locate our attention and channel our consequent activities in a high-value way. It frames a process we can adopt to enhance and maximize our trading performance.

When we make this separation into before, during, and after, what we want to think about in the *Before* time frame is the idea of High-Quality Preparation (HQP). There are certain things we can do in terms of our preparation, including activities we can focus on and engage in that are of high value to our trading, as well as mental or psychological skills relating to preparation that can be developed and that are also of high value to our trading. We'll briefly discuss the high-value activities and go into considerable depth on the mental skills associated with High-Quality Preparation.

Similarly, the *During* time frame is all about Effective Trading Execution (EE), and we will discuss the associated high-value activities and mental skills of Effective Execution. Our *After* time frame involves the psychological skills and activities of Constructive Self-Assessment (CSA). It is in this time frame that we intentionally evaluate our trading performance.

Once we understand the HVMSs and HVAs within each of the time frames, we can then assess ourselves on each domain and determine where we are strong or weak. From here, we can take steps to enhance our trading performance and our personal self-development. Not only do we have an inventory of HVMSs/HVAs and procedures to benchmark our trading performance, this same inventory also gives us a highly effective and practical process to follow. In this chapter we will focus on the mental elements and activities of High-Quality Preparation. Chapters 10 and 11 will be devoted to Effective Trading Execution and Constructive Self-Assessment, respectively.

Table 9.1 illustrates how the trading psychology framework is divided into the three major areas: High-Quality Preparation, Effective Execution, and Constructive Self-Assessment. Each of the three major areas is further divided into high-value mental skills. High-Quality Preparation, for example, is subdivided into the HVMSs of: Perspective, Personal Awareness, Self-Motivation, and Mental Discipline. We discuss each of these mental skills along with the specific trading activities that together form the process of High-Quality Preparation in this chapter. As we go through the details and discuss these HVMSs, think about how you might rank yourself on each of them. How consistent are you in each? The closer you score yourself to being fully consistent, the more dialed in you are for that high-value mental skill. Less consistency suggests you have some work to do in that area. The idea is to measure where you are in each of these mental domains. For each of the next three chapters, you are provided with a set of questions you can use to assess yourself in each of these important areas. These self-assessment tools come at the end of each chapter. Keep in mind we are evaluating ourselves in terms of mental and psychological skills specifically relevant to the mental side of trading and the trading process.

The credit for this framework belongs to Charles Maher, sport psychologist for the Cleveland Indians Major League Baseball team and professor emeritus at Rutgers

TABLE 9.1 **High-Value Mental Skills of the Performance Psychology Time Frames**

	Before	During	After
Psychological Time Frame	High-Quality Preparation	Effective Execution	Constructive Self-Assessment
High-Value Mental Domain	Perspective	Self-Confidence	Self-Esteem
	Personal Awareness	Emotional Intensity	Performance Accountability
	Self-Motivation	Focus	Perseverance
	Mental Discipline	Poise	Continuous Improvement

University's Graduate School of Applied and Professional Psychology. He developed this framework through his work with collegiate and professional athletes and professional sports teams and taught it to graduate students in psychology at Rutgers University, where I studied. I have adapted it for the trader, adding to it and modifying it somewhat for the specific context of trading, but the *Before-During-After* framework came from Charlie.

■ High-Quality Preparation

Before we start taking trades and before we start the trading day if we are day trading or the trading week if we are a swing trader, we engage in the core psychological principle of High-Quality Preparation. To a very significant degree, *preparation equals performance*. In other words, what we do to prepare for trading will be of substantial benefit to our actual trading. There are four high-value mental skills that form the basis of High-Quality Preparation. There are also specific HVAs that we can perform in the *Before* time frame of High-Quality Preparation that will be of substantial benefit to our trading.

When a trader has a clear approach and a clear process along with a defined set of procedures to prepare for trading, that trader will be better off both emotionally and performance-wise than those who lack these crucial essentials. If you can prepare yourself for trading the High-Quality way, that is, following a process, you will be standing on firm sands. You will be grounded and your process will keep the sands from shifting out from under your feet regardless of what the market does or how a trade turns out. As we noted above, process is key to those who operate within a probabilistic field, and trading is all about probabilities. When operating within a probabilistic field, it is consistency in the steps we take that will allow for the probabilities to materialize. When traders fail to follow a process and instead follow their gut, what their mind is telling them at the moment or how they feel, they end up missing trades, taking poor trades, overriding their system, cutting winners short, supersizing their position, holding when they should exit, and a whole host of other actions that fall under the category of erratic trading. Trading like this ensures that the probabilities of your trade setups or trading system will not play out. Without a solid trading process, every time you experience a loss or the market does something unexpected, you are subject to flounder. Having a clear approach and process is analogous to navigating by a GPS tracking system. You can lean against it and understand where you are when things get tough. Most importantly, it will help you further develop your trading knowledge, skills, and abilities when applied correctly.

At the heart of High-Quality Preparation are four high-value mental skills: perspective, personal awareness, self-motivation, and mental discipline. In addition, there are a range of associated, high-value trading actions. We detail both in this chapter.

Perspective

Perspective refers to how you view your trading in relation to the important roles and commitments you have made in the rest of your life. Balance is the key idea here. Trading places significant demands on the trader in terms of time and energy. Not only does the active trader work before the screen for much of the day, he or she also spends time and effort after the markets are closed to review performance, study charts, do research, scan markets, and develop plans for future trades. How one separates and balances the demands of trading with other important aspects of life is just as important as studying the markets. The trader who is clear on her roles along with the demands, expectations, and obligations as spouse, partner, parent, friend, sibling, daughter, employee or employer, student, community member, member of a spiritual community, and other important roles she may occupy as well as her role as a trader will be better off mentally and emotionally than those who are not clear on how trading is balanced with the rest of one's life. Educator and author on leadership and excellence Stephen Covey together with Roger and Rebecca Merrill have written on the importance of clarifying roles. People who have a clear sense of their roles and a strong sense of perspective are able to deal with events more effectively as they have the capacity to put them in their proper mental and emotional place. Overall direction and a peace of mind can come from this clarity, while frustration, anxiety, and the feeling of being overly burdened by claims demanded by one's roles can be the result if one is not clear and able to partition them.

> Michael is an experienced day trader in the currency markets. His elderly mother recently moved from her home to a nursing home due to failing health and declining mobility. It was a difficult decision, and Michael was reluctant to take this step, although he knew it was necessary. Michael was distressed at seeing his mother enter the nursing facility. He thought about her constantly. He was concerned about her health and wondered if she was all right and whether or not she was happy. He also felt pangs of guilt. As a result, his trading suffered. He missed trades, became distracted while in trades and managed them poorly, and made thoughtless mistakes. "I can't stop thinking about my mother," he said. "I worry about her and, of course, this is affecting my trading."

Michael's roles of being a son and a trader were clearly out of balance.

Being able to *mentally park* outside demands and concerns is a critical mental skill and part of the balance called for in perspective. As much as we need to be clear about our various roles, we also need to be able to separate our personal matters and concerns from trading so that we can trade with a clear and focused mind. Mental parking means that we separate from and set aside our other roles when we take on the role of the trader. Later, when trading is finished, we can pick up our parked roles and mentally park trading. Michael was unable to mentally park his concerns about his mother when trying to trade. For Michael, it would have been better to forego trading a few days until he was satisfied that his mother was in good care rather than try to trade through a difficult time. Once over the initial shock, specific steps could be taken to manage ongoing concerns. Simple scheduling of brief phone calls would help address his needs and allow him to actively park his familial concerns when he was engaged with the currency markets.

Even minor things can be disruptive. At the end of the trading day you turn your attention to your journal and begin to prepare for tomorrow. The phone rings and a friend asks, "Do you want to go out for a drink?" On the one hand, you have your preparation for the next trading day; on the other hand, you have the promise of a good time with a friend. You have a choice to make. Can you mentally park what isn't going to contribute to what's important to your trading and do what you need to do when you need to do it? Being aware of our various functions and responsibilities, making time for their demands, proactively managing them, and being able to mentally park concerns outside of trading are all part of perspective.

Everyone experiences distractions, of course. We want to be able to develop the ability to mentally and emotionally manage distractions so that they do not affect trading. Can you come into your trading room ready to trade and not be thinking about other aspects of your life? Mindfulness helps substantially in this regard. Mental parking is an application of mindfulness. Thoughts and feelings unrelated to trading are acknowledged, evaluated for their urgency, and, if not critically and immediately important, we set them aside and mindfully turn to the trading task at hand. This requires clarity of your roles, making the commitment to leave nontrading concerns outside the trading room, focusing your full attention on trading tasks, and then picking up your personal cares and interests and parking your trading as you leave the trading desk. Formal mindfulness practice will help build the mental muscle needed for mental parking. We have more examples of the essential HVMS of mental parking a little further in the chapter.

Part of perspective and the process of managing distractions is to understand your values, know what is important to you, and have clarity on how trading fits into your life and how it also supports the other important areas of your life. It helps to have a defined vision of yourself as a trader as well as your vision of yourself as a person with all the other important roles you play in addition to being a trader. You identified your vision of yourself as a trader by describing why you trade and the values you hold as a trader in Exercise 8.2 in Chapter 8. You can do the same for other important roles in your life. Creating a "mission statement" for yourself by identifying two to four key things you want to experience in that role and what you want to be known for or remembered for in that role will help you clarify those roles. Just as in trading, we can evaluate our actions by how well they hold up to and harmonize with our values and mission. Those actions that are not in sync with our values can be dropped or changed.

Trading is not the only important commitment in our lives. Attention needs to be paid to other important roles, too. Being clear on those roles, what you want from them and how they bring meaning to your life will help you do this efficiently and effectively. It also helps avoid one role having a distracting or otherwise negative influence on other areas of our life. It is a part of overall balance all traders need. True clarity on why you do certain things, why it is important to you, and how it fits with the rest of your life is one of the ingredients for high achievement. This perspective is an important *Before* activity for those who want to excel: see Exercise 9.1.

Exercise 9.1 will help you to clarify your roles and sharpen your perspective. This form provides a format for you to identify important roles in your life, what matters to you in that role, and HVAs associated with that role which you want to devote attention and effort to in order to maximize your experience in that role and to get what matters to you from that role. Two examples are provided. Begin by identifying all the important roles you have in your life. Under the column *What's Important to Me* list two to four things that you value or that matter to you in that role. Under *HVAs*,

Exercise 9.1 Important Roles in My Life

Role	What's Important to Me	High-Value Actions
Example 1: Father	Being a good role model and creating a loving family environment for my daughter and son	Actively showing interest in their lives (e.g., attending school plays and sporting events they are in); be a good listener and provide appropriate guidance
Example 2: Friend	Connecting with others in a meaningful way; have a strong social network	Be available for friends when needed; pitch in and help organize and participate in social activities

list two or three activities you can do to help you fulfill that role in a quality way and help bring about and actualize the values you hold dear in that role.

Trading Perspective

For traders, part of perspective also involves your view of the market. How will you trade it? What is your understanding of important market structure, like trends and trading ranges, and how do you define these? Where do you locate trades? What is your trading edge and where do you find it? What markets and time frames are you trading and how frequently are you in them? Are you basing your trades off support and resistance, price action and volume, candlesticks, indicators, fundamental benchmarks, or some combination of these? What are your money management practices, both for protecting your capital and for increasing position and account size over time? In other words, what is your trading plan?

You trading plan reflects your personal perspective of the market and how you will trade it. It is a foundational component of your trading that can change over time and experience, but should be your compass on how you view the markets, how you assess them, and how you extract money from them day to day. Your job as a trader is to find, execute, and manage high-quality trades. You need to be very clear on how you do this; if you are not, you will be subject to the vagaries of the market and the vagaries of your emotional state, both of which will change from day to day. Jason Alan Jankovsky, a well-known Forex trader and trading author, states that having a trading plan is a must for a trader. He writes that when he considered the various traders he had met or known and compared winning traders and the losing traders, he found that most were about equal in their knowledge of the markets and the skills they brought to bear on their trading. What differentiated the winning trader from the losing trader, however, was one thing: the winning trader had a trading plan. The winning trader had a clear perspective on how to trade the markets. The well-crafted trading plan, according to Jankovsky, helps to protect the trader from becoming reckless and from taking low probability trades. It also addresses what to do and what not to do when the unexpected happens. Overall, having a trading plan reflects your perspective of the markets and provides a set of guidelines for how you interact with them.

Another component of perspective for traders involves the ability to think in terms of probabilities. Every trade we take is a probabilistic event. Every trade—regardless of how good it is—has a probability of a winning result as well as a probability of a losing result. No trade setup escapes this. Because of this, traders must adopt a perspective about the market and their trading that is based on probabilities.

Many traders do not adopt a probabilistic perspective on the markets and their trading. They think in opposite terms. They want every trade taken to be a winner. This is understandable. We want to produce winning trades. We would like it if every trade taken turned out a winner. But this is not realistic. More importantly, thinking non-probabilistically directly and negatively impacts trading performance. Recall from Chapter 1 that neglecting base rates—that is, trade probabilities—is a cognitive error and a hallmark characteristic of the intuitive mind. This kind of thinking leads traders into erratic trading behavior such as taking unskilled steps to avert losses. It also keeps the trader focused on trade outcomes instead of his or her trading process. In trading and other probabilistic fields of endeavor, a results orientation undermines performance. Caring only about whether each trade is a winner or a loser with a strong bias toward a winning result causes us to act in ways to try and ensure a winning outcome. But those actions almost always run counter to our best interests as a trader and, most often, the best interests of the trade.

Traders want to think in terms of probabilities for every trade. As Mark Douglas and Hong Kong trader Ray Barros have pointed out, there is a paradox we need to understand when it comes to probabilities in trading. The paradox goes like this: For any given trade, we can never be certain about its outcome when we first put on the trade. It may turn out to be a winning trade or a losing trade. The outcome of every individual trade, therefore, is uncertain. In contrast, over a large number of trades, that trade's edge will prevail. A trade setup, for example, may have an edge of 60 percent. This means that on average 6 out of 10 trades will be winners and four will lose money. This is the trade setup's base rate. When putting on that trade, we never know whether this particular trade will result in one of the six wins or one of the four losses. We just can't know that in advance. But if we trade this setup consistently, and make, say, 100 trades over time, then our edge should prevail and we will have 60 winning trades and 40 losing trades. If the trade setup has a large win when it does succeed and a comparatively small loss when it doesn't, we will have a positive expectancy and a net profitable setup. Therefore, we want to take that trade each time it sets up according to its criteria. We want to be on the right side of the paradox and the right side of the law of large numbers. When traders are focused on whether this trade will be a winner or a loser (i.e., the trade outcome), they are operating on the wrong side of the paradox. And the wrong side is the scary side because, as we said before, we can never know whether any given trade will be a winner or a loser. We can never know its outcome. When our focus is on the trade's outcome and we want it to be a winner, we are thinking unrealistically and our actions are likely to be erratic. Therefore, the proper attitude is to be on the side of the paradox that says, over a large number of trades, the edge will prevail. Adopting this perspective is the same as "think like a trader," as shown in the research we discussed earlier on loss aversion. When study participants were instructed to "think like a trader" and that the sum of their trades was more important than any one trade, they were being instructed to keep their mind on the right side of the probabilities paradox and think about their edge playing out over a large number of trades. They did better than those not so instructed, significantly reducing the normal tendency toward loss aversion. That is why it is so important for traders to consciously embrace thinking in terms of probabilities and thinking in terms of process rather than outcomes as a critical part of perspective.

Personal Awareness

Personal awareness is the second mental skill in Charlie Maher's performance model of High-Quality Preparation. Personal awareness is about understanding your current strong points as well as your current limitations in all areas that affect your trading performance. You will be at an advantage when you are clear about the areas where you are strong and the areas where you are not so strong. Lacking this clarity, you run the risk of misleading yourself. Without a clear understanding of your current strengths and limitations, you are likely to believe you possess strengths where you do not. This, of course, can be costly in the markets.

A *strength* is something you do that is above average. It is a skill or ability that you can rely on and expect it to produce positive results. A *limitation* is something that keeps you from functioning effectively. You are below average here. A limitation is also something that, if overcome, will make you a more effective trader. A limitation that can be overcome with planning and effort through the development of additional knowledge, skills, or abilities becomes a *developmental need*.

In areas where you do fall short, you also want to distinguish between things you can avoid and not do and things that are a problem and need to be addressed. It is always easier and more efficient to simply avoid the things you don't do well if you can. It is always harder to change as change always takes energy and effort. If you can steer clear of a limitation and staying away from it does not adversely affect your trading, then this is the best route to take. Here's a case example:

> Emil is an active trader with a chief focus on select futures markets. He concentrates primarily on the S&P e-minis, crude oil, and the Euro currency markets in his day trading. He has a solid trading plan and a good understanding of market behavior. He recognized, however, that he was not producing the kinds of returns that reflect his trading knowledge, skills, and abilities. He was falling short. His assessment of his strengths and limitations revealed a few limitations, but one thing stood out prominently. In his day-to-day trading, he found that he made good trades during the morning sessions, but during the afternoon sessions he became careless. Much of what he made in the mornings was given back to the markets in the afternoons. By becoming aware of his strengths and limitations, he learned that although his skills were strong, he simply got tired in the afternoons and his concentration suffered. His trading became casual and sloppy. Emil stopped making trades in the afternoons, avoiding

Exercise 9.2 My Current Strengths and Limitations

Use an asterisk to denote whether the limitation is something you can easily avoid or if it is a developmental need.

	Current Strengths	Current Limitations
Mental		
Technical		
Other Considerations		

his limitation, and traded only during the morning sessions. Even though he traded less, Emil's overall profitability increased substantially.

Assessing one's strengths and limitations can often reveal insightful information as in Emil's case. Another trader who conducted this self-assessment immediately recognized that he is easily enticed by other trading methods even though he had a good knowledge of what works in the markets for him. Viewing this as a shortcoming to avoid, he applied the mindfulness skill of mental parking to remain focused on what was productive and to stay away from other new indicators and methods as they were essentially a distraction.

Use Exercise 9.2 to assess your personal strengths and limitations. When assessing your strengths and limitations, write down trading related mental and technical skills and abilities that you do well and things that need work. Under mental skills and abilities, consider your mindfulness skills and abilities at mental parking. Also consider how well you can hold a trade to its logical conclusion. Can you stick to your trading plan? Are you able to set aside losing trades? Can you maintain an overall even mental keel while trading? After you have completed the remainder of this chapter along with Chapters 10 and 11, return to this exercise so you can include your abilities in each of the mental domains we are discussing within the *Before-During-After* matrix.

For technical strengths, consider such things as identifying choice trade setups, being clear on entries and exits, ability to manage your trades while they are happening, your understanding of market behavior, level of expertise with respect to indicators you use, your abilities at trading in multiple time frames, and other technical considerations.

In the *Other Considerations* category, include things like social and family support (e.g., do you have good communication with your spouse or partner regarding your trading; how are you at sustaining your significant other's support), physical strengths and limitations (fitness, ability to sit in front of the screen), physical health, nutritional habits, and anything else that may affect your trading that does not fit into the mental and technical categories.

You need not be elaborate and overly detailed with this exercise. Just jot down the things that come prominently to your mind. Ask yourself, "What are my strong points mentally, technically, and otherwise? What can I rely on? Where do I have limitations mentally, technically, and otherwise? What do I need to work on?"

One caution to note in this exercise: Don't overlook your strengths. It is important to know your strengths as this knowledge has utility. You know you can rely on them. When a situation arises that calls upon one of your strengths, you can act with confidence. Limitations may be difficult to see and even more difficult to accept for some traders. It requires an open-mindedness that allows you to identify where errors are frequently made and also allows you to learn from the experience and not get down on yourself. A trader who previously played on the tennis pro circuit once said that when playing tennis, you could always tell who the most promising players were not by their strengths, but by their response to their limitations. When recognizing a shortcoming, these players didn't try to sweep it under the rug or hide it in any way. In fact, they responded in just the opposite manner. Upon recognizing a weakness, they went to their coach and said, "I'm having this difficulty. How can I get over this? What can I do?" Instead of getting down on themselves for discovering a weak point in their game, they got excited. They were excited because they knew they now had something by which they could improve. If they worked in this current limitation, they would better their skills and abilities in that regard and have a better overall game. Unlike many, top players are happy to discover personal shortcomings. Now they have something to work with. It is the same in trading.

As discussed, limitations need to be divided into things that you can practically avoid and things you need to work on. Those things that are adversely affecting your trading and that can't readily be avoided become a *developmental need*. A developmental need will relate to a current shortcoming in a trader's knowledge, skill set, or ability. Let's say, for example, that in your personal assessment of your current strengths and limitations, you realize that you tend to hold trades too long, looking for a home run, rather than taking profits when the trade is showing signs of a reversal. This is something you really can't avoid. If you can change this behavior, it will be of significant benefit to you, both profit-wise and psychologically. You'll make more money and feel better about your trading. Importantly, this is also something that is within your control. You can take corrective action. This is a developmental need that can be turned into a *developmental goal*, which we discuss in the next section on Self-Motivation.

Self-Motivation

Trading is a tough business. There is a fair amount of adversity and you need high levels of motivation to be able to sustain yourself when the chips are down and the market isn't offering trade opportunities or you've just had a series of losses. Motivation is a state that changes all the time. Have you ever wanted to lose weight or get fit? You get a little inspiration, maybe join a gym and buy some new exercise shoes, and for a few weeks you are there every other day working out. But, then, something happens. Maybe you get overly tired, or other things take priority. You get off schedule and suddenly a month or two later finds you no longer on the path of fitness. You've stopped going to the gym. What happened? As we discussed in Chapter 8, making changes like this require numerous daily decisions over a long period of time. You were inspired at first, and this gave you the impetus to get started. But, motivation ebbs and flows. You didn't sustain the same level of motivation. Perspective helps in this regard. Being clear about what you are all about helps when things don't go swimmingly. You also need the proper goals.

Self-motivation comes from our willingness and ability to commit to a process of setting important, relevant goals directly related to our trading and pursuing them with enthusiasm and dedication. This applies to both short-term and long-term goals. Simply put, motivation that is sustained day after day and week after week comes from the proper goals we set for ourselves, pursuing them, and in our pursuit making progress and becoming better and better.

A *proper* goal is a vital concept. You will recall that earlier I mentioned sport and human performance psychologist Zella Moore studied some of the traditional methods used in sport psychology and found that many of the traditional methods—including goal setting—are best considered as "experimental." There isn't much empirical evidence that traditional goal setting (as well as some other well-worn methods) significantly improves performance. Simple goal setting, therefore, is unlikely to enhance trading results. So why are we discussing setting goals? Because it is the *type* of goal you employ that is important. If we set simple goals that are related to trading outcomes, we are unlikely to achieve more than we already do. For example, if you are making $1,000 a week in your day trading activities, setting a goal to make $1,200 next week is unlikely to increase your performance such that you actually reach the goal and make $1,200 next week. This is an outcome goal and outcome goals are not the kind of goals we are interested in.

The type of goal for traders to focus on is a *process goal*. Process goals are vastly different from outcome goals. An outcome goal is associated with a number, a statistic, or a result. Here are some examples of outcome goals: achieving four points a day; making $10,000 a week; generating an average win rate of 65 percent on your trades; making a certain number of winning trades a week; producing a profitability expectancy of xyz per trade; and similar goals. All these are about results. While it is useful to maintain such metrics, turning measurements into goals has little value to the trader wishing to improve performance. A main reason for this is that we have very little direct control over them. If we have a goal, for example, of making five S&P points a day, it will be very hard to achieve that goal if the market we trade is trading flat and stuck within a narrow range. This can go on for days and even weeks.

Market volatility expands and contracts. There have been low volatility periods—sometimes lasting weeks and even months—in the S&P futures market where the average daily range narrowed and it was difficult to consistently earn a few points a day. If your goal was to take five points out of the market each day, you would have found it extremely challenging to reach. Because we have such little control over outcomes, goals like this can actually have dark-sided results. When a market isn't trading in a way that supports your outcome goal, you may try to compensate with your actions by overtrading it or taking unwise risks. Poor results are then likely and this can affect you psychologically. If your focus is on things outside of your control—such as the market's behavior, the profit you make, your win/loss ratio, your judgments about what other traders are doing, and the like—you can place yourself on an emotional rollercoaster that adversely affects your motivation as well as your trading. Obviously, we don't want our goals to be inducing these kinds of problems.

Rather than setting outcome goals which have uncertain efficacy, we want to set process goals. A process goal is entirely within the trader's control. It involves developing your knowledge, skills, or abilities, not trade results or statistical outcomes. A process goal helps you develop as a trader. When you have assessed your current strengths and limitations and have identified a current limitation that needs to be addressed, you have identified a developmental need. The next step is to create a process goal that will help you build your knowledge, skills, and abilities related to that need. This is how we become better as traders and how we achieve excellence in trading performance. Process goals that address a developmental need are called *developmental goals*, because they aid in your personal development as a trader. All of our goals should be developmental goals.

There are probably an infinite number of developmental goals that can be constructed. As long as the goal addresses a current performance limitation and is oriented to the process of trading, it is a proper goal. Let's say that when you took stock of your current strengths and limitations, you noted that you have a tendency to enter trades too early. The trade setups are sound; you just jump the gun before entries are triggered. Because of this, you often sit through an uncomfortable period as the market completes its last move. Sometimes, the trade is under water and you may close it at a loss only to see the trade trigger shortly thereafter. It is frustrating and it costs missed profits and the occasional loss. This is a clear developmental need. A process goal for this developmental need might be structured in two parts. First, you conduct research on all trades you entered over the past six months and determine the best entry trigger. It might be a specific type of price bar, a break of the last price bar's high or low, a specific indicator value, or some other relevant trigger. Whatever entry trigger you decide upon, you are process oriented and building your knowledge about solid entry tactics. Second, you put this into practice. Armed with distinct knowledge about how to best enter your trades, you focus day by day on waiting for your specific entry and take the trade at that point. Again, you are process oriented. You gauge your performance not on whether the trade is a winner or how many points or pips you make on the trade, but *how you entered the trade*. Here, you are building knowledge and skills with respect to trade entry and you are building your ability to wait for your entry to trigger. This, in turn, builds your ability to overcome a current limitation. This is what process is all about. The more the trader focuses on and strives to improve what can be controlled, the better the trader is likely to be. Do this, and see your performance improve. The trade results will take care of themselves.

Let's go a little deeper on developmental goal construction for some sound guidelines on how to put them together so that you begin to not only correct current limitations but maximize you performance ability. All goals should be put into the format originally created by George Doran, business consultant and management author. The format is known as the SMART Goal. The acronym stands for:

S – Specific: the goal should be stated in specific terms and be about a skill, action, ability, knowledge, or some other aspect of your trading.

M – Measurable: The goals should be able to be stated in such a way that you can easily monitor and measure your progress toward achieving them. This is of particular value because if we are seeing that progress is not being made, we will know this quickly and can make adjustments. Frequently, our measurement will simply be whether or not the task or action occurred or it didn't.

A – Attainable: The goal should be able to be realized by the trader. The goal may involve instruction, practice, coaching, and other forms of learning, but at some point the trader should be able to achieve the goal. Therefore, we want to have goals that are reasonably reachable. Avoid setting unrealistic goals that are unattainable or very difficult to achieve. While you may eventually achieve extreme goals, it is far better and far more motivating to break down large goals by setting and realizing a series of incremental, reachable goals.

R – Relevant: The goal should be applicable and appropriate to your trading. The best test of this is that once attained, the goal will contribute to and enhance your trading performance.

T – Time-bound: Achievement of the goal should occur within a reasonable time period. It is discouraging to have goals drag on with little progress being seen.

Let's look at a few examples of SMART trading goals. In Chapter 8, we discussed the mechanics of overcoming challenging trading situations involving mental and emotional reactions. We will frame one of the examples from that chapter into a SMART goal. You will recall that Ammar wanted to change his unconstructive behavior of increasing position size to make up for a recent loss. His plan involved taking a break from his trading desk after a losing trade and engaging in productive exercises that remind him of how he wants to behave on the next trade. We can state this as a SMART goal:

Over the next four weeks when I have a losing trade I will:

1. Acknowledge that I am now vulnerable to increasing position size on the next trade.
2. Leave my trading desk and do a 10-minute acceptance exercise.
3. Affirm my commitment to my trading values and how I want to act, even if I feel differently.
4. Place the properly sized position on the next trade.

I will do this after losing trades at least 70 percent of the time.

In terms of the SMART goal framework, it clearly meets the S criterion. It is quite specific. He will do three specific things after a loss. It can also be readily tracked and measured. As part of the goal, Ammar states that his objective is to achieve a minimum threshold of completing the specified mental routine and properly sizing his next trade after 70 percent of all losses. This seems reasonably attainable and he will clearly know whether or not he has achieved his goal. Ammar's goal is also highly relevant to his trading. Not only does his current limitation, reflected in his developmental need, cause him distress, but he trades outside the bounds of sound money management. Correcting this current limitation will serve to enhance his trading performance. Finally, the goal is time-bound. There is a specific period of four weeks.

Note also that this is clearly a process goal. Ammar does not have a "numbers" goal. It is not related to money won or improving his win rate or any other outcome goal. His goal has to do with what he can control: his actions. If Ammar works on the process he has developed to maintain sound money management in sizing his positions and achieves his goal, it will add to his trading performance. He should see positive results in his trading and in his stress levels over time.

We will discuss two additional SMART goal examples. The first concerns a trader who had difficulty exiting trades. She got into trades fine, but frequently thought they would run farther than they did. She thought she would be leaving money on the table, but often had to give back profits. Here is her SMART goal:

> I will establish a logical profit target for each trade. I will exit at least half of my position at the target. If I decide to let a portion of my trade run, I will employ Welles Wilder's parabolic SAR trailing stop to protect profits already made. I will do this on at least 80 percent of all trades over the next 20 trading days.

We can see that this trader's goal meets all the criteria of a SMART goal. It is specific in what she will do. It can be measured by recording whether or not she followed the goal's steps. It is a reasonably attainable goal in at least two respects. First, she is looking to achieve her goal on 80 percent of her trades. Although this is a substantial majority of trades, she isn't looking for 100 percent, at least in this initial goal. She can fall short 20 percent of the time and still be within the goal's criteria. More importantly, if she can reduce her erratic trading behavior by 80 percent, she is making strong progress. Secondly, she may hold one-half of the position for greater gains. These two features render it an incremental goal that she should be able to attain. The goal's relevance should be obvious: she will enhance her trading by learning to sharpen her exit skills. And, finally, her goal is bounded by a 20-day time period.

Here is a slightly different SMART goal written by a day trader:

> Each night, I will review the markets I trade and assess them for tomorrow's trading. Each night, I will identify the location of the first trade of the day for tomorrow. Within four months, I expect to be able to pre-identify the first trade location 60 percent of the time.

All the criteria of a SMART goal are included. See if you can identify why it is SMART. Note again that this trader has set a goal related to the process of trading—in this case, it has to do with preparing for trading the night before. Preparation is an integral part of a successful trader's process. Again, the goal is not looking to increase profits or make a higher win rate. The goal is about preparing to trade with a specific objective: identifying tomorrow's first trade area. This is highly relevant. If the goal is reached, this trader would be determining the first trade of the day on three out of five trading days each week.

Developmental goal setting along with the hard work needed to realize the goal is what addresses a trader's developmental need. The application of SMART developmental goals will help increase and sustain a trader's motivation. Setting appropriate goals to tackle personal challenges can make a real difference in the trader's performance. By working on the goal the trader sees steady progress being made, and, ultimately, meets those challenges in a timely way. All this not only helps sustain our motivation, but makes us much better traders.

Mental Discipline

The last mental domain in the *Before* framework is the mental domain of mental discipline. Sometimes, we refer to it as willpower. The terms are interchangeable. The idea of mental discipline is probably different from what you might imagine it to be. It is not enough to merely be strong mentally. In fact, that misses the point entirely. Traders who try to be robotic and mentally impervious will quickly find themselves in difficulty. We've discussed this throughout the book. In this framework, mental discipline does concern mental strength, but in a specific way. Mental discipline at its basic level is about the ability to follow a plan.

We have already discussed the necessity of a trading plan. In part, the trading plan informs your perspective on the market and how you will trade it. Your trading plan is also a significant part of mental discipline. Failure to follow a trading plan is a prominent cause of erratic trading and loss of capital, not to mention the psychological havoc it creates. Remember that Jason Jankovsky separates winners and losers by the sole criterion of a trading plan. You need one and you need to follow it. But there is more to willpower than merely following a trading plan.

Mental discipline is really about following a process, not just a trading plan. We are detailing a process here that successful traders as well as successful performers in other professions follow. This is the *Before-During-After* process where we logically separate high-value activities and the associated mental skills into what we do before trading, what we do during trading, and what we do after trading. Mental discipline, then, involves a commitment to preparation that results in a plan, following through on your plan, adjusting when your plan isn't working, and learning from both your successes and your mistakes. New learning then becomes a part of your preparation, which flows into execution, which you then evaluate and again make whatever adjustments may be necessary, which then flows into your preparation, and so on. This is the trading psychology process. Our willpower helps us commit to and follow the trading psychology process. It takes willpower to engage in the activities of High-Quality Preparation before trading. It also takes willpower to engage in the HVMSs and HVAs of Effective Execution during trading. And, finally, it takes willpower to assess your trading performance in an objective way (Constructive Self-Assessment) so that you can use that data to identify developmental needs and create SMART goals for continual improvement. This is the process of excellence in trading. It is available to anyone who follows it.

In the *Before* time frame, mental discipline is directed at pre-trading activities and routines that help ready you for trading. Such productive pre-trading activities can involve analyzing the markets you trade for support and resistance, signs of distribution or accumulation, the market's overall structure, and the current trending or congestion characteristics. Developing a game plan for the next day's trading (for day traders, or next week's trading for swing traders) is a High-Value Activity every trader should carry out. This would include the anticipated direction of the next trading period and key areas where a trade is likely to set up. Other High Value Activities in the *Before* time frame include such things as researching market behavior and trade setups, practicing trading, learning the key characteristics that appear as a market is about to turn, and other activities related to your trading that help you build your trading knowledge, skills, and abilities and that can later be put to use during trading.

In the *During* time frame, mental discipline is measured by the trader being able to follow through on the game plan developed the night before. This doesn't mean that if the game plan turns out to be wrong, that the trader stubbornly refuses to adjust. Making adjustments as needed is a feature of mental discipline. We are disciplined in that we look to execute our plan and not become cavalier or erratic in our trading. But it also implies that we be mentally flexible. No plan devised the night before will hold up 100 percent the next day. Often, if we are skilled in reading the chart, the game plan will provide a good map of tomorrow's trading. But many times it won't. We may have to throw it out right at the open. That's okay. This is actually the beauty of having a game plan. You know right away whether it is working and also if it is not working. When it isn't working, you adjust.

Here is a typical example of making adjustments. Last night, you viewed the market as being weak. You developed a game plan to sell the market short around today's high. The next day, however, the market does something unexpected. Instead of failing at the high, it pushes right on through. Immediately, you know your game plan is wrong and you adjust accordingly. Thus, instead of shorting yesterday's high, you look to buy the market as it comes back to test that high. The discipline comes in tracking the market against your game plan however the market acts the next day. We use the game plan as a guidepost and exercise the mental discipline to evaluate the market against it and then take the appropriate action.

Mental discipline also means adhering to our overall trading plan. We want to trade only within the context of the markets, trade setups, money management parameters, and other strictures we have established in our overall trading plan. Traders who find themselves frequently abandoning their plans have a developmental need to improve their mental discipline. The exercise in Chapter 8 together with the SMART goal format described above provides guidance on how to deal with lapses in mental discipline. We discuss this in more detail in the next chapter.

Finally, mental discipline is seen in the *After* time frame by committing to review trades taken and missed, maintaining our trading journal, and, as we will discuss in Chapter 11, assessing our trading performance. Mental discipline is reinforced by keeping good records and committing to a disciplined approach and routine after the trading is over by understanding the value of constructive self-assessment. You can see that mental discipline is more than just adhering to a trading plan. Mental discipline in trading is about maintaining the *Before-During-After* process of High-Quality Preparation, Effective Execution, and Constructive Self-Assessment.

The Daily Mission

One aid to maintaining mental discipline while trading is to prepare a daily mission. This is a concept borrowed from sport psychologist Ken Ravizza. The daily mission is a brief statement about your performance goal for the day.

> Thorsten sometimes hesitated on pulling the trigger on his trades. His trade setups were well-researched and provided a strong edge. At times, however, he didn't like the "look of the market" or had some other vague qualm, and this would cause him not to enter. Of course, the trades he didn't take worked nicely.
>
> He knew he had to take all the trades that met his criteria and not let his doubts keep him from opening a position when they appeared on his screen. Thorsten developed a mission he would follow to help

him enter valid trade setups. His daily mission was stated simply: "Take every trade that meets my plan."

He kept this on a note card at his trading desk. His daily mission reminded him of the high-value action of taking every setup that met his criteria. It also reminded him of how he wanted to act when a trade set up.

The daily mission can be about anything that contributes to your trading. Here are a few examples:

- Take every trade that meets my plan

- Stay focused; no distractions

- Remain patient; let the trade come to me

- Press my winning trades

- Stay aware of the higher time frame

- Scale out and bank profits

- Cut trades that aren't working

Simple and direct.

You can have a daily mission every day. It will give you direction and help you sustain focus and discipline. When used over time, they will help build confidence and reduce stress because they will keep you engaged in the tasks of trading and help keep you on a sustained level of intensity.

When creating a daily mission be sure to focus on your performance and your trading process, not trade results. Make them about things you can control, not things that are outside of your control. Keep them brief and specific, as illustrated above. Make them personal—whatever is important to you. Have just one or two daily missions. Trying to manage more than a couple of missions is likely to be too taxing. Write them down and keep them handy where you can see them. Finally, change them as needed.

The daily mission can be quite powerful when used to support any developmental (SMART) goal you are working on. The trader who develops a SMART goal to improve his trade entries might have a supporting daily mission of "Wait for my entry" to help him refrain from entering prematurely and wait for his trigger. By linking the daily mission to a developmental goal you augment that goal with mental discipline.

Limits of Mental Discipline

Roy Baumeister, social psychologist at Florida State University, and *New York Times* journalist John Tierney conceive of mental discipline, or what they call willpower, as a finite resource, much like a muscle, that becomes exhausted with use. We have but one source of willpower, according to Baumeister, and it is used for all manner of tasks requiring focus, concentration, and self-control. Thus, it can become easily depleted. As willpower becomes expended, our emotions, desires, and cravings are experienced more acutely. As our mental discipline erodes, we become vulnerable to emotion-driven decisions and the erratic trading behavior that follows. Although Baumeister and Tierney do not make this connection, it seems logical that, as mental discipline becomes depleted, room is made for the quick, unstudied, and superficial intuitive mind to move in and take over in decision making. Because it takes energy to engage our deliberative minds, as mental discipline wanes we can become more susceptible to the trading errors caused by cognitive biases and the use of heuristics. It is important, therefore, that we monitor our mental discipline closely and consider stepping away from trades when we feel it slipping.

Baumeister highlights other things that deplete willpower. Stress obviously affects our mental discipline. So do attempts to try and control our emotions and thoughts. We have spent a lot of time discussing the futility of attempting to control thoughts and feelings and embracing the acceptance of all thoughts and feelings, even the difficult ones, as a more effective way to reach goals and to maintain poise and composure even when facing a difficult situation. When we try and control emotions and struggle with them, we can rapidly use up our stores of willpower. This is another good reason to stop the struggle with thoughts and emotions.

Illness and chronic physical pain also diminish mental discipline, as does making numerous decisions. One way to help save your stock of willpower is to have as many decisions as you can already addressed by your trading plan. How you enter a trade, where and how you exit it, the amount you will risk on each trade, and where you set your stops are examples of decisions that can be made in advance. You will preserve less of your mental discipline if, as you are about to take a trade, you are trying to figure out whether you should be entering on the close of a key reversal bar or a break of the high of the last bar and whether or not you should be scaling in or putting on the full position at entry. Decide on your trading mechanics ahead of time and protect your limited storehouse of mental discipline.

Interestingly, mental discipline may be correlated with blood glucose levels. This makes sense because mental activity requires a lot of energy. The body converts the sugars contained in carbohydrates into glucose which supplies fuel to the brain. Neurons in the brain cannot store glucose; they must get it continuously from the bloodstream. If your blood sugar levels drop, you may fall prey to impulsivity and lack of self-control. The straightforward habit of eating a nutritious breakfast before starting the trading day is commonsensical in this regard.

Stanford University health psychologist and expert in willpower Kelly McGonigal notes that when we practice mindfulness meditation the brain gets better not just in meditation but in a wide range of self-control skills. She says that those who practice mindfulness meditation develop their brains over time into "finely tuned willpower machines." Part of the reason for this is that the brain's prefrontal cortex—an important brain region we have discuss earlier—is associated with mental discipline.

In addition to mindfulness meditation, McGonigal notes that physical exercise may just be the "the closest thing to a wonder drug that self control scientists have discovered." We have already discussed how exercise reduces stress, emotional reactivity, and increases our tolerance of discomfort. Exercise also promotes mental discipline. As we exercise over time, the brain experiences positive changes in both grey and white matter, with the prefrontal cortex gaining the most. Research has shown, according to McGonigal, that study participants who exercised three times a week showed improvements in attention and the ability to ignore distractions, reduced addictive behaviors (i.e., reduced tobacco, alcohol, and caffeine intake), ate less junk food, ate more healthy foods, made fewer impulsive purchases, saved more money, and watched less television. All of these behaviors are associated with mental discipline and the only change was in exercise.

Kelly McGonigal describes a paradox concerning willpower with which every trader needs to be aware. It's called *moral licensing*. When we do something we believe to be good, we feel good about ourselves, naturally. But this means we are also more likely to become impulsive next. When we feel good about something positive we have done, it can give us permission to do something bad. As an example, if we feel particularly good about our diligence at work in the morning, we are more likely to slack off in the afternoon.

The key idea here is that we moralize our behavior. When we tell ourselves we are good when we correctly size a position and bad when we oversize it, we are more likely to oversize our next trade if the last trade was sized correctly. It is as if we are licensing our indulgences. The irony, McGonigal says, is that we actually feel in control of our choices and not feel guilty when we indulge ourselves. Instead, we feel as if we are earning a reward. But we are not. This trick of the mind can create self-sabotaging behavior. More than one seasoned trader has noted that significant psychological challenges often arise after a period of exceptional profits. The same can be true after an outsized win. It is more than just becoming complacent. We feel we have earned the right to act a little recklessly, carefree, or bold.

We can do this with goals, too. Making good progress on a goal can give us the license to hold ourselves back from ultimate success. Progress on a goal is motivating, but only when you view that progress as being committed to your goal. In other words, view the progress you are making as evidence that you highly value reaching that goal; you deeply care about that goal. Kelly McGonigal says that this is an important shift in perspective from "I'm good because I'm making good progress" to "I really care about my goal because I am making good progress." The former perspective will give you the psychological license to slack off; the latter perspective will motivate you to work hard to continue to advance toward achievement of your goal. Underlying the helpful perspective is the *why*—the reason you are engaged in the goal. It is helpful to remind yourself why you are working so hard to achieve your goal. This will add to your mental discipline.

The bottom line is that traders need to pay attention to their mental discipline and monitor it. Mindful self-monitoring begets self-control. The more you mindfully monitor yourself and your performance, the better your mental discipline will be. Avoid multitasking, as this disperses our focus and can affect our discipline. Get sufficient sleep and eat well-balanced meals. Avoid sugary drinks or snacks. These will cause glucose to rocket, but just as quickly also cause it to crash. Snack on complex carbohydrates that enter the bloodstream more evenly, such as fruit and raw vegetables during the trading day. Be sure to establish a game plan in advance for the trading day (or week for swing traders). If you skip it or otherwise fail to do it, your mind will naturally be thinking about how the next day is likely to trade and what you should do. Baumeister explains this as the *Zeigarnik effect*—the mind will continue to focus on an uncompleted task and this competes with other mental resources, potentially affecting willpower. The good news is that the effect abates once concrete plans are made. Having a game plan not just prepares you for trading, but helps keep you mentally fresh as well.

This completes our discussion of the first component of Charlie Maher's three-part *Before-During-After* trading process. Table 9.2 summarizes the mental domains (HVMSs) and several of the High-Value Actions encompassed in the *Before* principle of High-Quality Preparation. The next exercise provides a basic set of questions you can ask yourself that are specific to the HVAMS of High-Quality Preparation. When

TABLE 9.2	High-Value Mental Skills and Some High-Value Actions of High-Quality Preparation
Before: High-Quality Preparation	
High-Value Mental Skill	**Examples of High-Value Actions**
Perspective	Write a trading plan
Personal Awareness	Role clarification
Self-Motivation	Practice/simulation trading
Mental Discipline	Research
	Study market behavior
	Identify developmental needs
	Create and work on developmental goals
	Develop a game plan before the trading day or week
	Mentally park distractions
	Daily mission
	Maintain a daily practice of mindfulness
	Locate areas where potential trades may occur in advance
	Commit to and maintain high effort in following the *Before-During-After* trading process

Exercise 9.3 Mental Skills Inventory: High-Quality Preparation

Mental Domain		Rating
Perspective	I maintain a balanced perspective between trading and the other important roles in my life. I am able to mentally park non-trading–related concerns while I am trading.	
	I have a strong understanding of how I trade the markets which is reflected in my written trading plan.	
	I understand and act in concert with the laws of probability in trading, especially the idea that my trading edge will play out over a large number of trades.	
Personal Awareness	I am clear on my strong points and my limitations in the mental, technical, money management, and other important areas of my trading.	
Self-Motivation	I set and achieve goals with respect to my performance and development as a trader.	
	For my current limitations, I have developmental goals framed as SMART goals.	
	I focus on my trading process more than my trading results.	
Mental Discipline	I follow my trading plan, understand how my willpower can be strengthened and depleted, and take steps to preserve and increase my mental discipline.	
	I create a game plan for my trading.	

answering these, be objectively honest in your answers. Rate yourself on each question against a scale of 1 to 6 with 6 representing your performance in that domain at the highest level and superior in all respects; 4 being satisfactory with minor inconsistencies; and below 3 indicating inconsistency and a developmental need. Use these questions to assess your process and performance in the *Before* mental domains of High-Quality Preparation and where you might need to make adjustments. For ratings of 5 or 6, consider these mental strong points and continue to do what you have been doing in this area. Work to reduce inconsistencies for those areas you have rated 3 or 4. Make low ratings of 1 or 2 into developmental goals using the SMART goal framework to begin serious work on the process of High-Quality Preparation!

In the next chapters, we detail the remaining two components of the trading process—*During* and *After*—and their mental domains along with their associated high-value trading activities.

CHAPTER 10

The Trading Psychology Process: Effective Execution

In Chapter 9, we began discussing the process of psychological development and performance enhancement with the *Before-During-After* framework developed by sport psychologist Charlie Maher. We focused on the mental domains (HVMSs) and high-value actions (HVAs) associated with the principle of High-Quality Preparation. These are the main tasks in the *Before* time frame. In this chapter, we discuss the second component of the process, *During*, and the core principle of Effective Execution with its associated HVMSs and HVAs.

Before we get to Effective Execution, however, I want to spend a little time clarifying the process of a trader's psychological development and trading performance enhancement. Although we are discussing each of the three principles (High-Quality Preparation, Effective Execution, and Constructive Self-Assessment) separately, and we do want to keep them logically separate to help differentiate them in our minds, they do have some overlap. Some of the HVAs and especially the HVMSs are utilized in more than one time frame. The skill of mental parking is a good example. We discussed this in High-Quality Preparation as a skill and technique that helps us focus, for instance, on our nightly homework, as we mentally park other distractions such as watching TV or going out to the pub. But the utility of mental parking isn't limited to the *Before* trading activites of preparation. Mental parking is an HVMS that also applies *during* trading in execution. We want to mentally park, for example, a trading loss in the middle of the trading day in order to clear our mind and be able to focus

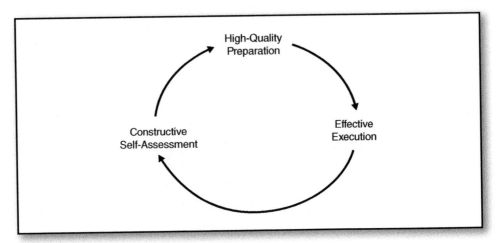

FIGURE 10.1 The Trading Psychology Process

on the next trading opportunity. In this way, what we learn to do well in preparation will flow into the other components of the process and vice versa.

Aside from the overlap, what will be of great use to the trader is to understand how the principles of *Before-During-After* work together. We are discussing each principle separately in order to clarify each of them for you, but it is important to understand how all three principles work together as a process to directly enhance your trading performance. Figure 10.1 illustrates this process.

It should be obvious that the activities of High-Quality Preparation will impact our performance during trading in Effective Execution. For an example, a day trader engages in High-Quality Preparation activities, including developing a game plan for the next trading day. She notes that the market has been trending higher. From her research, she knows that dips in the morning often put in the lows for the day in overall up trending conditions. She develops a game plan to buy a morning pullback if the volume and price action have indicated a minor reaction rather than a market changing into down trending conditions.

Can you imagine how she will trade the next day if what she anticipated in her preparation and game plan unfolds the next morning? She will immediately recognize what is happening, know exactly what to do, and act with confidence at the right time because she was well prepared through her process of High-Quality Preparation. Preparation gives execution a strong edge.

Once the trading day is over, the process-oriented day trader engages in the high-value activities of Constructive Self-Assessment discussed in Chapter 11. Perhaps she learned something new today about the market or maybe something new about her performance. This new information gleaned from reflective observations made post-trading will now influence the way she prepares. Constructive Self-Assessment leads to better preparation, which leads to better execution. This all adds up to better trading performance. Using the process of *Before-During-After* makes the trader's self-improvement systematic and reliable. Let's look at an example provided by Tony, a day trader.

Tony followed the *Before-During-After* process. From his daily Constructive Self-Assessment he learned that many of the trades he made were successful, but he often closed them early. This wasn't related to loss aversion; he wasn't closing trades prematurely due to fear of having a loss. In fact, he held his trades to profit objectives that he set; but many trades ran further than he anticipated. This recurrently caused him to miss profits, sometimes large profits.

Tony set his profit objectives at the next level of resistance or support, which seemed logical as the market often trades between support and resistance. He missed, however, the profits available when the market broke through his targets. As he studied this situation, he realized that sighting targets at support or resistance was generally valid as many trades did, indeed, end there. Those that continued further, however, produced outsized gains. Tony wanted to be a part of those trades that continued. "After all," he reasoned, "I figured out that a good trade existed and I was already in them. I should get paid for their full potential, not just a portion."

Tony recognized he had a developmental need. He set up a SMART goal to address his need. At first, his goal was structured to close only one-half of his position at support or resistance and hold the other half. He did this for the next three trading weeks. His assessment of this goal was not as he desired. He was earning too little on the trades that ended at the support/resistance target because the portion he held for a breakout didn't produce much profit when the breakout failed to occur. He needed to adjust his goal.

Upon further assessment, Tony realized that one of his indicators reliably told him when support or resistance was likely to break. It wasn't perfect, but it gave him the edge he needed. He, thus, revised his goal to hold one-half of his position when his indicator was signaling a breakout was more likely; otherwise he would close his entire position at his intial target. Again, he did this for three weeks. He was pleased with the results. He now had an effective way to address his developmental need. By following the *Before-During-After* process, he elevated his knowledge, skills, and abilities. He made an incremental change to his trading by adjusting an already successful method, and this took him to a new level of profitability.

We recap the process Tony followed next. The corresponding principle (High-Quality Preparation, Effective Execution and Constructive Self-Assessment) is highlighted in parentheses so you can track the process as Tony took action to improve his trading.

Tony identified missed profits when he assessed his trades (CSA). He recognized he could do better and therefore had a developmental need. He created a plan to improve using a SMART goal (HQP). He implemented his SMART goal plan over the next few weeks as he traded (EE). He found the initial results less than desirable (CSA) and revised his plan setting up another SMART goal (HQP). Once again, he implemented his revised plan (EE) and tracked the results. This time, his assessment (CSA) told him that he was achieving his goal.

By following the *Before-During-After* process Tony elevated his trading. Note carefully that this was a process-oriented effort. His primary goal was not to make more profit, but to improve his trade exit strategy. He did use trading results to measure and evaluate the effectiveness of his strategy, but it was his strategy that he looked to improve. He knew that if he could develop a better exit strategy, profits would take care of themselves. By applying the *Before-During-After* process, Tony now has refined his trade exit procedure for greater trading performance, greater profit, and greater personal satisfaction.

Before-During-After is a powerful approach for self-improvement. It encompasses the entire process of trading—both in terms of mental skills and abilities required for trading as well as the high-value actions that demonstrate and reflect excellence and achievement in trading. The process offers those who embrace it a continuous cycle where, through preparation, execution, and assessment, increasing competence and, eventually, excellence and mastery in trading can be realized. The *Before-During-After* process paves a royal road to excellence in trading performance.

During

When we consider the *During* time frame, we are concerned about Effective Execution. The underlying principle of Effective Execution is that a trader will be able to trade most effectively when experiencing constructive psychological states while trading. These advantageous mental states will allow the trader to execute high-value trading actions (HVAs). When a trader is able to both sustain beneficial high-value mental skills (HVMSs) and implement HVAs, that trader is putting herself in the best possible posture to maximize her trading performance. Further, the principle of Effective Execution also asserts that traders can learn the mental skills needed to trade in a capable and dependable manner.

Like High-Quality Preparation, the principle of Effective Execution is composed of key psychological domains or high-value mental skills. These domains or HVMSs are: Self-Confidence, Emotional Intensity, Focus, and Poise. We discuss each of these next.

■ Self-Confidence

Every trader wants self-confidence and every trader seeks to gain more of it. As one trader said after missing a trading opportunity, "If I just had more confidence, I would be trading better. I wouldn't have hesitated in taking that trade." This is a common refrain. So what exactly do we mean when we refer to self-confidence? Like everything in trading psychology, it helps to begin with clarity.

There are two kinds of confidence in trading: external confidence and internal confidence. Externally confident traders base their confidence on things outside of themselves, such as the money they make or the number of winning trades they have. Tying our confidence to external factors, however, can be problematic. For example, a trader is flying high emotionally because he just had a banner day making significantly more money on this day than he did on any day of the past few months. He feels great and his confidence is soaring. In fact, he feels invincible, as if he cannot lose. But this kind of confidence is hollow because it comes from outside the trader. His confidence comes from the amount of money won on an extraordinary day. What will happen the next day if he doesn't make as much money or the day ends in loss? Where will his confidence be then?

When we allow our confidence to be based on things outside of ourselves we subject our confidence to the vagaries of things beyond our control. It's like basing confidence on the weather. It's great when the sun is shining in a bluebird sky, but we feel down when it is overcast, and absolutely terrible when stormy. The prudent trader will not want her confidence to be dictated by unpredictable or eccentric changes. Yet that is exactly what happens when confidence is placed in the hands of things like how much money was made today, how many winning trades we have, whether we are up or down on the day, and other results-oriented numbers and statistics.

When your confidence is tethered to the results of your trading it will rise when results are positive and fall when they are negative. Traders—like any performer— can experience a temporary slump. If your confidence is attached to outcomes, it will make it harder to break out of your sagging performance. Lashing your confidence to money, winning trades and other things not under your control puts you in psychological trouble. You place yourself on an emotional roller coaster that will be thrilling at times when your trades are working, you are making money, and the market is behaving favorably, and harrowing and emotionally distressing when trades are not working or the market is acting unfavorably. With confidence misplaced on external factors you are much more likely to act erratically (e.g., force trades, overtrade, and the like) when things aren't going so well as you try to regain the positive, confident feelings you had when your trading was better. Note once again that you are trading your emotions not the market as you try to recapture confident feelings. But forcing trades, overtrading, and other erratic actions will only serve to further erode self-confidence. Given that there are many trades that don't work out, markets that behave erratically, and many events in the market that seem capricious and unpredictable, it doesn't make sense to base confidence on external factors. Relying on external factors for our confidence is shaky at best.

Internal confidence, on the other hand, is not based on the outcome of your trading results. Internal confidence is process based. It comes from three things you have complete control over: the knowledge you acquire, the skills you develop, and the ability to apply your knowledge and skills in the market. Internal confidence comes from within as a discernment of self-efficacy in your ability to organize yourself and take the necessary actions to trade. The self-confident trader believes that she can competently interact with the market and be successful in her interactions in the *During* time frame. She believes in her ability to see sound trade setups, she has developed the capability to follow through and to act on what she sees. She is able to execute the trade, manage the trade and its associated risk, and exit the trade according to her trading plan. In this way, *self-confidence arises as a sense of mastery in performing the tasks of trading*. A self-confident trader would say with conviction, "I am confident in my trading knowledge, skills, and abilities. I am confident I can trade without making unforced trading errors. I have confidence in my ability to assess the market, select appropriate trades, size the trades properly, control risk, execute and manage those trades, and exit at the proper time."

Self-confident traders are effective traders who do not base their self-confidence on their last trade or how many points or pips they won on a given day. Self-confident traders feel confident on their winning days and they know they were successful because they had the knowledge and skills to trade a favorable market well. But they also feel confident on the days when the market trades narrowly because they are able to say, "I feel good today because I didn't get whipsawed in the narrow range. My knowledge and skills told me this wasn't a great day to trade and I was able to sit on my hands." Self-confident traders do not tie their confidence to what is outside of themselves.

True confidence is based on what matters over the long haul. Remember, trading is all about probabilities. What works over the long term in probabilistic fields of endeavor is developing and adhering to a process which you can control, rather than focusing on results, which cannot be controlled. For traders, fostering confidence has to be based on the process of developing, honing, and applying your trading knowledge, skills, and abilities—both mental and technical, in other words, the *Before-During-After* process. True self-confidence, therefore, is grounded in process not results. In a very real sense, *when you focus on process, you are in control of your self-confidence.*

Building self-confidence requires a mindful approach to your trading. For example, if you end the day down due to several losing trades, there is a mental choice to be made. You can choose to damage your confidence by feeling bad about the loss. Alternatively, you can choose to build your confidence by stepping into your process of *Before-During-After* and working to understand why it happened and how to improve. You can mindfully choose to learn from the experience—even though painful—and work to improve your knowledge, skills, and abilities. By mindfully choosing what is productive and constructive, you will learn to avoid repeating unconstructive behavior in the future. Taking this positive step serves to add to your self-confidence because you are augmenting your trading knowledge, skills, and abilities. The ability to deal with poor results in this way is a mental skill in Constructive Self-Assessment, discussed in the next chapter. For now, it is important to know that the *Before-During-After* process guides us in the development and maintenance of our self-confidence.

True confidence comes from within. Any self-assurance that comes from external factors will always be temporary, unstable, unreliable, unpredictable, and offer only insecurity. This is why traders who link their confidence and self-belief to trading results are always looking for self-confidence. There are many activities you can engage in to develop self-confidence. The practice of mindfulness will help your trading in uncountable ways. The practice of mindfulness helps develop your focus and awareness and helps you engage in value-directed actions that support your trades (e.g., holding a sound trade) by keeping you from succumbing to avoidance behaviors (e.g., cutting a sound trade) that address your internal state and which serve only to undermine confidence. Observation of other traders who perform competently and confidently is a useful exercise. You can lock into their vision and see how they implement it. Watch how they execute and manage a favored trade setup. See how they handle a trade that is failing to produce. How do they handle a loss? How do they handle a win? What can you glean from their expertise that you can use that will also add to your confidence? It helps to see others trade when you know what to look for.

> Early in my trading career I was fortunate to be able to sit with an expert trader and watch him trade. He was highly skilled in reading a chart and executing trades, and he had a healthy self-assurance that was easy to see. He entered a short trade, which quickly turned down. Profit built rapidly. I almost jumped out of my chair with glee. He looked at me with a bemused expression and said, "Why are you so excited? It's only a trade." I realized that he would have reacted the same whether the trade was profitable or not. Although he didn't say it, it was clear that his confidence came from his knowledge, skills, and abilities, not from the profit he made on any given trade.

It is also useful to observe yourself in confident states. This can be any time, not just in trading. Pay particular attention to your self-talk. What does your mind do and say to you when you are confident and how are your emotions? Notice when in a confident state how you handle the task at hand. Are you engaged in the task when you notice yourself in positive, confident states of mind? What about when you are agitated, and not in a confident state of mind. How is your task focus then? Usually, when we are not in a confident state, the mind will be giving us negative self-talk, emotions will run hot, and we will be distracted, focusing on our internal state rather than on the trading task at hand. Use mindfulness skills to help yourself return to task engagement. You will find that if you practice mindfully returning to the task and allowing—not fighting—your thoughts and emotions to be as they are, you will develop a new level of confidence that you hadn't had before. It is a confidence that you can bring yourself back to, a poised and composed state you can experience even in difficult trading situations. We discuss this in more detail shortly.

Rehearsing specific situations is also useful in developing self-confidence. This is different from merely imagining yourself to be a good trader. Broad, vague imagery is unlikely to be helpful. Rehearsing specific situations, in contrast, will add to confidence. For example, let's assume you have identified a potential trade location in well-defined support for the next day's trading. Rehearse what you expect to see as the market comes to that support and triggers the trade. How will price act? What will volume do? How will your indicators respond? See in your mind's eye what you will be looking for as this trade sets up and see how you will act when it sets up well. Then rehearse what the market should do after the trade is entered. Again, how will price, volume, and indicators respond as the trade goes in your direction? If you rehearse this ahead of time and then see it unfold on your charts, you will be more confident in taking and managing this trade. You can also do the same kind of rehearsal when a trade goes against you. Again, what would it look like for a trade to not be working? Rehearse what you will do about that. Be sure to note in your rehearsal what your mind is doing. If you are rehearsing correctly, your mind will be engaged with the trading task. It won't be focused on extraneous thoughts and feelings such as "What if the market suddenly goes against me" or "I can't take a loss." Your mind will be focused on the market, what you anticipate next, and what needs to be done next. Again, confidence is not built by money won but in your knowledge, skills, and abilities to handle different trading situations. This is what is being developed through rehearsal.

Emotional Intensity

Emotional intensity refers to the ability of the trader to trade at a level of emotional energy that is effective for the trader. Everyone will be a little different in this regard. Some may require more energy to trade well, others may require less. You want to be able to recognize when your emotions are too high, too low, or just right to trade. Just as important, you need to be able to make adjustments that help you "psych yourself up" when energy is running too low and tone yourself down when it is running too high.

Some traders come into the trading day with a positive level of emotional energy. They are eager, they feel good about their preparation, and they are ready to trade. Their energy is sustained throughout the morning session and they trade well. The afternoon, however, is a different story. Energy drains, trading becomes prone to errors, and money made in the morning can be given back in the afternoon. Notice that the traders' skill set hasn't changed, but their energy level has changed. Being strong in the morning but drained in the afternoon is common with many traders. Others can be just the opposite. The mornings are experienced with flagging energy but something turns on in the afternoon. Once the lunch period is over, these traders become energized and alert and carry their trading throughout the afternoon and into the end of the day.

The key idea is to know when your energy level wanes, when it is at an effective level for trading, and also when it is too strong. This requires that you monitor your emotional energy. Identify those periods when emotions are productive and when they are not productive for you. You may find that they coincide with specific periods of the trading day, as described above, or you may find emotional energy tied to specific actions or events. You may, for example, become bored when the market is trading sideways and feel your energy drop. Conversely, you may become overly excited when about to take a trade or when in a trade. Whatever the case may be, begin to pay attention to your emotional energy level and how it varies.

Be sure to pinpoint differences in thoughts and feelings when monitoring emotional intensity. Often, your self-talk (thoughts) will affect your emotions and energy. Note your self-talk when a trade is coming up. Are you hearing yourself say, "There's a great trade setting up," and feeling more alert and a bit excited? This is positive intensity reflecting confidence. On the other hand, if the market is in a narrow range and you feel your emotional intensity has drained, be wary of making "boredom trades" that try to change the sideways trading situation. It is as if you are trying to get the market to move and get some excitement going, which, of course, won't happen. The idea here is that our energy level can directly influence how we act. Note once again that unwarranted actions are addressing the trader's internal state, not market conditions. If the market suddenly takes off and our emotional energy soars with the market, we may be subject to jumping into an unplanned trade. Similarly, if the market is pushing strongly in one direction and we are in a trade, excitement can run high and cause us to miss the exit, holding on because we feel the market is going to "run forever." When energy is low we may miss trades, and if in a trade and we become agitated and overexcited, it may feel overpowering and we exit prematurely. Being aware of our level of emotional intensity, how it can affect our trading, and using the mindfulness and defusion techniques we have learned can help us to keep our energy at a constructive level.

Traders can also use rehearsal to create individual scenarios for preparing to trade and for actual trading with effective emotional intensity. As we discussed regarding self-confidence, rehearsal has you visualize what you expect to see and how you will act in advance in taking and managing trades. In addition to rehearsing your actions, rehearse what you say to yourself, and what energy level you want to experience. This will help you be aware of and adjust your emotional energy to a beneficial level. One rehearsal scenario, for example, would involve a sideways market that suddenly starts to move. Rather than feel your emotional energy levels become swept up in the market excitement, a trader might rehearse patience and waiting for a confirming pullback, seeing in advance how price, volume, and indicators would be expected to act, along with using calming techniques (discussed below under poise and composure) to keep emotional intensity on an even keel. Virtually any trading situation that affects emotional intensity can be rehearsed in this way. It is a form of exposure which, as discussed earlier, is a powerful technique.

Developing routines is another excellent way to manage emotional intensity. Mental parking is a technique the reader is already familiar with from previous discussion. Having a routine to mentally park trading losses or errors you make during the course of trading will help you maintain your psychological balance while trading. We do not want to sweep errors or losses under the rug, but during the middle of trading is not the time to deal with them. We will want to wait until after trading is over to address losses and errors and mental parking is an excellent way to do this.

In mentally parking errors and losses, we are taking a page directly out of sport psychology and applying it to trading. Athletes use mental parking as a foundational technique for mental focus and energy management during play. A tennis player, for example, hits an errant shot and loses the point. You will often see her pick up an extra tennis ball after the point is over, look intently at it mentally placing the error into the ball, and then hit the ball off into the opposite court. She is mentally parking her error. You might see a baseball pitcher grind his foot into the dirt after throwing a poor pitch. He is parking the miss-thrown ball. A basketball player might be seen wiping his hand across the leg of his shorts wiping away an error. The physical action of mental parking is useful as it tells the mind to set the mistake aside for now and return our focus to what's important at that moment. The error is best dealt with later, after trading is over. That is the proper time to carefully and objectively review what happened and learn from it. During trading is not the time for this.

Traders can mentally park a mistake or a loss by taking a moment to write it down in their journal. The physical action of writing it down is just like the tennis player mentally placing the error onto a tennis ball. We then close the cover on our notebook and signal the mind that it is time to return to the market and our trading, not dwell on the loss or mistake. Because we have written it down, the error will be there for us to review after trading is over. Mental parking is a useful psychological tool for traders.

Another routine traders can use to support their trading is getting ready for a trade. Again, we borrow from sport. We see athletes get ready for the next ball all the time. A baseball batter will take a few practice swings before stepping into the batter's box and, once in the box, he will set his feet and take a slow swing or two just before the next ball is pitched. This is the batter's 'get ready.' Outfielders will lean forward, assume an athletic stance, and hold their hands out in front of their body in anticipation of the ball being hit so they can spring into action immediately if the ball is hit near their field. A tennis player about to serve will bounce the ball a few times as they ready themselves to make a serve and the receiver will assume an athletic stance and take a small hop known as the split step just as the server hits the ball to ready themselves to return the serve. Getting ready puts the athlete's mind and body in sync with the game and gives them an edge in making the next play.

A trader can get ready by planting both feet squarely on the floor and leaning forward in their chair. Some traders like to wear a hat while trading and this could be put on as a part of the get ready. An alternative is to adjust your glasses, take hold of the computer mouse, and bring up your order entry window ready to place an order. If you have a daily mission related to entry or managing trades, now is a good time to remind yourself about what your mission is for today by stating your mission either silently or out loud, for example, "Patience. Let the trade come to me." Done as a routine, this series of actions helps you mentally prepare for taking the trade, putting your body and mind on alert that you want their complete focus and attention.

Focus of Attention

Focus is a huge part of trading. When we think of focus in trading we are talking about the extent to which we are paying attention to the factors that matter in trading. These include the high-value actions of trade identification and selection, trade entry and management, and trade exit. How good are we at maintaining our focus? How good are we at staying on task? Of course, everyone loses their focus some of the time. We can never stay 100% focused for lengthy periods of time. Accepting this very human fact, we then want to know how good we are at detecting that we have lost focus and how good we are we at getting it back. Lacking these mental skills will lead the trader to being vulnerable to distractions. When distracted—especially by mental chatter—our performance, and, therefore, our trading, will definitely suffer.

Charlie Maher identifies several factors that can influence what he calls our "competitive focus." As we review these influential factors, see how you might become distracted and lose your focus when challenged by these factors. Use the form in Exercise 10.1 to write down when you are most vulnerable to losing focus. Being aware of what and when you are likely to become distracted is the first step in better focus.

The immediate performance situation can certainly affect our focus. We might be down on the day and feel pressure to make up for losses and get positive on the day. Or it might be missing the last trade which would have resulted in outsized gains. We may be kicking ourselves for missing the trade and now look anxiously to compensate for the missed profits. In both cases, we are focused on something other than

Exercise 10.1 Factors That Affect My Focus

Factors	My Personal Examples			
	Example 1	Example 2	Example 3	Example 4
Market and performance situations	*Dull, narrow range days. It is hard to sit and do nothing. I check e-mail or surf the web and wind up missing trades. Often, I look at markets I don't trade to see if one is moving. I am anxious to get in. I usually don't trade that well.*			
Location of my thoughts in past or future	*I am looking for the big win. I see trades running much farther than they usually do. I can almost see it in my mind, so it seems real, but it's a future projection, not reality.*			
People, places, and things	*In chat rooms I want to show others that I'm a good trader. This can keep me from closing a trade when I should. I don't want to have a losing trade in front of my friends.*			

what we need to be focused on. There are a lot of trading situations that can trigger distractions. Even positive trading situations can challenge our focus. Some traders, for example, find maintaining focus difficult when in a profitable trade as their attention can be drawn into an internal debate about whether or not to close the trade rather than keeping their concentration on how price is moving. Market conditions can also affect our focus. Narrow range trading often sees traders surfing the net out of boredom and missing the moment when the market breaks out of its range-bound activity into a trending move. High volatility can also affect focus. We see over and over that news and scheduled reports trigger high volatility, excessive movement, and high trading activity. Many traders lose focus in these situations.

The location of our thoughts and feelings is another aspect of distraction. It is always how we perceive a situation that will determine how we respond. We measure our perception by what we tell ourselves about it and how we feel. A straightforward way to track our thoughts and feelings is by recognizing whether they are in the past, in the future, or focused on the present. If we are stuck in the past—perhaps a loss or even the last market movement, we are missing what is happening now. Thoughts and their associated feelings about the past are a distraction to sound trading performance during trading. The same is true for projections about the future. A trader may believe that his trade will unfold in a certain, imagined way, and this affects his trade management. The location of our thoughts and feelings needs to be in the present moment for effective trading. When in the past or the future, we are not in contact with what is actually happening presently in the market and our trade. We create a mental map of the past or the future and then attempt to fit it to the present terrain. It is far better to maintain contact with the present moment and the present reality as best we can. Mindfulness helps the trader stay focused and in touch with the present.

There will always be noise. We will have mental chatter about the two losses in a row we just had or concerns about the potential for a future loss in a trade about to be taken. Our minds will naturally dip back into the past and fast forward into the future. The key question for the trader to ask, however, is this: Can I develop the mindfulness skills to recognize when I am distracted and bring my focus back to the trading task at hand in the present moment, as needed, or do I allow my mind and feelings to hijack me into the past or into the future?

Other distracters include people, places, and things, which can occur within or outside of trading. Examples of things that are distracting might involve a new indicator you have just purchased and, instead of studying it outside of market hours (a High-Quality Preparation activity), you install it on your charts and use it during trading. Uncooperative software and internet connectivity can be a distraction, as can visits to favored websites when the market turns dull. All of these *things* are distracters. They steal your focus and diminish your trading performance. An obvious place that causes a distraction is the pub for some traders. It can take away the focus on review and preparation for the next day's trading. Chat rooms can be another distracting place. Many traders find themselves chatting rather than focusing on their markets and their trading.

People can also be distracting. An argument with a spouse or partner can carry over into the trading day. Mental parking is a high-value skill that will help bring focus back to trading tasks. Aaron had this experience when trading one of the currency futures markets while with friends on vacation:

> Aaron had gone to Australia with friends for a much needed vacation. He brought his trading computer to keep on top of the markets and perhaps make a trade or two in the Australian Dollar—a market he rarely traded due to the low trading activity when he normally traded in a distant time zone. Soon after arriving in Australia, he placed a trade. His friends—none of whom were traders—were naturally curious. Later that day when Aaron's trade had a few hundred dollars in profit, one of his friends said, you should take your profits before going to bed. The next day, when the trade was in the money by a few thousand dollars, his friends were excited talking about the money made and joking about how Aaron could now take them all out for dinner. This put Aaron under pressure. "I was really distracted," he said. Aaron said that

his mind was thinking, "If I take this trade off now, I'll be a hero in my friends' eyes." This was difficult for him because there was no reason to take the trade off. "I had to fight hard not to close the trade. This wasn't my process. My process was to let the trade run until there was a reason to take it off. I hadn't seen that yet."

In Aaron's case, both the situation and the people were distractions. He was also projecting himself into the future. "If I took the trade off, it would be profitable. I'd impress my friends. I could see myself taking them out to dinner. This stroked my ego, and I liked that." Aaron had distracting demands on his trading coming from his friends and the way in which he perceived the situation. None of these were relevant to his trade. His loss of focus on what mattered to his trade—his process— could easily disrupt his trade and undermine his performance.

You can learn to trade mindfully and keep your focus on the appropriate trading task. The basic elements of the mindfulness practice examples described throughout this book can be brought to bear in helping yourself keep your focus on what's important. Sport psychologist Charlie Maher has a step-by-step "Mind in the Moment" tactic you can use any time you feel your focus sliding down the slippery slope of distraction.[1] Here is my adaptation of the Mind in the Moment technique:

1. Be sure you know and understand the current trading task. It might simply be monitoring the market for a trade opportunity. The trader's current task might also be trade selection, position sizing, trade entry, setting a stop, managing the trade once entered, scaling out, trade exit, or other tasks relevant to the current market or trade situation.

2. Recognize when the mind has slipped off the trading task and onto an irrelevancy. A feeling (e.g., anger, anxiety, sadness, joy, etc.) or bodily sensation (e.g., tension, sweatiness, queasy stomach, etc.) may be more noticeable. Scan your feeling state and body and notice any shift in feelings as a signal that you may have lost focus. After detecting a change, observe what your mind might be telling you. This is the basic mindfulness skill you have been practicing. Remember, your thoughts are merely thoughts and feelings just feelings. They come and go and are not commands that you must obey.

3. Bring yourself momentarily into a neutral state. This takes a little effort and can be aided by changing your physical position. If you are sitting down, stand up and stretch. If you have time, take a short walk or go get a glass of water. Take yourself out of the distracted state and into a neutral state.

4. Use a key phrase such as "Back on task" or "Get back to the trade." Something short and to the point that will help to remind you to refocus your attention onto what is important.

5. Execute the trading task at hand.

Sometimes distractions, and especially our mental chatter, make it difficult to refocus. We need to do more. This brings us to *poise*.

■ Poise

We use the definition of poise from sport and human performance psychologists Frank Gardner and Zella Moore: the trader's ability to act in accordance with their goals and values, despite unpleasant feelings, thoughts, and sensations. In other words, to do what matters most for the trade and for yourself as a trader, even though emotions and bodily sensations may be uncomfortable and your mind is telling you to do otherwise. The illustration that comes easiest to mind is the experience of loss aversion while in a winning trade. The trade is in profit and you know it has more to run, but your mind and body are fearful of a loss and are urging you to exit the trade with a small profit. Exhibiting poise, the trader in this situation would acknowledge the uncomfortable thoughts and feelings and act in the service of the trade (and himself as a trader) by remembering that his internal state is fleeting and not a reflection of reality, and what matters is to be consistent in his execution and hold the trade to the planned exit.

Another way to think about poise is composure. We want to remain composed when in the heat of trading and not allow the mental and emotional chatter that naturally emerges in challenging situations to derail us in our pursuit of what matters. We can use the terms poise and composure interchangeably. Poise and composure are closely related to focus. In fact, whenever we lose our focus, it is a key indication that we can be about to lose our composure. When we lose focus we become vulnerable to cognitive biases and errors. We also become vulnerable to an emotional hijacking. Whenever emotions are allowed to take over (meaning we allow our attention to be drawn to our internal state), we become subject to erratic trading behavior and poor trading performance. This relationship is depicted in Figure 10.2

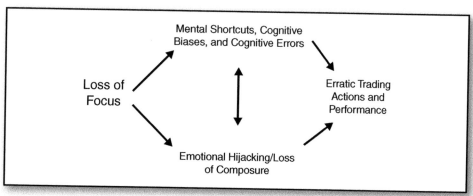

FIGURE 10.2 Focus, Cognitive Bias, Composure, and Trading Performance

Losing poise or composure is likely the biggest trading psychology challenge for traders in the *During* time frame. It has a direct and immediate effect on trading performance and therefore trading results. It can also render traders disconsolate and feeling miserable about their performance and even themselves. To be able to maintain poise and composure, it is vital that traders recognize what it is like to be in a poised state while trading, know what trading situations are most likely to provoke a loss of focus and an emotional hijacking, have a psychological routine to aid in coping with these demanding trading situations, and have a procedure to regain one's poise once it is lost.

Make sure that you know what it is like when you are trading in a poised state of mind. You will likely find that you are *responding* to the market or a situation rather than *reacting* to it. There is a difference. When poised, we are engaged in the situation and guided by our values and what is important to us as a trader. We are able to pause to consider the situation and look for the best option. We may feel uncomfortable, but we are mindful and know that our discomfort is only temporary and how we act in this situation is far more important than how we feel. When poised, we tend to act with integrity toward our values and goals and not just give in to emotion-driven demands. Because of this, our outcomes are more likely to be positive, though that is not our focus. In contrast, when we are reacting we typically perceive that we are at a disadvantage, feel compelled to act, and have no other viable choices available to us. We are defensive and guided by emotions and self-talk. When we merely react, a challenging situation often turns negative.

Identifying the kinds of trading situations that bring about a loss of focus and prompt an emotional hijacking is critical for the trader operating in today's challenging markets. As we have discussed previously with regard to fear, knowing the situations and the tell-tale signs that you are losing focus and are vulnerable to a loss of composure can help keep you one step ahead of the mental game. If you know the specific signs and symptoms that you are about to lose composure, you can take immediate and direct countermeasures and bring yourself back to a focused and poised state of mind. Exercises in previous chapters help the trader identify challenging situations and their psychological components. You can also use your journal to identify those times and trading situations that are particularly challenging for you and can cause a mental hijacking. Briefly note the situation and the usual consequences that occur when you face the taxing situation. Think carefully about what your mind tells you and how your emotions react. Also write down bodily sensations that reflect tension, fear, anger, or other hot emotions. Note if there is any progression in your thoughts and feelings. Do they start out comparatively mild and then grow to more unrestrained levels? You want to know this because you are in a better position to handle them and respond more effectively if you can recognize them early when they are mild than later when they are going full force.

One effective routine for maintaining poise when facing challenging situations involves a series of five mental steps designed to help remind you that you always have a choice to respond rather than react and to open up your options in responding. This will give you greater psychological flexibility than a maladroit, rigid reaction driven by emotions:

1. **What's important?** Recall your values and consider how the current situation and especially how you are about to respond fits into what matters for you as a trader and for the given trade.

2. **What are my choices?** Consider your options. What is the best decision you can make for this trade right now? Consider what HVA is most appropriate for the trade at this moment

3. **Can I accept my feelings?** Make room for your emotions; don't try to squelch them. At the same time, allow facts and critical thinking to emerge. Engage your deliberative mind.

4. **Can I respond, not react?** Ask yourself: *Am I simply reacting or am I responding to this challenging situation?* Are you simply reacting because it's the easy choice or to address discomfort, or are you responding based on the best choice available to you? Often, traders are able to boil down this mental routine to this one fundamental question.

5. **How will I feel later?** If you are inclined to merely react, think about how you will feel when the situation has past. How will you feel if instead of reacting, you respond in a way that is congruent with what is the best option for the trade or situation and the best option for you as a trader?

It helps to have more than one way of coping with difficult trading situations. Here is another routine that is effective for maintaining poise when facing challenging situations. It involves a series of mental steps designed to help remind you that you always have a choice to respond rather than react. This helps to open up the options you have in responding to challenging trading situations. We call this the Mindful S.T.O.P.[2] It was created by Australian mindfulness expert Russ Harris who we met earlier. I've adapted it for traders. This brief mental routine is grounded in mindfulness and will help give you greater psychological flexibility than a rigid reaction driven by emotions. You can write this brief mental routine down as a checklist and keep it on your trading desk. After you practice it several times, it can become a natural part of your trading. Here is my adaptation of Russ Harris's Mindful STOP:

S – Slow down. Take a deep breath and slow down your breathing. For just a moment or two, bring your awareness to your breathe and consciously slow down your breathing. You can even say to yourself in a quiet, silent voice, "Slow down."

T – Take Note. Notice what your mind is saying to you. Notice also any feelings you have and how they seem to reinforce your thoughts. No fighting with thoughts and feelings (i.e., don't feed the baby tiger), just notice them.

O – Open up. Make room for all your thoughts and feelings as we have discussed previously. They are just thoughts and feelings, nothing more. Allow them to exist and use any defusion skill you like from Chapter 7.

P – Pursue High-Value Actions. You have a choice in how you respond. Rather than reacting, choose to affirmatively respond with the HVA that is the best option for the trade or situation and also the best option for you as a trader.

Sometimes, even the most mentally skilled traders will lose their poise. Here is a quick and effective routine developed by sport psychologist Charlie Maher to bring yourself back when on the verge of losing composure.[3] Keep in mind this will be most effective if you recognize you are losing your poise in the early stages, though it is also helpful when composure has been lost. Below is my adaptation of Maher's composure routine:

Ask yourself these three questions:

1. How is my **breathing**? Typically, when a person is on the threshold of losing composure, breathing will be shallow, high in the chest, and rapid. We want to slow it down and breathe deeply. This will help activate the *parasympathetic nervous system*, which will dampen tension and anxiety arising from the flight-fight response (see Chapter 2) and help calm you down.

   Instructors at the Kripalu Center for Yoga and Health in Western Massachusetts teach a very effective breathing technique to bring about rapid calmness. It is called *Dirgha Pranyama*, which means three-part rhythmic breathing. Here is how you do it. Part 1: breathe deep into the belly and fill the lower lungs. Part 2: continuing with the same breath, fill the lungs and feel your ribcage expand. Part 3: top off the lungs with the last bit of breath and feel your upper chest swell slightly. Breathe slowly and smoothly on a slow count of three, pause for a moment or two, and then exhale slowly and smoothly in reverse order emptying the top, middle, and lower lungs. Repeat this a few times and you will notice yourself quickly reducing tension and becoming calmer. Practice will strengthen the effect.

2. How **anxious** am I? This is most easily felt in body tension. Do a quick scan of the areas where you personally experience tension, such as the neck, shoulders, hands, and legs. You can physically *shake off* the tension or mindfully breathe into the tension as a direct means to release any physical tightness.

3. What is my **mind** saying? Most likely it will be telling you about the past or the future. Activate a mindful, observing stance, make room for all thoughts, and bring your awareness and focus back into the present moment.

You can use the acronym BAM to help you remember this short routine: **B**reathing, **A**nxious, **M**ind. If you have actually lost your poise, you may need to step away from your trading station, take a break, and conduct this routine for a few minutes until composure has returned.

Traders who want a psychological edge during trading and trade with a poised, self-confident focus can spend time practicing mindfulness, mental parking, the three-part rhythmic breathing, progressive relaxation of body tension, rehearsal of challenging situations, using key phrases such as "focus on the task at hand" as real-time reminders of what matters, and developing SMART goals in these areas. If persistent loss of composure is experienced, then the trader is encouraged to review Chapter 8 and apply the methods discussed in that chapter to deal with strong emotions and difficult trading situations. They may also benefit from getting focused assistance from a qualified trading psychologist.

Table 10.1 summarizes the mental skills in Effective Execution and some of the associated HVAs. As we have done in Chapter 9, an inventory of the key elements of Effective Execution is provided. This is found in Exercise 10.2. You can rate yourself on each of the high-value mental skills. Use the rating scale of 1 to 6 with 6 representing your performance in that HVMS to be at the highest level and superior in all respects; 4 being satisfactory with minor inconsistencies; and below 3 indicating inconsistency and a significant developmental need. Consider ratings of 5 to 6 to be mental strong points. You can confidently continue to do what you have been doing in this area. Work to reduce inconsistencies for those areas you have rated 3 to 4. Make low ratings of 1 or 2 into developmental goals using the SMART goal framework and begin the necessary corrective work.

TABLE 10.1	High-Value Mental Skills and Some High-Value Actions of Effective Execution
	During: Effective Execution
High-Value Mental Skills	**Examples of High-Value Actions**
Self-Confidence	Identification and selection of choice trade setups
Emotional Intensity	Sound trade entry, protection, management, and exit techniques
Focus	Observing other traders
Poise	Rehearsal
	Mental parking
	Mindfulness and defusion
	Being clear on current trading task
	Daily mission
	Mindful S.T.O.P.
	Mind in the Moment tactic
	Use checklists and routines to center yourself
	Breathing-Anxious-Mind routine

Exercise 10.2 Mental Skills Inventory—Effective Execution

Mental Domain		Rating
Self-Confidence	I believe in and trust my abilities in interacting effectively with the markets, especially executing, managing, and exiting my trades. I am clear about the things that I can control. I focus on these and not on things that are not within my control.	
Emotional Intensity	I trade with an effective level of energy and emotional intensity. I monitor my energy and emotional intensity while trading and make adjustments as needed.	
Focus	I maintain effective focus on the trading task at hand. I know the factors that can be distracting and use mindfulness routines when I am vulnerable to distractions. I focus on process rather than results.	
Poise	I remain poised while trading, even in challenging situations. I can recognize when I am vulnerable to losing composure and take the necessary steps before losing it.	

■ Notes

1. Charlie Maher, *Sport Psychology Resource Guide: Building Performers through Programs, Services, and Systems* (Unpublished manuscript, 2003).

2. Russ Harris, "The Art of a Mindful S.T.O.P.," Happiness Trap Newsletter, October, 2013, accessed July 8, 2014, http://contextualscience.org/post/the_art_of_a_mindful_stop.

3. Charlie Maher, *Sport Psychology Resource Guide: Building Performers through Programs, Services, and Systems* (Unpublished manuscript, 2003).

CHAPTER 11

The Trading Psychology Process: Constructive Self-Assessment

251

Jenna traded the popular commodities, including Crude Oil and Gold futures. She had developed good technical skills and was a net profitable trader. Although enjoying success and profits, Jenna could be a better trader than her results reflected. What held her back was that she did not know that she frequently committed similar errors. For example, Jenna liked to test her reflexes at the beginning of the trading day by putting on an aggressive trade to see how she and the market responded. Being aggressive, these trades often went against her. At times, the market went swiftly through her mental stop. When this occurred, she froze and took a much greater loss than anticipated. This would adversely affect her trading the rest of the morning, making her much more cautious.

Like many traders, at the end of the day Jenna recorded her trades. She never made more than a cursory review of her trades or her performance for that day, however. Therefore, she was blind to the fact that she was making the same errors over and over again. Not only was she committing trading errors described above, she was also committing an error with respect to process.

W hat was missing in Jenna's process was Constructive Self-Assessment. Without this critical procedure, which includes a review of her trading performance, she kept herself in the dark—she didn't realize she was making the same errors. Without knowing why, Jenna was stuck and unable to move her trading to the next level.

Constructive Self-Assessment is a critical step in the trading process, which occurs in the *After* time frame of Charlie Maher's human performance framework we have been discussing in the last two chapters. It is after trading has concluded that we evaluate our trading performance and our trades.

As we discussed earlier, trading is a performance-based activity. To get good at trading, traders need to engage in a trading process that includes an assessment component to promote personal development and continuous improvement. However, such a trading process has not previously been defined and there are no systematic guidelines for traders to follow. Most traders are left to themselves to find ways to learn and improve their trading performance. Unlike athletes who work closely with coaches, or corporate execs and other professionals who enjoy mentorships and developmental training, the majority of traders do not receive structured guidance. Most have no trainers, mentors, or coaches. Traders are left on their own to coach themselves. This is one compelling reason why a trader's process should include self-assessment.

To achieve excellence and mastery in trading, traders not only need to systematically review and evaluate their performance and trading results, they also need to conduct those reviews in an honest and objective manner. Constructive Self-Assessment grounds traders in enacting focused, truthful, and open-minded reviews about how they traded and performed. Constructive Self-Assessment also encompasses the key mental skills traders need to help keep themselves on an upward path of self-improvement and self-development.

It is not easy, however, for everyone to conduct an honest, open-minded self-assessment. Our natural inclinations can work against us when it comes to honest self-assessment. As human beings, we like to see ourselves in a favorable light. This is such a strong trait that it can be hard to be truthful and objective about ourselves and our performance. Assessing ourselves in an impartial way that uncovers our limitations and performance flaws does not come naturally. For many of us, our ego would prefer to neglect our shortcomings. We think of evaluation as judgment and criticism, which is usually associated with disapproval and admonishment. As with many things in trading, we have to go against our natural inclinations if we want to advance. This becomes difficult psychologically, however, because in trading there are a lot of failed trades along with human errors: misreading of the charts, misinterpretation of the markets, and sometimes unforced and unskilled actions. In other words, frequent adversity is the norm. It is tough on the ego to confront this.

Our ego doesn't like to be challenged and uncovering our limitations and performance flaws challenges and threatens our egos. In this regard, it is helpful to view constructive self-assessment as the *high-value pursuit of self-advancement* rather than a search for inadequacies and flaws. It is also helpful to understand how our ego can work against our better interests when even mildly challenged. To illustrate how entrenched our ego can be and the problems it can cause, psychologists Liqing Zhang and Roy Baumeister (Roy Baumeister being the same psychologist we met earlier when discussing mental discipline and willpower) undertook a series of studies where participants' egos were mildly challenged. After filling out assessment inventories, one-half of the participants were subject to a mild threat to their ego. This varied by study. In some of the studies, participants were advised that "if you are the kind of person who chokes under pressure or don't think you have what it takes to win the money, then you might want to play it safe. But it's up to you." In other studies, some of the participants were given a very difficult creativity test on which it was impossible to score well, and then given feedback on their poor performance. The feedback set them up psychologically as a mild threat to their ego. All participants then engaged in various activities where the influence of a threatened ego on their comportment could be assessed. These activities included investing, puzzle completion, and auction bidding.

Zhang and Baumeister found that when people's egos were threatened, they became consistently entangled in losing endeavors. When people felt their self-image was in jeopardy, their decision making took a distinct turn for the worse and their performance as well as their outcomes suffered. When the researchers suggested to some persons that they might choke under pressure, those participants invested and lost greater amounts of money compared to participants who were not told they might choke. Those who were given negative feedback on a creativity test subsequently spent and lost more money in an auction, bidding significantly more than the actual value of items, indicating that an irrelevant ego threat (results on a creativity test have nothing to do with skillful bidding in an auction) engages the ego in an all out effort to win as a way to soothe a wounded self-image, despite negative consequences. Entrapment occurred for activities based on luck and chance, skill and ability, and interpersonal competition. Gender, personality traits, and mood states had little bearing on whether or not people felt their sense of self was threatened and their performances compromised. Those in the study who did not have their ego mildly challenged showed the opposite. They performed well.

The egoistic drive to protect our favorable view of ourselves can be so great that we can go well beyond avoiding a hard look at the poor decisions that we made. There is substantial research showing that people whose decisions turn sour tend to commit more resources to the failing endeavor. This is known as *escalation of a losing commitment*. "Throwing good money after bad" can be seen in the trader who takes a long position in a market, sees the market go against her trade, and begins to "average down" the trade's basis by adding additional capital at lower prices. Each additional commitment extends the risk. The decision to add to the losing trade is made not because the trade is a good one—it's underwater, but for other reasons. These reasons are primarily psychological, and there are several to consider, according to

Theresa Kelly and Katherine Milkman at the University of Pennsylvania's Wharton School. Escalating one's commitment in the face of a failing trade can occur because the trader attempts to avoid a loss. This is a behavioral expression of loss aversion, which we discussed in Chapter 2. It can also occur due to confirmation bias. Once people make a commitment, they are more likely to notice and respond to information that supports their decision and underweight contrary information. In the case of averaging down a losing trade, a trader may discount the fact that the market has fallen and at the same time be convinced that the market remains bullish because it hasn't fallen too far.

Kelly and Milkman note that self-justification can play a large role in commitment escalations. A trade that is failing can be hard to acknowledge when there is a strong desire on the part of the trader to see herself as skilled and competent. It creates an internal conflict between what is believed about the self and what is represented by the trader's behavior. A failing trade conflicts with one's identity as a skillful trader. One way to remove this conflict is to add to the failing trade, convinced that once it turns around, it will prove the original trade idea was valid and the trader competent and skillful. Being right is more important than being objective. This is also true in *impression management*, another psychological need that interferes with sound trading performance. When a trader feels the need to maintain a favorable impression with peers while in a losing trade, she may escalate her trade commitment as a way to justify the trade and circumvent any doubts others may have about her. Traders become especially vulnerable to impression management in online chat rooms, trading forums, and trading in a public setting. There has been more than one trading educator taking live trades before an audience that have resulted in averaging down, significant overcommitment, and substantial losses due to the need to manage one's impression on others in an attempt to protect the ego, rather than execute sound trade management.

It is difficult for us to set aside our ego, but we must if we are going to create the mental space within which we can address our shortcomings and maximize our trading skills and abilities. The trader's objective is to make money and this is best done by following a process in a rational, mindful way that leads to actions that are performed in the interest of the trade. By now, readers know, however, that a trader's choices can be strikingly influenced by other, less rational motives. This includes actions taken not in the service of trades, but to defend one's ego and one's self-esteem. Avoiding a review of one's trading performance and trade results may be a choice made to protect one's ego. Traders need to develop the ability to defuse from their egos to improve their trading results and to stimulate personal growth. Engaging in the process of Constructive Self-Assessment and reviewing one's performance is an excellent way to start. We will discuss the high-value mental skills that are a part of Constructive Self-Assessment, including Self-Esteem, Personal Accountability, Perseverance, and Continuous Improvement.

■ Self-Esteem

Self-esteem is an important mental domain within the context of Constructive Self-Assessment. Sport psychologist Charlie Maher refers to healthy self-esteem as being positive and humble about oneself no matter what the performance. This means that on a really good day when many points or pips were won and money was made, the trader remains humble and accepts the good day as a gift of good fortune rather than bragging about it, getting a big head about it, or believing one is invincible and somehow special because of the fortuitous performance. Conversely, if the trading day or week turns out to be poor, the mentally skilled trader does not get down in the dumps or try to hide from the world. We discussed how external factors can influence our outlook in the last chapter when talking about self-confidence. Those same considerations apply to self-esteem. Both the good day and the bad day are only a small part of the hundreds of trading days in a year and the thousands of trading days over a career. We never want to put much emphasis on any given day, either up or down.

The same holds true for individual trades. A day trader may make an average of three trades a day. Many will make more than this and some less, but for this discussion we will assume three trades per day. With approximately 250 trading days a year, the day trader in this example is making about 750 trades over the course of a year's worth of trading. One trade out of 750 has little significance. It has even less significance when viewed against the 22,500 trades one makes during a 30-year career averaging three trades a day. If you hang your self-worth on any given trade or any given trading day, you are in psychological trouble. You have lost perspective. The numbers help you see this.

Traders run the risk of self-disapproval and even self-scorn when they fail to pay attention to self-esteem. For many, the self-critic enthusiastically emerges when we lose perspective on losing trades and trading days that are less than optimal. We might hear our internal critic say things like "You'll never be a good trader" or "How stupid can you be. You ought to just give up trading." It becomes easy to fuse with what the self-critic is saying in our heads. We feel bad and believe it wholeheartedly. The self-critic can dish out quite toxic commentary that we would never think of saying to another person, yet we buy into it hook, line, and sinker. This, of course, is fusion. We uncritically consent to the negative evaluations and condemnations. Such unbridled criticisms make us feel worse and send our self-esteem plummeting deep into the abyss when we fuse with them. As we have talked about throughout this book, the bad feelings and toxic mental chatter encourage us to then avoid acting upon what is important to us because we fear that approaching what is important will cause further discomfort. We may, for example, stop assessing what might have caused the losing day, because we already feel down and want to avoid feeling worse. Not facing the situation, however, does us a great disservice. We can't learn from mistakes if we are unwilling to confront them.

When we are assessing our trades and trading performance, it is best to pay less attention to the results and much more to the process involved in the decisions made. Evaluate your process. Did you make sound decisions fitting the trading situation? Did you behave as you want to behave as a trader, or were you making careless or emotion-driven decisions intended to relieve yourself of some unpleasant feeling or distressing thought? Addressing these key questions about your decision-making and the trading process you followed will be of far greater value than hiding from your results or getting down on yourself because of your results.

Attitudes

There are certain attitudes, skills, and abilities that traders can adopt that are conducive to developing and maintaining positive self-esteem and that also assist the trader in his or her ability to adhere to the trading performance process of High-Quality Preparation, Effective Execution, and Constructive Self-Assessment. One of these attitudes is a respect for the market and for trading. The markets represent an extraordinary opportunity for financial independence and self-expression. A person can be his or her own master in trading. It is really a wonderful thing when you think about it. Possessing a genuine respect for the markets and trading and the tremendous opportunities they provide is a beneficial attitude for the trader to adopt.

Sometimes, traders become upset at the market and its participants. They may feel that the market had turned against them or that the so-called 'smart money' took their trade away by hitting their stop. They make it personal. They may blame the market for a loss and reprove the market for not trading well. This is faulty thinking. The market isn't concerned with individual traders. The market is unaware of you as a participant making trades. Blaming the market and the smart money is like shouting at the wall. It can't hear you and won't offer any response no matter how much you scream and yell. Traders committing this basic error in thinking are putting themselves above the market. It is subtle, but this is an action of the ego. The market is wrong, or others are to blame, not me. Blaming the market or the smart money may make the ego feel better, but you actually disrespect your true interests because in the act of assuaging the ego, an opportunity to learn is surrendered. In this regard, your ego is keeping you from becoming a better trader. Respect the market for what it is and avoid the side street of blame. It's a dead end.

Being humble about your trading is another mental virtue that will help promote as well as reflect self-esteem. There will be good days and not so good days, and once in a while a very good day and a very bad day. We want to be humble about our role and place within the larger context of the market and trading. No one dominates the markets. This includes hedge funds and larger players, least of all the smaller traders. We want to be humble about our successes and feel humility about it all. It is counterproductive to overinflate the importance of what we are doing as a trader and the importance of our accomplishments. We are simply traders. Likewise, not getting down on ourselves and allowing the inner critic to chastise and deride us for days that don't go so well is another facet of maintaining self-esteem. A hypercritical evaluation of ourselves rarely adds to our experiences. When we buy into these critical self-evaluations and fuse with them, we lose contact with reality. Our focus turns inside to our internal, depressive state. If we fuse with our internal state, making it appear real and overwhelming, we are highly likely to avoid contact with what is important to us. We will consequently stay mired and stuck in fault-finding thoughts and pessimistic emotions. Mindfulness and defusion will help the trader maintain self-esteem.

Mental Parking

Mental parking, as in the *Before* and *During* time frames, is also helpful in the *After* time frame with respect to self-esteem. Mental parking has multiple uses. Being able to park nontrading concerns and personal predicaments to clear your head for trading is a mental asset. So is being able to mentally park a trading error or loss during trading. We want to park the loss or error until after the trading is over. We can then make an assessment with fresh eyes in a calm and objective manner with the aim of expanding our knowledge, skills, and abilities.

Mental parking also directly adds to our self-esteem. If we do have an error while trading and we mentally park it for review after trading is over, how will we feel about ourselves? We should feel good that we have been able to do this and not become distracted by the mistake. Our self-esteem will rise from this action. This is in direct contrast to the effect on our esteem should we continue to fuss about the error, become distracted, miss or misread other trading opportunities, make additional mistakes, and spiral downward psychologically.

Being able to mentally park a loss or error is not an easy task. If you are finding it difficult, you may want to make it part of your daily mission. Here is an example from Emily, an active Forex day trader:

> I know trading is difficult. There is a lot to know about the market, how to manage trades, and how to deal with what goes on inside my head. It's not easy, but then, it probably shouldn't be for what you can accomplish. If it were easy, everyone can do it, right? I knew I had to be different. I had to think differently about my approach to the mental side of trading.
>
> Part of how I measure my success is how I face up to and handle the daily difficulties: the losses, the mistakes, the missed trades, the bad trades. A key indicator for me is how I am able to mentally park that

error, set it aside for now, and stop the crazy stress going on about it. Often, my daily mission is: "Park the error, adjust, and refocus back on the trading." Sometimes it feels impossible to do, but I force myself. *I know this is as important to my success as the money I make*, so that's why I do it. This has helped me immensely.

Roles and Values

In a larger sense, having healthy self-esteem also refers to the ability to separate yourself from trading. You are a person who has values and worth outside of trading. You can have a bad trading day, but you are still a worthy person. Some traders find this difficult. They have defined their entire identity as a trader. When they aren't successful, it hurts. Their self-esteem sinks.

Your roles, your values, and what's important to you outside of trading will help serve as protective factors for you when trading falls short of expectations. You may be a spouse, a partner, a fiancée, a mother, father, friend and confidant, sibling, child, teacher, employer, employee, community member, and more. You have all kinds of roles above and beyond trading. You are not just defined by your role as a trader. As we discussed in Chapter 9 in perspective, we want to be able to park non-trading—related concerns when we enter our trading room and sit down to our trading desk and take on the role of the trader. Likewise, we park our trading when we are outside of trading and are involved in the other important roles of our life. If we place all of our eggs into the basket of being a trader and trading is not going so well, then where will our self-esteem be?

You are a trader, but you should also keep in mind that away from the trading desk, you have other roles. You get feedback, identity, and sustenance from your other roles, not just from trading. You might, for example, have had a tough day trading. You might have missed the big move on that day and tried a couple of trades that didn't work out. You feel a bit down and frustrated. That's understandable. But there is no need to let this bleed over into the rest of your life. When you help your child work through a challenge she is facing later that day, you are acting as a parent. You have parked the trading day where it belongs and turn your full attention to another value—helping develop and nurture your child and being a good parent. If you fail to park your trading, the rest of your life can suffer as a result. Moreover, if all you do is focus on trading, you are shutting out other aspects of your life that give you richness, meaning, and vitality. Having and knowing the other roles in your life along with being clear on your values and what is important to you in those various roles helps keep the role of trading in perspective and our self-esteem in balance. As mentioned earlier, before his death Stephen Covey wrote worthwhile material on roles and values and how to organize yourself around them for a meaningful life. You are encouraged to consult his books.

Finding Opportunity

Part of self-esteem also has to do with how you evaluate yourself. We have already noted that allowing the inner critic free reign is usually not a good idea. Yet we do need to evaluate our trading performance. This has to do with evaluating ourselves accurately, not punitively and hypercritically. We certainly need to be open to the reality of what is happening in our trading and accept feedback. The market will give us feedback and it is critical that we be willing to accept the feedback.

In this regard, it is also useful to adopt the attitude of finding opportunity in the feedback you get from mistakes and losses. Paradoxically, this is precisely where self-esteem can be enhanced. When confronted by adversity, find opportunity. When a mistake is made and you recognize it, you now have something to work with. You should be excited about this. Heretofore, you weren't aware of your limitation. By making the mistake and acknowledging it, you can now address it. If you do this correctly, you can turn a mistake into an asset. You have identified a developmental need. You prepare a plan of action centered around a SMART goal, execute it, monitor and adjust for new information, repeat your execution and evaluation as needed. In this way, you develop new knowledge, skills, and abilities and turn them into a new strength. With proper effort, you will come to 'own' the limitation. Self-esteem will rise when you follow this vital process. In trading, *opportunities for personal growth come from the adversity we face and the mistakes we make.* It is exactly why this trading psychology process of Preparation/Execution/Self-Assessment provides traders with such a powerful edge.

Benefits of Self-Esteem

A few last words about self-esteem. Roy Baumeister has done a substantial amount of research on self-esteem. He and his colleagues have found that the correlation between self-esteem and performance is rather modest, and that high self-esteem probably doesn't lead to strong performance. In most cases, it is the opposite. Strong performance promotes high self-esteem, but not vice versa. In other words, high self-esteem does not lead to good trading performance; trading success boosts self-esteem. That is why in this book I have not focused on methods and techniques to boost self-esteem. We have, instead, continued to focus on skills and methods that will help improve your performance. Doing so will, in turn, promote self-esteem.

There is significant value in possessing high self-esteem. Baumeister points out that high self-esteem is beneficial because it helps us to feel good. It feels good to believe we are a good person and a good trader. Low self-esteem is more likely to lead to depression and persistent sadness. Feeling down affects our abilities not just in trading but in the rest of our lives as well. High self-esteem is of obvious value in this regard. It also promotes long-term happiness.

In addition to happiness, Baumeister's extensive research also found that self-esteem promotes initiative. Traders with high self-esteem are more likely to persevere when things become difficult. They are more likely to find ways around their current limitations and find solutions to their problems. Some of the research also shows that people with high self-esteem are more likely to bounce back after a failure compared to those with low self-esteem. These are important attributes for traders. We want to carefully attend to our self-esteem.

■ Performance Accountability

Performance accountability refers to the ability of a trader to track and use information about their trading performance. This includes both positive and negative performance information. By positive performance information, we mean trading performance that adheres to the trader's process of trading, that is, trading by his or her trading plan, applying sound money management practices, and also adhering to the *Before-During-After* trading psychology process. Negative performance information refers to the trader's deviations from trading her plan, failing to apply money management procedures, and disengaging from the *Before-During-After* trading psychology principles. Notice again that we are not looking at trading results as a primary performance indicator. It is especially important to understand that even though you may have made money and had positive results, your performance could still have fallen short. For example, money may have been won on a trade but the trade was outside the scope of the trader's trading plan or money management principles were violated because the trader oversized her position. We want to review all performance data—both the good and the not so good and then learn from our performance. This is a critical part of our trading psychology process. It is the best way for traders to consistently improve their trading.

Being able to consider what we did well and where we fell short in our trading requires that we have the capacity to accept responsibility for our trading performance results. We have already discussed the ego and how fusing with it can undermine our best interests. In the same vein, acknowledging responsibility for our trading performance can be a challenge for some traders. And yet, there is no one else upon whom the responsibility falls. Trading is different from some other professions where decisions may be shared by a group of people. In corporations or other organizations, you can get others to be involved in important decisions so that you are not the only one taking on the responsibility. This is not the case in trading. In trading, it's just you. Hence you are responsible for all your trading decisions and actions. This sometimes can be tough to accept.

As we discussed earlier, we are limited by our natural inclinations and we likely view ourselves in a favorable light. In fact, research shows that we tend to view ourselves more positively than objectively. When people were asked to rate themselves on their driving ability, for example, New Zealand psychologist Ian McCormick and colleagues found that only a small minority rated themselves as below average drivers.

Confirming prior research in this area, 80 percent of the respondents said they were above average on important driver characteristics. In fact, they were nine times more likely to rate themselves as above average than below average. It should be obvious that the vast majority in a group of randomly selected people will have to be average in driving skills. Nevertheless, because of our tendency to view ourselves with positive attributes, we see ourselves as better than average. This may, in part, explain why we find assuming individual accountability to be at least mildly abhorrent. We find it hard to reconcile data that does not conform to our positive view of ourselves.

Most of us also have an optimistic view of ourselves. This is a robust finding in the psychological literature. Researchers Neil Weinstein and William Klein summarized what are sometimes called 'positive illusions' that people have about themselves: People not only tend to believe they are superior to others, they also believe that they are less likely than others to experience negative events and negative consequences. Psychologists refer to this latter characteristic as *optimism bias*, another cognitive bias of importance for traders. A cigarette smoker, for example, expresses optimism bias when he discounts the likelihood of contracting illness from tobacco use and avoids taking precautions to reduce his elevated risk. Traders with optimistic views of themselves and their situations can take on more risk than is wise in their trading. It can also cause us to avoid taking responsibility for our actions, especially wrong choices.

When choices are made that don't work out, people will tend to disconnect from those choices by reducing or disregarding the negative consequences of their actions. They might disconnect by viewing the negative consequences as trivial or even flat out deny them. A trader may make an impulsive trade that turns into a loss, for example, and the loss is disregarded or minimized as unimportant. This is done as a way to save face. It also can be an unspoken reason not to review your trading at the end of the day and avoid performance accountability. People with low self-esteem were found to adopt such mental sleight-of-hand strategies by Rob Holland and his colleagues. Dr. Holland is a researcher of human behavior at Radboud University, Nijmegen, the Netherlands. He found that people with lower self-esteem will use external excuses to separate themselves from their actions when their action doesn't converge with how they view themselves. When a trader, for example, overconfidently views himself as skillful, but makes a poor trade and has a loss, he may overlook his part and place the blame on larger traders who engineered a move against him. The excuse helps him save face. His action remains justified and he maintains a favorable self-view. Unfortunately for this trader, by protecting his ego and not taking responsibility for the trade, he foregoes the opportunity to learn from the experience. Notably, Holland also found that people with higher self-esteem are less likely to employ self-justifying strategies because they experience less discomfort from threats to the self. This is another good reason to maintain self-esteem by using mindfulness and defusion to be humble, remain on an even keel, and not let egoistic needs take over your trading.

As we take responsibility in reviewing our trading, keep in mind that certain factors that can influence our trading results are outside of our control. These are things for which we are not responsible. We should note these as external factors that can have a varying effect on our trading performance. It is useful to note these factors because when we are able to recognize them in future trading, we can adjust our behavior accordingly. Although we can never have true control over these factors, there is one aspect that we can control and that is how we respond to these external factors. The external factors we refer to include the market and how it is trading. We are unable to control whether a market will have good range and volatility or be dull and narrow. We are also unable to control whether or not price will reach a support area, or if it will push through or bounce off that support. We can control our response, however, to a dull day and exercise patience when price is trading just above support. We are unable to control news and how a market reacts to that news, and we are unable to control how far a market will run in a given direction, or whether it will run at all. Likewise, we are unable to direct the outcome of any given trade. Again, what we are in command of is how we respond to all of these external factors. It is our response in terms of our actions that we do have power over.

There are a lot of specific factors that are within your direct control. These factors have a direct influence on our trading performance and can be clearly listed, observed, measured, and evaluated. A responsible trader will keep these factors in mind when reviewing and appraising her trading. Factors within your control include the quality of your preparation before you start trading, the caliber of your thoughts and feelings during trading, the actions you take or do not take, and how resourcefully you are using your trading performance review data. If you are a responsible trader, you would want your preparation to be high quality, complete in every way, and inclusive of new skills and abilities you are working on to improve your trading. As thoughts and feelings start to become distracting when trading, you want to bring mindfulness and mental parking skills to bear. This involves acknowledging unwanted thoughts and feelings, centering yourself mentally, mindfully turning your attention toward the things that are important for the trade and for you in your growth as a trader, and taking the appropriate high-value actions in the service of the trade. And, finally, taking responsibility for your trading performance, using your trading journal or your personal Trader's Performance Assessment (Exercise 11.1), and creating a solid self-development program using your trading performance as continuous feedback for your personal development and growth as a trader.

Exercise 11.1 provides a set of questions, which together form a personal trading performance assessment you can use to review and appraise your trading performance. It is based on a performance tool for athletes developed by Charlie Maher, which I have modified for traders. These are simple, key questions that get directly to the heart of trading performance. When used routinely and systematically, they provide a guide for you to discover your developmental needs and develop a way to address them. In the process, you will become a more knowledgeable, skilled, able, and responsible trader.

Exercise 11.1 Trader's Performance Assessment

1. What were my trading strong points? Why were these strengths?

2. What were my trading limitations? Why were they limitations?

3. What have I learned about myself and my trading?

4. What steps can I take based on what I have learned?

When using the Trader's Performance Assessment, keep in mind that we are less concerned about results than the trading process. Making three winning trades in a row would not be considered a trading strength on its own, for example. It is much more important to know what you did to select three winning trades and how these three winning trades reflected your personal strengths. This might exhibit several specific abilities, including identifying high odds trades, waiting patiently for them to fully set up, pulling the trigger in the right place, and holding them to their logical profit objective.

When using this assessment protocol, keep in mind that both technical and mental factors are important and should be noted. When identifying limitations, for example, you might recognize that, although your profit target on a long trade was higher, you closed the trade after it reached only 60 percent of its objective because you were fearful that price looked threatening. As you consider why this was a limitation, you might recognize both technical and mental limitations: technical in that you were not reading the market well. The minor threatening price action you saw while in the trade was not evidence of strong supply hitting the market. Mentally in that trade you were anxious, worried about keeping profits you made, and feeling averse to giving any profits back. Thus, for this trade at least, you have learned that you need more work on both the mental and technical sides of trading when in a profitable trade that has more to run. Should you learn from multiple reviews like this over multiple days or weeks that this same issue keeps occurring across different trades, then you know you have a developmental need. You can now concentrate on the steps you need to take to effectively address this and begin to develop the knowledge, skills, and abilities to hold your trades to their profit targets.

To help you understand how best to use the Trader's Performance Assessment we will look at one of Ian's self-evaluations. Ian is a skilled day trader who focuses primarily on the S&P e-mini, crude oil, and gold futures markets:

What were my strong points? Why were these strengths?

My strong points in today's trading included really good preparation the night before and good clarity in my mind and emotions. Because I identified strong support last night, I didn't hesitate in taking the first trade this morning. I was able to initiate trades in two markets (S&Ps and crude oil) at almost the same time, as they were in sync today, which I anticipated in my preparation. Because the S&Ps were expanding out of a narrow range from yesterday, I was prepared for trending conditions and able to reenter two additional trades in the direction of the trend.

What were my limitations? Why were they limitations?

I want to be able to put on a core position when it becomes clear that the market is in a strong trend. Instead, today I made multiple trades but all resulted in small profits. I am still reluctant to give profits back to the market and won't allow a trade room to pull back.

What have I learned from this day's trading?

I can identify early in the day when trending conditions are occurring. I was hesitant about this in the past, but I have worked on this as a developmental need and I now know exactly what to look for. I now have this defined. It has become a strength for me. I have also learned that I have a new developmental need with respect to trading trending conditions. If I can next develop in myself the skills and abilities to trade the trend by holding a core position throughout the day, I will further develop as a trader and improve my overall trading results.

What steps can I take based on what I have learned today?

Develop a SMART goal for keeping a core position during trend days. To do this, I will initiate a core position equivalent to one-half my normal position size as soon as I identify that conditions favor trending conditions. I will hold that one-half position through the end of the day. I can trade in and out of the trend on pullbacks (entries) and extension of swings (exits), but will strive to hold the core position. Because this will be mentally challenging, I will use deep breathing, mindfulness, and defusion techniques while managing the trade. Since true trending conditions occur only two to three times a month, I will work on this for the next six months with an objective of holding a core position throughout the day on 70 percent of actual trend days.

Ian has been using the Trader's Performance Assessment in his personal development. Earlier, he used this tool to understand that he needed to be able to recognize early in the trading day when trending conditions were occurring. He knew that although they occur only a few days a month, trending days gave the trader the potential for outsized profits compared to all other days and capturing them would add to his trading results. Although he learned to identify them, he has also been limited in his trading of trend days and not making the kind of profits available on these days. He has thus identified a developmental need and has created an action plan with a SMART goal to address this need. The approach recognizes that he will be challenged psychologically, and he has prudently incorporated mental skills into his plan.

During the six-month period, Ian will continue to assess his execution of this SMART goal by using the Trader's Performance Assessment to evaluate strengths he is building as well as any barriers that arise as he works on his goal. This will give him the opportunity to make any necessary adjustments to his SMART goal that may be warranted. This way, Ian continues to work on his goal and to work on himself, assessing his progress, staying motivated, and developing valuable trading skills—including necessary mental skills—in the process. Once again, the reader should take careful note that Ian is working on his process of trading a trend day. He is not focused on his trading results. His goal does not target money or S&P points. Ian's goal is about his trading process: holding a core position and applying mental techniques to build the skills and abilities to trade a trending day. Ian is focused on process, not outcome, exactly as he should be.

■ Perseverance

Perseverance refers to the trader's capacity to work tirelessly and purposefully toward goals and challenges, sustaining their interest and effort over long periods of time despite adversity and failures. Angela Duckworth, a University of Pennsylvania research psychologist and a 2013 MacArthur Fellowship recipient, calls this vital capacity "grit."

Duckworth's research has shown that perseverance, or grit, can be more important than talent, IQ, conscientiousness, and other factors commonly associated with success across a range of different endeavors and professions. Grit and perseverance involve sustained effort over long periods of time—what we might think of as stamina. It also involves concerted effort and an intensity of attention, along with the ability to commit to and follow through on important, specific, trading-relevant activities. Notably, the capacity of perseverance, as measured by Duckworth's grit scale, tends to increase over the life span with older individuals having more grit than their younger counterparts.

A trader working on her charts each evening to understand how trend changes occur, how the charts appear when trends are sustained, what choice trade setups look like, and the different, nuanced patterns of each, over many days, weeks, months, and years is an illustration of perseverance. Hard work is a virtue that is understood by most people. "Nothing worthwhile comes easily" and "the more effort you put into something, the more likely you will achieve it" are familiar axioms in this regard. What may not be so familiar, according to Duckworth, is that it is far better to concentrate and focus one's efforts than it is to be constantly changing one's objectives. A person who changes jobs frequently from one kind of job or field to a vastly different other job repeatedly, for example, is less likely to achieve the same levels of success as the person who finds his niche and concentrates his efforts on developing skills in that area. Success comes from concentrating on one thing. In trading, this would mean, for example, knowing a trade setup deeply and intimately. It would include knowing deeply what market conditions favor that trade setup, what favorable price action looks like as the trade is setting up, how the indicators behave, and also how far it can run in varying market conditions and other considerations.

While trading requires an early exploration of different methods of technical market analysis (e.g., Elliott Wave, Fibonacci, Japanese candlesticks, pivot points, support and resistance, statistical indicators, Wyckoff Method, chart patterns, Market Profile, signal processing methods, etc.), continuously jumping from one indicator or method to another at some point becomes counterproductive. A trader will find success by settling on a single method and sticking with this, learning all about it, how to properly use it, along with its nuances and its limitations.

Intensity of effort is a significant aspect of perseverance leading to success. Intensity here means the extent to which our attention is engaged during practice periods. When we are reviewing charts, for example, or learning a new trade setup, we want our attention focused and concentrated on that activity. Allowing attention to wander and become distracted is detrimental to learning and acquiring expertise. The better we are at sustaining attention over time, the better we position ourselves to achieve success. Mindfulness is one of the best methods available to develop and sustain focused attention. Attention must be sustained over weeks, months, and years for the development and deepening of expertise and mastery. Mindfulness teaches us how to sustain attention moment-by-moment, and also helps us maintain mental clarity over the long haul.

Follow through is critical to grit. Sustained and purposeful commitment to specific trading-related activities is much more likely to lead to trading success than sporadic effort in different unrelated areas. Spending only an hour here and there is too intermittent and casual to be conducive to developing optimal performance abilities. Frequent switching of methods, as already discussed, will not lead to success in trading. Spending inordinate time on unproductive areas such as Internet trading forums and chat rooms will provide less personal development of knowledge, skills, and abilities than doing your homework and studying your charts. In research reviewed by Duckworth, this kind of follow through is noted as the single best predictor of accomplishment across a range of endeavors, including sport, art, science, communication, and other fields. Trading is no different.

Lastly, when considering grit, it is important to note that stamina is involved. We want to work not only with intensity, but also with endurance. You can think about it like a road race. A marathon requires both intensity and endurance. A sprint requires only intensity. Traders want to be marathon runners, having a level of intense effort that is sustained over the long term. Excellence requires years of focused work. It also requires that we experience and overcome failures and adversity, pick ourselves up, and get back into the trading arena. As we noted earlier, sustaining a level of intense effort over many days, weeks, and longer requires numerous decision to be made. It is easy to say, "Gee, I'm tired. I think I'll just skip the work tonight." Developing mindfulness skills and keeping in mind what is most important to you go hand in hand with perseverance. Most people have had at least one experience in their lives where they have wanted something bad enough to have sacrificed and put sustained effort into achieving it. They have persevered and dealt with whatever obstacles got in their way to obtain something of personal import. This is perseverance. We continuously make decisions and choices that get us closer and closer to what we value.

The epitome of grit and perseverance is what psychologists call *deliberate practice*. Deliberate practice is a specialized form of high-quality practice in which you engage in planned, highly focused training activities that cause you to train just outside your reliable level of performance. It is a training activity that pushes you to perform outside your comfort zone. Extensive research by K. Anders Ericsson, professor of psychology at Florida State University and a world authority in expert performance and deliberate practice, shows that *deliberate practice is the single most important factor in developing mastery and expertise in performance-based activities such as trading*.

Deliberate practice can be thought of as "deep practice." Practicing our craft at a very deep level—concentrated and intense—for a sustained period of time brings us in contact with learning subtleties and nuances that can take our knowledge, skills and abilities to a mastery level. Deliberate practice is done alone. Immediate feedback about the performance is available and trainees can repeat the performance task or a similar performance task with an aim to correcting or improving upon previous responses. It is a structured way of taking a current limitation and turning it into strength.

Continuous, solitary deliberate practice over lengthy periods of time has been found to be the main ingredient of expertise and mastery regardless of the field of endeavor. Whether we are talking about an Olympic athlete, elite level lawyer, neurosurgeon, actor, trader, chess master, Navy pilot, or dart thrower, it is deliberate practice that sets the elite apart from the also-rans. With the exception of physical size, which can make a difference in some sports such as in basketball and horse racing, mastery of a given discipline or field isn't explained by personality, IQ, innate talent, physical characteristics or even years of experience. World-class levels of mastery and expertise are accomplished by thousands of hours of high-quality training that involves pushing your personal envelope of competence. In other words, working beyond the edge of your abilities with respect to a given skill, failing, trying again, failing, putting in more effort, failing, and then working at it again until you finally achieve success is how deliberate practice works and how it leads to mastery. It is daunting and truly hard work. Frankly, most people won't do it.

Readers may have heard of the 10,000-hour rule popularized by social science writer Malcolm Gladwell: that is, it takes about 10,000 hours or about 10 years of nearly daily, deep, deliberate practice in a given field to become expert in that field. This is true. It was first uncovered by Carnegie Mellon University professors Herbert Simon (a Nobel laureate in economics) and William Chase in their research on world-class levels of expertise in chess. It is a lot of dedicated work. Deliberate practice is also not perceived as pleasant by those who engage in it. It is experienced as difficult, though they do it anyway, day after day. Working alone trying to perfect skills you don't currently have and experiencing failure over and over, day in and day out is felt as difficult and unpleasant by those who do it. This is one reason why there are so few elite level performers.

This is not to say that a trader requires a minimum of 10,000 hours of practice to become profitable. To operate on a world-class level requires that amount of work. Traders can develop a level of competence to profitably trade the market in less time. Competence can be profitable, though it is not at the level of elite. Deliberate practice will bring you to competence more quickly than other forms of practice, and if you want to operate at an elite level, nothing else will. Nevertheless, compared to other ways of learning such as reading, attending webinars, seminars, and casually reviewing charts, deliberate practice is experienced as effortful and unpleasant. And this is where grit comes in. It turns out that people with the ability to persevere against difficult challenges are those with the grit to commit to unending hours of improving their performance. Those who have a real passion for trading, who can sustain their passion and not lose interest in it, and are not thwarted by setbacks, possess the grit needed to be successful in deliberate practice and, ultimately, trading.

If you are like most traders, you have experienced trading as exceptionally difficult, more difficult than just about any other endeavor you have tried. It takes time to develop the knowledge, skills, and abilities to trade competently. But this is true for any worthy endeavor. It takes serious passion and dedicated effort to be good and an exceptional commitment to be great.

■ Continuous Improvement

Continuous improvement is what every trader would like—getting better every day. To get better requires a high level of commitment. It also involves a strong desire and dedication to learning to be the best trader you can be, not just today or tomorrow, but over the long term. In other words, it requires effort, and lots of it.

A useful way to think about continuous improvement is to imagine that you have had a long and successful trading career, and you are now about to retire. You are ready to hang up your charts and entry platform and do things you've never had the time to do. The trading world is holding a testimonial dinner for you on Saturday night. All your peers and people you respect will be there. What would you like them to say about you as a trader over your years and decades of trading? We explained a similar exercise in Chapter 8 where you noted what a reporter might say about you and your trading. If you haven't done this exercise, it is useful to pause for a few minutes and jot down what comes to mind.

What comes to your mind when you think about how you would like to be remembered for your trading? These are a set of your long-term objectives from which you can construct SMART goals, work on, and actualize. These are the things you most value in the profession of trading and the things you most value in yourself as a trader. Do you want to be remembered for cutting winning trades short, for example? Probably not. Instead, you may want to be remembered for excellence in reading a chart, creating unique trade setups from your research, and demonstrating sound trading performance when executing and managing trades.

Keep in mind that what you want to be remembered for is more than just money. Of course you want to make money and provide a solid financial foundation for yourself, your family, and your loved ones. That's a given. But there are other things, too.

At your retirement dinner, people may stand up and say things like, Marcia was one heck of a chart reader. She could read almost any chart just by the price bars and volume. John had a great sense of trade management. He always had a target in mind and once in a trade he would hold it to its target. Juan knew how to enter trades well; he rarely sat through pressure. He also knew when a trade wasn't working and was quick to cut it and get out before it could do damage. These and other things we value as a trader are the kinds of things we want to think about when we make a commitment to trading and to becoming the best trader we can be.

When we are thinking about continuous improvement, it is helpful to consider the professional athlete. Even though they may have been in their sport for 10 or more years (and most—depending on the sport—will play their sport for 20 or more years, starting as a youth and retiring in their late 20s or early 30s), they get up early every day and put in several hours of practice. They get coached every day while in training. During their competitive season, they continue to practice and think about their sport, planning their strategies and maintaining their optimum level of fitness. They are constantly doing continuous improvement.

In sport, continuous improvement is structured for the athlete. Whether they function as an individual athlete as in tennis or are part of a team such as in football or baseball, they are on a schedule. They are coached, work on their mental game with a sport psychologist, and have access to trainers, dieticians, and other supportive structure. Virtually everything the player does is about their sport and it is all well organized for them. This is not the same for most traders. Those who work on a trading desk with a trading firm do have some structure and have training. But the vast majority of traders operate without external structure. We have to structure our own program of self-development if we want to truly achieve in trading.

You can use this same *Before-During-After* framework of High-Quality Preparation, Effective Execution, and Constructive Self-Assessment to structure your continuous trading performance improvement. This means you are oriented to continuous learning about the markets and yourself as well as your trading through study, journaling, personal research, seminars, mentorships, deliberate practice, and other forms to improve your trading knowledge, skills, and abilities. It also means you are committed to making adjustments in your preparation and your execution from what you learn in Constructive Self-Assessment.

Here is how you conduct Constructive Self-Assessment. Use the Trader's Performance Assessment to identify developmental needs. Once a developmental need has been identified and seen as something that, if changed into a strength, would add significantly to your trading performance, you begin planning for that change. Prepare for change in a high-quality manner by developing SMART process goals to address your developmental needs. Although you may have multiple needs and multiple goals, it is best to focus on only one or two at a time. Concentration of effort is almost always a better approach. SMART goals are then implemented through Effective Execution. Progress is monitored through the procedures of Constructive Self-Assessment and by applying the Trader's Performance Assessment to your preparation and execution of the SMART goal. As you take action on your plan in Effective Execution, you gather more performance data, which you then evaluate in Constructive Self-Assessment. This takes you once again into High-Quality Preparation where you adjust your plan and prepare for the next round of trading where you again implement your plan and then assess how you did. The cycle is repeated until you achieve the goals reflected in your developmental need and you have turned a limitation into a personal trading strength.

To achieve excellence and mastery in trading, you need to be mindful throughout the process of High-Quality Preparation, Effective Execution, and Constructive Self-Assessment. Engage mindfully and fully in the cycle of continuous improvement. As you work with this process of self-development and improvement over time, you will gain a sharper perspective on your trading psychology and your trading, embracing its probabilistic nature and the role it plays in your life. Your personal awareness of your strengths and limitations will expand and your motivation will improve. You will become better at mental-discipline and have more self-confidence because you will be focusing on the things that lead to improvement and you will see improvement happening. You will develop a more balanced emotional intensity as you perform the tasks of trading, experiencing fewer emotional whipsaws and fewer emotional hijackings. You will have improved your focus and poise and be able to maintain your composure. Self-esteem will grow as you assume responsibility for your trading and you make the effort to practice it deliberatively. You will add significant value to your trading through continuous self-improvement. These are the true elements of trading psychology. And, as you may have noticed, they work not just for trading, but for life, as well.

Table 11.1, High-Value Mental Skills and Some High-Value Actions of Constructive Self-Assessment, provides a summary of Constructive Self-Assessment. The four high-value mental skills are listed and examples of HVAs are provided.

We end this chapter as we have ended the previous two chapters with a Mental Skills Inventory for Constructive Self-Assessment in Exercise 11.2.

TABLE 11.1	High-Value Mental Skills and Some High-Value Actions of Constructive Self-Assessment
After: Constructive Self-Assessment	
High-Value Mental Skills	**Examples of High-Value Actions**
Self-Esteem	Defining roles and values outside of trading
Performance Accountability	Maintaining a trading journal
Perseverance	Regular review of charts
Continuous Improvement	Seek feedback and advice from experienced traders
	Concentrate on one trading method
	Regular use of Trader's Performance Assessment
	Seek feedback from mentors and trading psychologists
	Engage in deliberate practice
	Create developmental plans to address developmental needs
	Keep good records

Exercise 11.2 Mental Skills Inventory: Constructive Self-Assessment

Mental Domain		Rating
Self-Esteem	I know my self-worth and am able to keep myself on an even keel no matter how my trading goes. I neither get excited when I have a strong trading performance nor get down on myself when my trading performance is less than I would like.	
Performance Accountability	I take full responsibility for my trading performance and am willing to confront the factors that affect my performance, including my performance shortcomings.	
Perseverance	I do the work necessary without distraction and strive to be the best trader I can. I maintain my intensity of effort even when things aren't going my way.	
Continuous Improvement	I use the information about my trading performance to improve as a trader, making adjustments in my trading. I constantly seek ways to develop and improve my trading knowledge, skills, and abilities.	

CHAPTER 12

Final Thoughts

This is the first book that integrates mindfulness skills with performance psychology to present traders with a structured trading psychology process. Our focus has been on the mental and emotional challenges traders face and the cutting-edge psychology that can address and help the trader deal with the mental side of the game. Two things stand out. One is the importance of practicing mindfulness. The other is committing to the *Before-During-After* trading psychology process.

Although trading is replete with psychological challenges, if there is a secret to greater consistency and proficient performance in trading, it is developing the skill of mindful self-awareness. Mindfulness research reveals enormous benefits for traders. The practice of mindfulness trains the mind to be aware of ourselves and what our mind is telling us and, most importantly, mindfulness enables us to see that we have a choice in how we act in any given trading situation. Mindfulness helps us notice when we have become emotionally hooked by a demanding trading situation and also that we do not need to take action to appease the mind's chatter. Mindfulness, acceptance, and commitment help us remember and choose what is of value to us in our trading and perform the high-value activities that lead to optimum performance and profitable trading results.

The high-value mental skills and high-value actions (HVMS and HVAs) associated with optimal trading performance and profitable trading results are honed through the *Before-During-After* trading psychology process. Preparing for trading in a high-quality way, taking our preparation into trading to maximize our trading abilities, and assessing our trading performance and results with the intent to improve our preparation and execution is the royal road to developing, advancing, and enhancing our trading. It is a purposeful, systematic method that guides you in making attainable goals while at the same time helps you develop new skills so that you can actualize the trader you desire to be.

Whether or not you have been sampling the exercises presented in the book as you have been reading it, you need to understand that just reading the book and doing the exercises once will not equip you with competence in these skills. Mindfulness and other cutting-edge mental skills are skills and, as with acquiring any new skill, they require practice and effort. Engage in practicing mindfulness regularly and systematically follow the trading psychology process. Those who routinely do mindfulness, in fact, refer to it as "mindfulness *practice*," and they do so for a reason: developing mindful self-awareness skills requires application, with an underlying sense of devotion. The same is true with the *Before-During-After* trading psychology process. Act on what you have learned and put it into practice for yourself. You can read all about swimming, for example. You can study how the body remains buoyant in water, how the legs and feet should kick to propel the body forward, how the arms move to direct and pull the body, and how the head rotates to allow breathing between strokes. You can study all of this diligently; even take a written test on the material and pass with flying colors. But you won't be able to actually swim until you get wet.

Both mindfulness and the trading psychology process require regular, preferably daily practice. It is wise to schedule time and practice various exercises described in the book and routinely follow the trading psychology process laid out in Part III. This requires effort and commitment. Resolve for yourself a level of commitment that is right for you, jump into the water, and start practicing mindfulness and the trading psychology process. The benefits can be enormous.

Expanding on this theme of actually doing, one of the intentions of this book is to go beyond the mere explanations of techniques and methods. The book provides a platform from which you can teach yourself something about yourself and your trading challenges. The exercises sprinkled throughout the book enable you to look deeper into your own trading situations. Take the time to do them. They require thought, a little diligence, and an open honesty with ourselves—exactly the same as in trading. Use these exercises to develop your own understanding of yourself within the context of trading. They will guide you as you develop your own personal trading psychology edge.

Trading psychology is only one aspect, though a crucial one, for success in trading. There are three fundamental aspects to trading well. A trader must: (1) unlock the secrets behind the technical aspects of the market, (2) develop an understanding of sound money management and risk practices, and (3) develop a trading psychology edge. This is depicted in Figure 12.1. By itself, psychology will not turn you into a great trader without technical and money management proficiencies. Consider a club-level tennis player, for example. She may have great mental skills and be as cool as ice on the tennis court. But if she hasn't developed the knowledge, skill, and ability to play professional-level tennis, she won't make it very far at Wimbledon. The same is true in trading. This being said, psychology is crucial. It underpins both

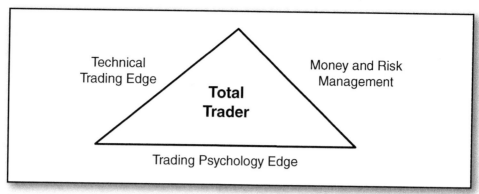

FIGURE 12.1 Fundamental Abilities of the Competent Trader

technical skill and money management practice. Without a strong sense of one's psychology, which we define as a psychological edge, technical strategies can easily be compromised and money management practices may be left by the roadside. The mental side of the game and especially the trading process described in this book can help you both develop and use your technical skills to their greatest advantage.

■ Next Steps

As this book draws to a close, you will want to begin thinking about what to do next. Each individual is different. Although there are commonalities among traders, we each experience the trading world from our own unique perspective. This is the beauty and joy of being human. As we conclude, reflect on what you personally have learned from this book. What has changed or is beginning to change for you with respect to your emotions, your mind, and trading psychology? Has your perspective changed about your trading psychology? Do you see new opportunities for yourself in trading? If so, what are they?

Consider what has been most useful for you in reading and practicing what's presented in this book. Was it how intuitive and deliberative minds work? Mindfulness and defusion? Understanding what's of value to you in your trading and committing to what really matters to you? Maybe it was the idea that we can't really control our thoughts and emotions and it's time to stop the tug of war with them? How about the trading psychology process of *Before-During-After*? What can you now use in your trading?

Was there anything that surprised you? The mind is complex and its workings are relatively hidden from us all. Perhaps one of the paradoxes described within the book was an eye-opener and gave you some new insight into yourself and your mental world. Was there anything that stood out as an "ah-ha" moment for you? It is important to note that.

As you begin to think about what you will be using in your own trading, keep the trading psychology process firmly in mind. Prepare a plan of action, execute it, and evaluate how you did and how your plan is working, and then make adjustments. Start with small, incremental steps. They quickly add up. Keep your mind open and be willing to learn new things about yourself and about your trading. Above all else, have a little compassion for yourself when things don't go as planned or you fall short. No one gets to master it right off. And, remember what matters most to you. Keep your values as your beacon toward which you direct your actions and you will be tacking along the right course. Practice mindfulness and trade mindfully to achieve your optimum trading performance and reach excellence in your trading.

Alcoholics Anonymous. 2001. *The Big Book*, 4th ed. New York: Alcoholics Anonymous World Services.

Barros, R. 2008. *The Nature of Trends: Strategies and Concepts for Successful Investing and Trading.* Singapore: John Wiley & Sons (Asia).

Baumeister, R.F., J. D. Campbell, J. I. Krueger, and K. D. Vohs. 2003. "Does High Self-Esteem Cause Better Performance, Interpersonal Success, Happiness, or Healthier Lifestyles?" *Psychological Science in the Public Interest* 4: 1–44.

Baumeister, R. F., and J. Tierney 2011. *Willpower: Rediscovering the Greatest Human Strength.* New York: Penguin Press.

Benson, H. 1975. *The Relaxation Response.* New York: Harper Collins.

Bechara, A., H. Damasio, and A. R. Damasio. 2000. "Emotion, Decision Making and the Orbitofrontal Cortex." *Cerebral Cortex* 10: 295–307.

Bechara, A., D. Tranel, and H. Damasio. 2000. "Characterization of the Decision-Making Deficit of Patients with Ventromedial Prefrontal Cortex Lesions." *Brain* 123: 2189–2202.

Bollinger, J. 2001. *Bollinger on Bollinger Bands.* New York: McGraw-Hill.

Blonna, R. 2007. *Coping with Stress in a Changing World*, 4th ed. New York: McGraw-Hill.

Blumenthal, J. A., M. A. Babyak, P. M. Doraiswamy, L. Watkins, B. M. Hoffman, K. A. Barbour, S. Herman, W. E. Craighead, A. L. Brosse, R. Waugh, A. Hinderliter, and A. Sherwood. 2007. "Exercise and Pharmacotherapy in the Treatment of Major Depressive Disorder." *Psychosomatic Medicine* 69: 587–596.

Bourquin, T., and N. Mango. 2013. *Traders at Work: How the World's Most Successful Traders Make Their Living in the Markets.* New York: Apress.

Braboszcz, C., S. Hahusseau, and A. Delorme. 2010. "Meditation and Neuroscience: From Basic Research to Clinical Practice." in *Integrative Clinical Psychology, Psychiatry and Behavioral Medicine: Perspectives, Practices and Research*, edited by R. A. Carlstedt, 755–778. New York: Springer Publishing.

Brewer, J. A., P. D. Worhunsky, J. R. Gray, Y. Y. Tang, J. Weber, and H. Kober. 2011. "Meditation Experience Is Associated with Differences in Default Mode Network Activity and Connectivity." *Proceedings of the National Academy of Sciences of the United States of America* 108: 20254–20259.

CBS News: 60 Minutes. 2009. *Flight 1549: A Routine Takeoff Turns Ugly*, February 8 (rev. July 4, 2009). Accessed December 20, 2012 at www.cbsnews.com/8301-18560_162-4783580.html.

Chiesa, A., and A. Serretti. 2010. "A Systematic Review of Neurobiological and Clinical Features of Mindfulness Meditations." *Psychological Medicine* 40: 1239–1252.

Christoff, K., A. M. Gordon, J. Smallwood, R. Smith, and J. W. Schooler. 2009. "Experience Sampling During fMRI Reveals Default Network and Executive System Contributions to Mind Wandering." *Proceedings of the National Academy of Sciences of the United States of America* 106: 8719–8724.

Cooper, M. J., O. Dimitrov, and P. R. Rau. 2001. "A Rose.com by Any Other Name." *Journal of Finance* 56: 2371–2388.

Cooper, M. J., A. Khorana, I. Osobov, A. Patel, and P. R. Rau. 2005. "Managerial Actions in Response to a Market Downturn: Valuation Effects of Name Changes in the Dot.com Decline." *Journal of Corporate Finance* 11: 319–335.

Covey, S. R., A. R. Merrill, and R. R. Merrill. 1994. *First Things First: To Live, to Love, to Learn, to Leave a Legacy*. New York: Free Press.

Creswell, J. D., W. T. Welch, S. E. Taylor, D. K. Sherman, T. L. Gruenwald, and T. Mann. 2005. "Affirmation of Personal Values Buffers Neuroendocrine and Psychological Stress Responses. *Psychological Science* 16: 845–851.

Csikszentmihalyi, M. 1990. *Flow: The Psychology of Optimal Experience*. New York: Harper & Row.

Damasio, A. 1994. *Descartes' Error: Emotion, Reason and the Human Brain*. New York: Penguin.

Damasio, H., T. Grabowski, R. Frank, A. M. Galaburda, and A. R. Damasio. 1994. "The Return of Phineas Gage: Clues about the Brain from the Skull of the Famous Patient." *Science* 264: 1102–1105.

David, S., and C. Congleton. 2013. "Emotional Agility." *Harvard Business Review Online*, November. Accessed December 15, 2013 at: http://hbr.org/2013/11/emotional-agility/ar/1.

DeMartino, B., C. F. Cramerer, and R. Adolphs. 2010. "Amygdala Damage Eliminates Monetary Loss Aversion." *Proceedings of the National Academy of Sciences of the United States of America* 107: 3788–3792.

DeMartino, B., D. Kumaran, B. Seymour, and R. J. Dolan. 2006. "Frames, Biases, and Rational Decision-Making in the Human Brain." *Science* 313: 684–687.

Dickenson, J., E. T. Berkman, J. Arch, and M. D. Lieberman. 2013. "Neural Correlates of Focused Attention During a Brief Mindfulness Induction." *Social Cognitive and Affective Neuroscience* 8: 40–47.

Doran, G. T. 1981. "There's a SMART Way to Write Management's Goals and Objectives." *Management Review* 70: 35–36.

Douglas, M. 2000. *Trading in the Zone: Master the Market with Confidence, Discipline and a Winning Attitude*. New York: New York Institute of Finance.

Duckworth, A. L., T. A. Kirby, E. Tsukayama, H. Berstein, and K. A. Ericsson. 2011. "Deliberate Practice Spells Success: Why Grittier Competitors Triumph at the National Spelling Bee." *Social Psychology and Personality Science* 2: 174–181.

Duckworth, A. L., C. Peterson, M. D. Matthews, and D. R. Kelly. 2007. "Grit: Perseverance and Passion for Long-Term Goals." *Journal of Personality and Social Psychology* 92: 1087–1101.

Eifert, G. H., and J. P. Forsyth. 2005. *Acceptance and Commitment Therapy for Anxiety Disorders: A Practitioner's Guide to Using Mindfulness, Acceptance and Values-Based Behavior Change Strategies.* Oakland, CA: New Harbinger Publications.

Elder, A. 1993. *Trading for a Living: Psychology Trading Tactics Money Management.* New York: John Wiley & Sons.

England, E. L., J. D. Herbert, E. M. Forman, S. J. Rabin, A. Juarascio, and S. P. Goldstein. 2012. "Acceptance-Based Exposure Therapy for Public Speaking Anxiety." *Journal of Contextual Behavioral Science* 1: 66–72.

Ericsson, K. A. 1996. *The Road to Excellence: The Acquisition of Expert Performance in the Arts and Sciences, Sports and Games.* Mahwah, NJ: Lawrence Erlbaum.

Ericsson, K. A., N. Charness, P. J. Feltovich, and R. R. Hoffman. 2006. *The Cambridge Handbook of Expertise and Expert Performance.* New York: Cambridge University Press.

Faulds, R. 2006. *Kripalu Yoga: A Guide to Practice On and Off the Mat.* New York: Bantam Dell.

Fenton-O'Creevy, M., E. Soane, N. Nicholson, and P. Willman, P. 2011. "Thinking, Feeling and Deciding: The Influence of Emotions on the Decision-Making and Performance of Traders." *Journal of Organizational Behavior* 32: 1044–1061.

Forsyth, J. P., and G. H. Eifert. 2007. *The Mindfulness and Acceptance Workbook for Anxiety: A Guide to Breaking Free from Anxiety, Phobias and Worry Using Acceptance and Commitment Therapy.* Oakland, CA: New Harbinger Publications.

Frederick, S. 2005. "Cognitive Reflection and Decision Making." *Journal of Economic Perspectives* 19: 25–42.

Gardner, F., and Z. Moore. 2006. *Clinical Sport Psychology.* Champaign, IL: Human Kinetics.

Gardner, F., and Z. Moore. 2007. *The Psychology of Enhancing Human Performance: The Mindfulness—Acceptance—Commitment (MAC) approach.* New York: Springer.

Germer, C.K., R. D. Siegel, and P. R. Fulton (Eds.). 2013. *Mindfulness and Psychotherapy.* New York: Guilford Press.

Gladwell, M. 2008. *Outliers: The Story of Success.* New York: Little Brown & Company.

Goleman, D. 1995. *Emotional Intelligence: Why It Can Matter More than IQ.* New York: Bantam Books.

Graham, B., and D. L. Dodd. 2009. *Security Analysis: Principles and Technique*, 6th ed. New York: McGraw-Hill.

Hanin, Y. L. (Ed.). 2000. *Emotions in Sport.* Champaign, IL: Human Kinetics.

Hänsel, A., and R. von Känel. 2008. "The Ventro-Medial Prefrontal Cortex: A Major Link between the Autonomic Nervous System, Regulation of Emotion, and Stress Reactivity?" *Biopsychosocial Medicine* 2: 21.

Harlow, J. M. 1869. *Recovery from the Passage of an Iron Bar through the Head.* Boston: David Clapp & Son.

Harris, R. 2013. *Dipping Your Toes into ACT*. E-course. Melbourne, Australia: Author.

Harris, R. 2013. "The Art of a Mindful Stop," *Happiness Trap Newsletter*, October 2013, accessed July 8, 2014, http://contextualscience.org/post/the_art_of_a_mindful_stop.

Harris, R. 2006. "Embracing Your Demons: An Overview of Acceptance and Commitment Therapy." *Psychotherapy in Australia* 12: 1–8.

Harris, R. 2009. *ACT made simple: An Easy-to-Read Primer on Acceptance and Commitment Therapy*. Oakland, CA: New Harbinger.

Hartranft, C. 2003. *The Yoga-Sutra of Patanjali: A New Translation with Commentary*. Boston: Shambhala Publications.

Hasenkamp, W., C. D. Wilson-Mendenhall, E. Duncan, and L. W. Barsalou. 2012. "Mind Wandering and Attention during Focused Meditation: A Fine-Grained Temporal Analysis of Fluctuating Cognitive States." *Neuroimage* 59: 750–760.

Hayes, S. C., and C. Shenk. 2004. "Operationalizing Mindfulness without Unnecessary Attachments." *Clinical Psychology: Science and Practice* 11: 249–254.

Hayes, C. S., and S. Smith. 2005. *Get Out of Your Mind and Into Your Life: The New Acceptance and Commitment Therapy*. Oakland, CA: New Harbinger.

Hayes, S. C., K. D. Strosahl, and K. G. Wilson. 1999. *Acceptance and Commitment Therapy: An Experiential Approach to Behavioral Change*. New York: Guilford Press.

Hayes, S. C., K. D. Strosahl, and K. G. Wilson. 2012. *Acceptance and Commitment Therapy: The Process and Practice of Mindful Change*, 2nd ed. New York: Guilford Press.

Hoffman, B. M., M. A. Babyak, W. E. Craighead, A. Sherwood, P. M. Doraiswamy, M. J. Coons, and J. A. Blumenthal. 2011. "Exercise and Pharmacotherapy in Patients with Major Depression: One-Year Follow-Up of the SMILE Study." *Psychosomatic Medicine* 73: 127–133.

Holland, R. W., R. M. Meertens, and M. van Vugt. 2002. "Dissonance on the Road: Self-esteem as a Moderator of Internal and External Self-Justification Strategies." *Personality and Social Psychology Bulletin* 23: 684–692.

Hölzel, B. K., J. Carmody, K. C. Evans, E. A. Hoge, J. A. Dusek, L. Morgan, R. K. Pitman, and S. W. Lazar, 2010. "Stress Reduction Correlates with Structural Changes in the Amygdala." *Social Cognitive and Affective Neuroscience* 5: 11–17.

Hölzel, B. K., J. Carmody, M. Vangel, C. Congleton, S. M. Yerramsetti, T. Gard, and S. W. Lazar. 2011. "Mindfulness Practice Leads to Increases in Regional Brain Gray Matter Density." *Psychiatry Research: Neuroimaging* 191: 36–43.

Holzel, B. K., S. W. Lazar, T. Gard, Z. Schuman-Oliver, D. R. Vago, and U. Ott. 2011. "How does Mindfulness Meditation Work? Proposing Mechanisms of Action from a Conceptual and Neural Perspective." *Perspectives on Psychological Science* 6: 537–559.

Jacobson, N. S., K. S. Dobson, P. A. Truax, M. E. Addis, K. Koerner, J. K. Gollan, E. Gortner, and S. E. Prince. 1996. "A Component Analysis of Cognitive-Behavioral Treatment for Depression." *Journal of Consulting and Clinical Psychology* 64: 295–304.

Jamieson, J. P., M. K. Nock, and W. B. Mendes. 2011. "Mind over Matter: Reappraising Arousal Improves Cardiovascular and Cognitive Responses to Stress." *Journal of Experimental Psychology: General* 147: 417–422.

Jankovsky, J. A. 2007. *Trading Rules that Work: The 28 Essential Lessons Every Trader Must Master*. Hoboken, NJ: John Wiley & Sons.

Kabat-Zinn, J. 1994. *Wherever You Go, There You Are: Mindfulness Meditation in Everyday Life.* New York: Hyperion.

Kahneman, D. 2011. *Thinking, Fast and Slow.* New York: Farrar, Straus and Giroux.

Kahneman, D., and G. Klein. 2009. "Conditions for Intuitive Expertise: A Failure to Disagree." *American Psychologist* 64: 515–526.

Kahneman, D., P. Slovic, and A. Tversky (Eds.). 1982 *Judgment under Uncertainty: Heuristics and Biases.* New York: Cambridge University Press.

Kahneman, D., and A. Tversky. 1979. "Prospect Theory: Analysis of Decision under Risk." *Econometrica* 47: 263–291.

Kaliman, P., M. J. Alvarez-Lopez, M. Cosin-Tomas, M. A. Rosenkranz, A. Lutz, and R. J. Davidson. 2014. "Rapid Changes in Histone Deacetylases and Inflammatory Gene Expression in Expert Meditators." *Psychoneuroendocrinology* 40: 96–107.

Kang, D. H., H. J. Jo, W. H. Jung, S. H. Kim, Y. H. Jung, C. H. Choi, U. S. Lee, S. C. An, J. H. Jang, and J. S. Kwon. 2013. "The Effect of Meditation on Brain Structure: Cortical Thickness Mapping and Diffusion Tensor Imaging." *Social Cognitive and Affective Neuroscience* 8: 27–33.

Kaustia, M. 2010. "Disposition Effect." In *Behavioral Finance: Investors, Corporations, and Markets*, edited by H. K. Baker and J. R. Nofsinger, 171–189. Hoboken, NJ: John Wiley & Sons.

Keller, A., K. Litzelman, L. E. Wisk, T. Maddox, E. R. Cheng, P. D. Creswell, and W. P. Witt. 2012. "Does the Perception that Stress Affects Health Matter? The Association with Health and Mortality." *Health Psychology* 31: 677–684.

Kelly, T. F., and K. L. Milkman. 2013. "Escalation of Commitment." In *Encyclopedia of Management Theory*, edited by E. H. Kessler, 257–260. Thousand Oaks, CA: Sage Publications.

Killingsworth, M. A., and D. T. Gilbert. 2010. "A Wandering Mind Is an Unhappy Mind." *Science* 330: 932.

Knutson, B., G. E. Wimmer, S. Rick, N. G. Hollon, D. Prelecand, G. Loewenstein. 2008. "Neural Antecedents of the Endowment Effect." *Neuron* 58: 814–822.

Lo, A. W., and D. V. Repin. 2001. "The Psychophysiology of Real-Time Financial Risk Processing." *Journal of Cognitive Neuroscience* 14: 323–339.

Lo, A. W., D. V. Repin, and B. N. Steenbarger. 2005. "Fear and Greed in Financial Markets: A Clinical Study of Day-Traders." *American Economic Review* 95: 352–359.

Logue, A. C. 2011. *Day Trading For Dummies*, 2nd ed. Hoboken, NJ: John Wiley & Sons.

Longmore, R. J., and M. Worrell. 2007. "Do We Need to Challenge Thoughts in Cognitive Behavioral Therapy?" *Clinical Psychology Review* 27: 173–187.

Lynch, P. 1994. *Beating the Street.* New York: Simon & Schuster.

Maher, C. 2003. *Sport Psychology Resource Guide: Building Performers through Programs, Services, and Systems.* Unpublished manuscript.

Maher, C. 2011. *The Complete Mental Game of Baseball: Taking Charge of the Process, On and Off the Field.* Bloomington, IN: AuthorHouse.

Mauboussin, M. J. 2006. *More than You Know: Finding Financial Wisdom in Unconventional Places.* New York: Columbia University Press.

Mayer, J. D., P. Salovey, D. K. Caruso, and L. Cherkasskiy. 2011. "Emotional Intelligence." In *The Cambridge Handbook of Intelligence*, 3rd ed., edited by R. J. Sternberg and S. B. Kaufman, 528–549. New York: Cambridge University Press.

Mayer, J. D., D. R. Caruso, and P. Salovey. 2000. "Emotional Intelligence Meets Traditional Standards for an Intelligence." *Intelligence* 27: 267–298.

McCormick, I. A., F. H. Walkey, and D. E. Green. 1986. "Comparative Perceptions of Driver Ability: A Confirmation and Expansion." *Accident Analysis and Prevention* 18: 205–208.

McGonigal, K. 2012. *The Willpower Instinct: How Self-Control Works, Why It Matters, and What You Can Do to Get More of It*. New York: Avery.

Moore, Z. E., and F. L. Gardner. 2011. "Understanding Models of Performance Enhancement from the Perspective of Emotion Regulation." *Athletic Insight: The Online Journal of Sport Psychology* 13. Accessed July 24, 2013, at www.athleticinsight.com/Vol13Iss3/Feature.htm.

Nhat Hahn, T. 2009. *The Blooming of a Lotus: Guided Meditations for Achieving the Miracle of Mindfulness, revised*. Boston: Beacon Press.

Odean, T. 1998. "Are Investors Reluctant to Realize Their Losses?" *Journal of Finance* 8: 1775–1797.

Otto, M. W., and J. A. J. Smits. 2011. *Exercise for Mood and Anxiety: Proven Strategies for Overcoming Depression and Enhancing Well-Being*. New York: Oxford University Press.

Pfister, H. R., and G. Böhm. 2008. "The Multiplicity of Emotions: A Framework of Emotional Functions in Decision Making." *Judgment and Decision Making* 3: 5–17.

Plous, S. 1993. *The Psychology of Judgment and Decision Making*. New York: McGraw-Hill.

Pollack, S. M. 2013. "Teaching Mindfulness in Therapy." In *Mindfulness and Psychotherapy*, edited by C. K. Germer, R. D. Siegel, and P. R. Fulton (133–147). New York: Guilford Press.

Ratey, J. J. 2008. *Spark: The Revolutionary New Science of Exercise and the Brain*. New York: Little, Brown and Company.

Ravizza, K., and T. Hanson. 1995. *Heads-up Baseball: Playing the Game One Pitch at a Time*. New York: McGraw-Hill.

Roese, N., and K. Vohs. 2012. "Hindsight Bias." *Perspectives on Psychological Science*, 7: 411–426.

Rolls, E. T., J. Hornak, D. Wade, and J. McGrath. 1994. "Emotion-Related Learning in Patients with Social and Emotional Changes Associated with Frontal Lobe Damage." *Journal of Neurology, Neurosurgery, and Psychiatry* 57: 1518–1524.

Rosenbloom, C. 2011. *The Complete Trading Course: Price Patterns, Strategies, Setups, and Execution Tactics*. Hoboken, NJ: John Wiley & Sons.

Ruscio, A. M., T. A. Brown, J. Sareen, M. B. Stein, and R. C. Kessler. 2008. "Social Fears and Social Phobia in the United States: Results from the National Comorbidity Survey Replication." *Psychological Medicine* 38: 15–28.

Russo, J. E., and P. J. H. Schoemaker. 2002. *Winning Decisions: Getting It Right the First Time*. New York: Currency Doubleday.

Schwager, J. D. 1993. *Market Wizards: Interviews with Top Traders*. New York: Harper Business.

Sedlmeier, P., J. Eberth, M. Schwartz, D. Zimmermann, F. Haarig, S. Jaeger, and S. Kunze. 2012. "The Psychological Effects of Meditation: A Meta-Analysis." *Psychological Bulletin* 138: 1139–1171.

Simon, H. A., and W. G. Chase. 1973. "Skill in Chess." *American Scientist* 61: 394–403.

Skinner, B. F. 1953. *Science and Human Behavior.* New York: Macmillan.

Sokol-Hessner, P., C. F. Camerer, and E. Phelps. 2012. "Emotion Regulation Reduces Loss Aversion and Decreases Amygdala Responses to Losses." *Social Cognitive and Affective Neuroscience*, e-publication ahead of print. Accessed June 9, 2013, at http://scan.oxfordjournals.org/content/early/2012/02/15/scan.nss002.full.pdf+html.

Sokol-Hessner, P., M. Hsu, N. G. Curley, M. R. Delgado, C. F. Camerer, and E. A. Phelps. 2009. "Thinking Like a Trader Selectively Reduces Individuals' Loss Aversion." *Proceedings of the National Academy of Sciences* 106: 5035–5040.

Soros, G. 1998. *The Crisis of Global Capitalism: Open Society Endangered.* London: Little Brown.

Steenbarger, B. N. 2003. *The Psychology of Trading: Tools and Techniques for Minding the Markets.* Hoboken, NJ: John Wiley & Sons.

Tang, Y. Y., Y. Ma, J. Wang, Y. Fan, S. Feng, Q. Lu, Q. Yu, D. Sui, M. K. Rothbart, M. Fan, and M. I. Posner. 2007. "Short-Term Meditation Training Improves Attention and Self-Regulation." *Proceedings of the National Academy of Sciences of the United States of America* 104: 17152–17156.

Teper, R., and M. Inzlicht. 2013. "Meditation, Mindfulness and Executive Control: The Importance of Emotional Acceptance and Brain-Based Performance Monitoring." *Social Cognitive and Affective Neuroscience* 8: 85–92.

Terasawa, Y., H. Fukushima, and S. Umeda. 2011. "How Does Interoceptive Awareness Interact with the Subjective Experience of Emotion? An fMRI Study." *Human Brain Mapping* 34: 598–612.

Tharp, V. K. 1998. *Trade Your Way to Financial Freedom.* New York: McGraw-Hill.

Toplak, M. E., R. F. West, and K. E. Stanovich. 2011. "The Cognitive Reflection Test as a Predictor of Performance on Heuristics-and-Biases Tasks." *Memory and Cognition* 39: 1275–1289.

Tversky, A., and D. Kahneman. 1974. "Judgment under Uncertainty: Heuristics and Biases." *Science*, 185: 453–458.

Wegner, D. M. 1994. "Ironic Processes of Mental Control." *Psychological Review* 101: 34–52.

Wegner, D. M., and S. Zanakos. 1994. "Chronic Thought Suppression." *Journal of Personality* 62: 615–640.

Weinstein, N. D., and W. M. Klein. 1996. Unrealistic Optimism: Present and Future. *Journal of Social and Clinical Psychology* 15: 1–8.

Wenzlaff, R. M., and D. M. Wegner. 2000. "Thought Suppression." *Annual Review of Psychology* 51: 59–91.

Weir, K. 2011. "The Exercise Effect." *Monitor on Psychology* 42 (December): 48–52.

Wilder, J. W. 1978. *New Concepts in Technical Trading Systems.* Greensboro, NC: Trend Research.

Wilson, K. G., and T. Dufrene. 2010. *Things Might Go Terribly, Horribly Wrong: A Guide to Life Liberated from Anxiety.* Oakland, CA: New Harbinger.

Wilson, K. G., and A. R. Murrell. 2004. "Values Work in Acceptance and Commitment Therapy: Setting a Course for Behavioral Treatment." In *Mindfulness and Acceptance:*

Expanding the Cognitive-Behavioral Tradition, edited by S. C.Hayes, V. M.Follette, and M. M.Linehan, 120–151. New York: Guilford Press.

Wood, J. V., W. Q. Perunovic, and J. W. Lee. 2009. "Positive Self Statements: Power for Some, Peril for Others." *Psychological Science* 20: 860–866.

Zhang, L., and R. F. Baumeister. 2006. "Your Money or Your Self-Esteem: Threatened Egotism Promotes Costly Entrapment in Losing Endeavors." *Personality and Social Psychology Bulletin* 32: 881–893.

REFERENCES

Printed and bound by CPI Group (UK) Ltd, Croydon, CR0 4YY

03/01/2025

14620130-0001